Dimensions of German Unification

Published in cooperation with
The Robert Bosch Foundation, GmbH,
and
The Robert Bosch Foundation Alumni Association

Dimensions of German Unification

Economic, Social, and Legal Analyses

EDITED BY
A. Bradley Shingleton, Marian J. Gibbon, and Kathryn S. Mack

Westview Press

BOULDER • SAN FRANCISCO • OXFORD

Copyright © 1995 by Westview Press, Inc.

Published in 1995 in the United States of America by Westview Press, Inc., 5500 Central Avenue, Boulder, Colorado 80301-2877, and in the United Kingdom by Westview Press, 36 Lonsdale Road, Summertown, Oxford OX2 7EW

A CIP catalog record for this book is available from the Library of Congress.
ISBN 0-8133-8875-9

Printed and bound in the United States of America

The paper used in this publication meets the requirements
of the American National Standard for Permanence of Paper
for Printed Library Materials Z39.48-1984.

10   9   8   7   6   5   4   3   2   1

*To the Kuratorium of
the Robert Bosch Foundation
in grateful appreciation of a decade
of support for the promotion of
German-American relations*

Contents

Foreword

For each of the past ten years, the Robert Bosch Foundation has invited fifteen highly qualified young Americans for a nine-month stay in Germany. The fellows have educational backgrounds and professional experience in law, business, public administration, and international relations. Their stay in Germany is not academic but, rather, allows them to acquire practical experience in the German federal and state government, business, and media.

Since 1989 the Robert Bosch Fellows have shown a special interest in the realities of life in unified Germany and have frequently selected internships in the new federal states. In the past, issues of security policy and the Atlantic Alliance occupied their interest. They have now become increasingly involved in issues of environment, immigration policy, education, health care policy, and intersocietal conflict—areas that offer opportunities for fruitful interaction between the United States and Germany.

The 130 former fellows constitute a notable group, many pursuing successful careers not only in the United States but also in Germany and Europe. Many have remained personally and professionally involved with promoting and improving German-American relations.

Through the fellowship program, the Robert Bosch Foundation has demonstrated its thankfulness to the American people, who have magnanimously helped the Germans to overcome two dictatorships and to return to the community of free and democratic nations.

We thank the editors of this book, A. Bradley Shingleton, Marian J. Gibbon, and Kathryn S. Mack, for publishing the third volume of essays by Bosch Fellows on the occasion of the tenth anniversary of the Bosch Fellowship Program. I would also like to thank Dr. Gale Mattox for her coeditorship of the first two volumes and A. Bradley Shingleton for his coeditorship of the second volume. On this anniversary of the Fellowship Program I also wish to thank the dedicated members of the Fellowship Selection Committee under the initial leadership of Martin Hillenbrand, former U.S. ambassador to Germany, under the subsequent leadership of John Rielly, president of the Chicago Council on Foreign Relations, as well as Wolfgang Linz, Steven Muller, Peter Pechel, and Maria Ramirez.

Without the personal engagement of the officials of the Robert Bosch Foundation and CDS International, Inc., in New York the Fellowship Program would not have been implemented successfully. To all of them, in particular Dr. Rüdiger Stephan, Gunter Gerstberger, and Jacqueline von Saldern, I extend my sincere thanks.

Dr. Ulrich Bopp
Robert Bosch Foundation

Preface

Though Germany's political unification occurred extremely rapidly, its economic and social unification are being gradually and, in some respects, laboriously consummated. In this sense, unification has been a process rather than an event. The economic, cultural, and psychological dimensions of unification have, each in their own way, proven to be complex challenges to the energies and resources of the German people, their political leaders and policymakers. Unification has also been complicated by a series of external developments. A wrenching economic recession, the Gulf War, the massive task of recreating the economic and political systems of eastern Europe and the Commonwealth of Independent States (CIS), waves of cross-border immigration, the movement toward a more integrated Europe, the need to redefine security alliances: any single one of these developments alone would have created difficulties for Germany in the midst of dramatic change. Collectively, these and other developments have rendered German unification a greater challenge than it first appeared in 1990.

In spite of these difficulties, Germany has achieved a great deal through perseverance and sacrifice during the past four years. Although the new federal states may not yet be the "blooming landscape" Chancellor Helmut Kohl predicted in 1990, there is broad agreement that the geographic area they encompass will have the most modern economic infrastructure in Europe within this decade. Our hope is that this book will illuminate the challenges unification poses for Germany in economic, political, and social terms, and convey a sense of the achievements, and the costs, of unity.

This book is divided into three parts. The first part, introduced by Marian J. Gibbon, is concerned with the challenges of unifying the German economy while integrating it into the European Union and maintaining its competitive edge in the global economy. The second part, introduced by Kathryn S. Mack, addresses some of the social and cultural dimensions of unification. The final part, initiated by a brief overview of the legal dimension of German unification by A. Bradley Shingleton, includes chapters on three fields of German law. Although these chapters are not directly concerned with the process of unification, they provide insight into some of the philosophical presuppositions that underlie not only German law but also the German concept of a social market economy *(Sozialmarktwirtschaft)*.

The Robert Bosch Foundation selects fifteen fellows each year on the basis of expertise in a particular field to spend nine months in Germany working in both federal and state government. Each fellow is required to produce an essay on a topic of his or her choice. The contents of this book were selected from papers submitted between 1991 and 1993.

•

The objective of the Robert Bosch Alumni Association in publishing this volume is to reinforce and further the purposes outlined in the association by-laws, which include:

- providing a continuing education for former Bosch fellows on current German and European social, political, and cultural issues
- supplying a forum for maintaining personal and professional contacts with German counterparts
- creating and fostering contact and communication among successive groups of Bosch Fellows
- encouraging and fostering any other such activity that promotes the long-term improvement of German-U.S. relations

The editors wish to thank the authors for their diligent work on their chapters. Their tasks have been complicated by the press of time, but they admirably met the challenge.

In dedicating *Dimensions of German Unification* to the Board of Trustees of the Robert Bosch Foundation, we wish to recognize, on behalf of all former and future fellows, the enormous and generous contribution they have made to mutual understanding between our two countries.

A. Bradley Shingleton
Marian J. Gibbon
Kathryn S. Mack

Acknowledgments

The editors owe a debt of gratitude to a number of people for their assistance in the publication of this volume. The Alumni Association and the authors have benefited from the financial support and encouragement of the Robert Bosch Foundation, its executive director Dr. Ulrich Bopp, and the Robert Bosch Foundation Board of Trustees. The authors submitted their chapters as papers to the Foundation from 1991 to 1993, and their contributions reflect their professional experiences as Bosch Fellows in the Federal Republic of Germany. The Bosch Foundation's deputy director, Rüdiger Stephan, and other staff members, particularly Jacqueline von Saldern, in addition to CDS International, Inc., deserve special thanks as well for their assistance.

A board of outside experts, including Lily Gardner Feldman, Werner Hein, Richard Smyser, and Ronald Bee, reviewed the chapters. We thank them for their time and efforts. We also express our thanks to Dr. Gale Mattox, coeditor of the first two volumes in this series, for her indispensable help. Carmen Paige provided invaluable assistance in preparation of the manuscript.

The views expressed in the volume are those of the authors and do not represent the views of the institutions with which they are affiliated, the Robert Bosch Foundation, or the Robert Bosch Foundation Alumni Association.

A. B. S.
M. J. G.
K. S. M.

Acronyms

CIS	Commonwealth of Independent States
CSCE	Conference on Security and Cooperation in Europe
EC	European Community
ECB	European Central Bank
EFTA	European Free Trade Area
EMU	European Monetary Union
EU	European Union
FRG	Federal Republic of Germany
GATT	General Agreement on Tariffs and Trade
GDR	German Democratic Republic
IGC	Inter-Governmental Council
NATO	North Atlantic Treaty Organization
THA	Treuhandanstalt
TQM	Total Quality Management

PART ONE

German Unification:
Economic Aspects

Introduction

Marian J. Gibbon

In the early 1990s European alliances and borders shifted and changed for the first time in nearly half a century. As they did, many feared that the Germany which emerged in the new Europe would be a force to reckon with: the combined strengths of the Eastern Bloc's most advanced economy, and the West's most stable, would result in an economic power-house, ready to dominate a unified Western Europe and an opening Eastern Europe.

At the outset of unification few predicted that the process of creating one Germany would be anything other than smooth, its results anything other than beneficial. Yet after the first giddy days of post-Border, post-Wall Germany, reality struck, bringing with it unemployment, government deficits, higher taxes, and general malaise. It soon became apparent that the East's most advanced economy had little more than noncompetitive industries to offer, and that significant sacrifices would be required from the West's most stable economy in order to make unified Germany the economic powerhouse that most had expected it to become. With this revelation came resentment, recriminations, and a severe countrywide recession, the worst the Federal Republic has seen in the postwar period.

In early 1993 Germany's leading economic institutes published grim predictions for the country's expected performance during the coming year. Following three years of drastic contractions in the eastern industrial base and growing federal deficits borne out of shoring up the eastern economy, the overall economic outlook was poor indeed. For the western *Länder* (Germany's equivalent of states) the best predictions foresaw GNP growth of 0.9 percent. The worst predicted a contraction of 0.5 percent. In reality, 1993 was even worse than predicted, with the economy shrinking by 2 percent, exports dropping off by 8.5 percent, and imports falling by 10.5 percent. At year's end it appeared that unemployment, which had averaged 2.28 million throughout the year, would soon reach 4.0 million (which it did in March 1994). Predictions for 1994 were not much brighter, at best calling for 1.0 percent growth in the west and 7.5 percent in the east.[1] Both westerners and easterners were left to grapple with a general sense of dislocation as they found their economic security—be that defined by capitalist or socialist terms—turned on its head.

The start of the 1990s has indeed been trying for the Federal Republic's economy. But in assessing the situation, one must ask two fundamental questions: Without unification, would the economic situation have been that much better? Will unification hold the German economy back in the long run? The answer to both questions is "No."

Consider the economic condition of the Federal Republic's primary allies, trading partners, and economic competitors during the same time period. Britain, Canada, France, Japan, and the United States—all have been struggling with changing economic rules and imperatives, as they lose precious investment dollars to low-wage nations in Latin America, Southeast Asia, and Eastern Europe. All have suffered through a recession, which has led to increased unemployment and sluggish spending patterns. And most have seen unemployment in the ranks of white-collar workers, as company's downsize, looking to cut costs and adjust to the realities imposed by higher overhead costs and tougher international competition. Each country has struggled to redefine its area of industrial strength and prowess and to identify areas of high-tech competitive advantage.

To a certain extent these issues worldwide have been driven by the collapse of the Eastern Bloc, as states have been forced to alter their economic focus moving away from from a Cold War orientation defined by goods produced, primary trading partners, or both. The changes have also been driven, however, by the simple reality that it is cheaper to undertake heavy industrial tasks with low-cost labor or with the assistance of productivity-boosting robots and machines. With these changes, jobs have been lost, and the whole production schema of advanced states have been shifted towards a service economy and away from the industrial sector, the traditional backbone of Germany's economy. Thus, to lay all of the blame for Germany's economic woes at the feet of unification costs is an unfortunate oversimplification. With or without unification, western Germany, one of the highest-cost production locations in the world, would have been struggling with many of the same issues it faces today.

What of the eastern states, with raging unemployment and a decimated industrial base? Are they not worse off in postunification Germany? Although their difficulties are severe, the answer remains "No." Eventually, the east's economy, with its rotting core of industrial machinery and equipment, had to collapse. Its goods were noncompetitive, and the need for upgrading capital equipment was intense.

Although the pain of transforming the economy of the *neue Bundesländer* may be great, it is analogous to that of removing a bandaid: the pain can be short and sharp, or long and drawn out. There is no question that the transition is and has been painful. Unofficial unemployment estimates for the five new states remain in the 40 percent to 50 percent range, and transfer payments continue to sustain living standards throughout the region. Some positive signs, however, suggest that the pain may soon be abating. In 1993 per capita investment was 140 percent higher in the east than in the west. While Germany's overall GNP shrank in 1993, in the east alone GNP grew 7.1 percent, and predictions for growth in 1994 range from 6.0 percent to 7.5 percent.[2] Infrastructure is being rebuilt at a state-of-the-art level in the five new states and many of the country's ultra hightech investments are being located there.[3] These facts and figures indicate that the worst part of the transition period in the east may soon be over.

To imply that unification has been without cost—east and west—would, however, be shortsighted. One of the most pressing issues challenging policymakers at this time is Germany's growing budget deficit. During the postwar period officials in the Federal Republic of Germany were loath to undertake debt-incurring government spending. With unemployment nationwide at record levels, however, and with the *neue Bundesländer* demanding significant levels of investment and transfer payment assistance, the government's deficit has been on the rise. It is predicted to reach 2.5 percent of GDP in 1995.

Quite suddenly, Germany, with its world-renowned social safety net and high level of public services, is finding itself squeezed, trying to cut corners, and to identify sources of additional revenue. As a result, taxes are increasing, health care, welfare, and educational programs are being scaled back, and a number of key state-owned enterprises, such as the post office and rail system, are being privatized. Policymakers are struggling to bring expenditures and revenues back into line.

Again, however, what is apparent is that the current economic situation in Germany is not that different from that of many other industrialized nations. While there is indeed an added drain because of the east's need to rebuild, overall, Germany is facing the same set of challenges confronting policymakers elsewhere. Thus, the proper question is, can Germany and its partners effectively address these issues, both individually and collectively. With sufficient political will, they certainly can.

The successful conclusion of negotiations on the General Agreement on Tariffs and Trade, progress in strengthening the European Union, greater ties with the economies of Eastern Europe—all are steps which Germany is taking towards focusing economic strength at home on ties with the global economy. In addition, the issue of Germany as an investment location—the so-called *Standort* debate—gives policymakers a focus which is independent of east-west divisions. As this issue becomes of increasing concern, it will be a vehicle that truly unifies the approach of policymakers and businesses to the German economy. In the transition away from immediate postunification divisions, such a vehicle is necessary, positive, and timely.

Ultimately, there is and should be remarkable faith in the German economy's ability to rejuvenate and to survive the challenges of unification and industrial change as a strong and powerful economic locomotive. In a survey of more than 500 top European business leaders, performed by Harris Research in early 1994, Germany was judged to have the best chances of any European economy in overcoming untenably high production costs. The German respondents were particularly sure of their economy's resilience.[4] There is a clear belief among top managers that in the long run the hackneyed comparison to Germany's first *Wirtschaftswunder* (economic miracle) will once again prove true. As managers act on this optimism, and as policymakers tackle current issues with the same tenacity as they attacked the initial challenge of unification, a competitive Germany will indeed emerge.

The papers in this section provide an overview of key issues pertaining to Germany's economic situation and economic policy since unification. Frederick R. Fucci's paper begins Part 1 with "Whither the Treuhandanstalt?", a review of the state agency's fast-paced and controversial privatization of eastern enterprises. Mark J. Jrolf's case study of the privatization of a Treuhand enterprise follows. Entitled "The Politics of Restructuring Business Enterprises in the Former GDR: The Case of EKO Stahl," the paper illustrates the tensions emerging among Brussels, Bonn, and the new states as Germany works to mainstream the East.

Adam Posen's paper on Germany's banking system, "Less than a Universe of Difference: Evaluating the Reality of German Finance," argues that the country's vaunted "relationship banking" may not be as influential as once thought. Indeed, Posen cautions against emulating the contemporary German financial system given the changes and problems now buffeting the system.

In "Germany at Maastricht: Diplomacy and Domestic Politics," Collette Mazzucelli reviews Germany's role defining the European Monetary Union. Her discussion highlights not only the influence of the European Union on Germany's economic policies but, like Jrolf's paper, also illustrates the ongoing tensions among Brussels, Bonn, and the *Länder*. This tension is likely to remain in German policymaking, as the EU continues to take shape in the coming years.

Finally, in "Standort Deutschland" Michael Zumwinkle discusses Germany's efforts to retain and attract long-term productive investment. Ultimately, as noted above, this issue—more than any other—is likely to compel Germany to truly unify its economic policies and to move the country forward as one unit into the twenty-first century.

Notes

1. Thomas Hanke, "Schwerer Weg aus der Talsohle," *Die Zeit*, 7 January 1994, 9.

2. "Eastern German Investment Rises," *The Wall Street Journal*, 25 March 1994, A6; see also Hanke, "Schwerer Weg," 9.

3. As only one example among many, Siemens is reportedly planning to build one of the most modern microchip plants in Europe outside of Dresden. The project is expected to cost approximately DM 2 billion and create 1,200 jobs.

4. Nikolaus Piper, "Unternehmen Europa im Härtetest," *Die Zeit*, 4 March 1994, 12.

1

Whither the Treuhandanstalt?

Frederick R. Fucci

In the early days of her tenure as president of the Treuhandanstalt, THA, the state privatization agency, Frau Birgit Breuel was fond of observing that the agency was the world's largest holding company, but that it was the only one whose mission was to sell off all its assets and then dissolve itself as quickly as possible. Her audiences often greeted this statement with polite incredulity. Now that—according to the Treuhand's own reckoning—the lion's share of its privatization work has been accomplished, and it is preparing to dissolve the Treuhand structure that has been in place since German unification, it is time to take stock of what the Treuhand has accomplished, draw lessons from its policies and practices, and assess plans for continuing its unfinished work.

German Unification and the Founding of the Treuhand

The first version of the Treuhand was created in June 1990 pursuant to a law passed by the only democratically elected *Volkskammer* in the forty-year history of the German Democratic Republic (GDR).[1] The law was based on the premise that the command economic model had to be abandoned and created an agency that would regroup all of the GDR's industrial and other holdings and then attempt to sell them off to private investors. With so little private property in the GDR, few problems arose from transferring ownership to one trusteeship agency. The agency was housed in the seat of the GDR's House of Ministries on Leipziger Straße, against the east side of the Wall between Potsdamer Platz and Checkpoint Charlie.[2] Because the House of Ministries, complete with its Orwellian-sounding name, housed numerous GDR ministries with influence over economic questions, including the ministry responsible for planning, it was thought logical to locate the new privatization agency there.

At the time, some eight thousand separate industrial companies existed in the GDR. Organized into legal entities called *Volkseigentums-betriebe*, or "people's property companies" (VEBs), these companies were often huge industrial conglomerates integrated vertically to ensure the supply of inputs through the various phases of production. Most VEBs also had all sorts of ancillary activities and holdings not directly related to the production of their goods, such as kindergartens, canteens, vacation homes, and consumer goods outlets. Four million citizens (out of a total population of about 17 million) were considered "industrial" employees when the Treuhand was created, without regard to whether they were directly involved in the production of the company's products or in one of its ancillary activities. The Modrow government blithely assumed that the value of the GDR's enterprises and real property in the market economy was about DM 400 billion.

At first, the Treuhand was a comparatively small operation with only a few hundred employees. Because it was still a part of the GDR government, all of its employees were easterners. Negotiations with private investors were carried out very quickly and privatization contracts were extremely simple.

After the 1 July 1990 currency union, but before German unification on 3 October 1990, the *Volkskammer* passed a law that, subsequent to its incorporation into the German Unification Treaty, would serve to regulate eastern property questions.[3] After German unification in October 1990, control of the Treuhand was vested in the general German government, which meant that West Germans were put in all the Treuhand's positions of power and an attempt was made to build up a bureaucracy, in both senses of the word. In the good sense, it meant that administrative procedures, with the attendant checks and approvals, were imposed on the privatization process that tended to regularize the decision making. But it also meant that the Treuhand grew into a rather large organization commonly regarded as unwieldy both by the Treuhand's own employees and by outsiders having to deal with it. At the height of the Treuhand's privatization activity in 1992, it had about four thousand employees—two thousand in the central office in Berlin and some two thousand in the fifteen branch offices spread throughout the five new federal states.

Principal Privatization Work

In order to begin privatizing in accordance with Western business practices, the new Treuhand converted the eight thousand-odd VEBs inherited from the GDR into about thirteen thousand new legal entities, most of which were organized under the traditional West German corporate form of *Gesellschaft mit beschränkter Haftung* (limited liability company or GmbH), which is roughly equivalent to what American attorneys call a "closely held corporation." The Treuhand became either 100 percent or majority shareholder of these GmbHs. A few of the larger industrial enterprises were converted into *Aktiengesellschaften* (AGs), the German version of the joint stock company.

In addition to the VEBs mentioned above, the Treuhand also started out with real estate holdings in approximately half the territory of the former-GDR, large agricultural tracts consisting of the former agricultural production communes, forestry plots, numerous public utilities, and all the small shops and restaurants in the country.

As of mid-1994, practically all of the Treuhand's initial portfolio has been disposed of in one way or another, with the exception of about twenty large industrial enterprises and a significant portion of its real estate holdings.

The privatization work for the thirteen thousand industrial enterprises began very quickly while the former GDR was still in existence, but was then practically halted from September 1990 until March 1991 owing to questions relating to compensation for properties lost in eastern Germany since 1933. The West German government had paid substantial amounts in compensation for Nazi-era damages; no compensation at all had been paid by the GDR government. Thus the Bundestag, eager to provide for such compensation, passed a law[4] establishing the fundamental principle that persons who had property confiscated in the eastern part of Germany either during the Nazi regime, the Soviet occupation between 1945 and 1949, or during the existence of the GDR were entitled to restitution of their property rather than compensation.

Because practically every industrial enterprise in the GDR was affected by one or several property claims, the application of the principle of restitution before compensation cast doubt on the legal title of industrial enterprises, and buyers refused to move forward unless clear title could be passed to them. This situation was resolved by a law known popularly as the "Impediments Removal Law."[5] In effect reversing the "restitution before compensation" principle, this law required that persons with confiscation claims present, within stringent time frames, an investment plan for the properties affected. If their plan was equivalent to proposals submitted by other investors wishing to buy the property, they would be entitled to the property. If not, they would be entitled to compensation. In practice, the victims of confiscation, or their heirs, were almost never in a position to present competitive business plans. They therefore became entitled to compensation according to formulas to be set in the future by the Bundestag.

After this law effectively allowed unencumbered title to pass to investors, privatization began with stunning speed. This was, in fact, the result of the government's policy that the ownership of eastern industrial assets should be transferred to private hands and market principles introduced as quickly as possible. The "quick privatization" model, as it came be known, has proved to be controversial in Germany. Its theoretical underpinning seems to be a profound conviction on the part of conservative members of the Kohl government (and of the industrial interests that tend to support them) that subsidizing inefficient industrial enterprises in the east during an extended transition period was highly undesirable. Moreover, such state-supported industries would be competing with their western counterparts in many sectors.

Because the Christian Democratic Union (CDU)/Christian Social Union (CSU)/Free Democratic Party (FDP) coalition of Christian Democrats remained in power after the 1990 all-German elections, it was logical that this coalition should appoint the persons to control the Treuhand. Thus, the two western presidents of the Treuhand have both been CDU politicians. Although this consideration may not have been paramount when the coalition was riding high after the 1990 elections, as the international economic situation worsened, the coalition members may have realized their ability to appoint the people running the Treuhand would soon cease. Thus, the decision to sell enterprises quickly could well have been colored by the desire to ensure that the Social Democratic Party (SPD) have very little left to sell, if it should gain power after the 1994 elections.

Whatever the motivation, industrial enterprises were dissolved at the rapid rate of about twenty a day from March 1991 until mid-1993. This meant that either the enterprise was sold in total or in part to outside investors or to teams of incumbent managers under management buyout schemes, or that the enterprise was placed either in bankruptcy to be liquidated or into what is known as a "Management KG," which is a grouping of enterprises designated for subsidized restructuring in preparation for later sale.

As of 31 January 1994, some 5,914 enterprises had been sold to private investors in their entirety.[6] Majority stakes have been sold in 33 companies.[7] An additional 7,154 company divisions were privatized by the Treuhand. Since there often is not much viable left after a company division has been privatized by the Treuhand (unless it is a fairly large company), the remainder of the company is liquidated or its machinery is offered for sale separately.

Therefore, privatization solutions have been found in whole or in part for most of the original industrial companies in the Treuhand's portfolio.

In addition, the Treuhand has begun to liquidate some 3,219 of the companies or company divisions in its original portfolio. Eighty-five of these winding-up procedures are now complete. The Treuhand liqui-dates most companies according to a three-year procedure and that permits the Treuhand to continue to employ a certain percentage of its workers during the wind-down phase, as well as to continue to try to privatize divisions of the company.[8]

What has been the net financial result of this frenetic privatization activity? The Treuhand has realized DM 48.3 billion in sales proceeds in its portfolio. This is a far cry indeed from the DM 400 billion that was expected by the Modrow government in 1990. Moreover, covering the operating losses of the companies in the Treuhand's portfolio, subsidiz-ing their restructuring to make them salable, and paying their workers pending privatization has also cost the Treuhand princely sums of money. The debt incurred by the Treuhand for these purposes has amounted to close to DM 300 billion. It has been financed by short- and medium-term borrowing on Euromarkets at comparatively favorable interest rates; Treuhand debt is guaranteed by the full faith and credit of the German government. Although its debt is considered to be "off balance sheet" for the purposes of Germany's budget deficit, in practice, the Treuhand's work will greatly increase the German budget deficit because the debt is guaranteed by the government, and it is understood that the proceeds realized by the Treuhand by the time its entire portfolio is gone will never be enough to meet the obligations it has incurred.

Thus, on one level, one can view the privatization process in eastern Germany as a huge bailout, similar in scale and financing technique to the U.S. government's efforts to bail out insolvent savings and loan banks.

On the positive side of the balance sheet for the five new eastern states, however, the sale of companies in the Treuhand's portfolio has resulted in commitments from private investors to maintain almost 1.5 million jobs and to invest DM 188 billion in capital in the purchased com-panies.

Successor Organizations

Now that the operative task of the Treuhand is drawing to a close, will it really dissolve itself, as Frau Breuel has predicted? The answer is "yes," in a formal sense, but "not really," in a practical sense, although the number of people employed in privatization-related activities will decrease by more than half. The Treuhand structure as it has been known from 1990 will be dissolved at the end of 1994. The Treuhand's tasks and responsibilities will be transferred to several different successor entities. It is not difficult to imagine that these successor entities will be busy with privatization follow-up until at least the turn of the century.[9]

The plan for creating the most important Treuhand successor entities is discussed below—at least as they were envisioned at the beginning of 1994 (for implementation at the beginning of 1995).[10] The extent to which these plans will be implemented, of course, depends on whether the political branches approve them as proposed and whether the CDU/CSU/FDP coalition remains in power after the Fall 1994 Bundestag elections. The emphasis could be dramatically different if an SPD dominated coalition takes power after the election.

Bundesanstalt für Vereinigungsbedingtes Sondervermögen (BVG)

This agency is planned to be the main successor organization to the Treuhand. Like the Treuhand, the BVG will be an independent government agency. It will also assume the Treuhand's dual legal personality for being a debtor or a creditor and will assume responsibility for all the Treuhand's sovereign activities. It is projected that 450 persons will be employed by the BVG.

Gesellschaft für Vertragsmanagement, Abwicklung, und Reprivatisierung (VAR)

The Treuhand has proposed to create a private GmbH that would be responsible for managing the privatization contracts that have been entered into, for directing the liquidation process, for completing what is termed "reprivatization" and for environmental cleanup. These functions, as described below, are projected to require 650 employees.

Monitoring Contract Performance. Indeed, one of the most important aspects of the Treuhand's continuing work will be monitoring the performance of the contracts it has entered into with private investors. About two-thirds of Treuhand privatization contracts commit the investor to two major guarantees. One is the maintenance of a specified number of jobs for a term of two to five years after privatization, while the other is the making of a specified sum of monetary investment, again for a period of two to five years. The length of these commitments are negotiated points.[11]

Managing Treuhand contracts presents two different sorts of headaches—the first is that for fully a third of the approximately twelve thousand privatization contracts concluded with investors, there are no provisions for monetary or other sorts of penalties if the investor does not keep his or her commitments. These were the earlier form of Treuhand contracts, which were exceedingly simple. In cases like these, the persons responsible for contract management must decide whether it is worthwhile for the Treuhand to use the courts to pursue legal remedies. Generally speaking, in these instances the Treuhand can do very little if the investor has not kept its commitments and has placed the company into voluntary bankruptcy.

The situation is different for contracts concluded after March 1991. According to the Impediments Removal Law, sale or lease contracts concluded by the Treuhand are legally binding only if the purchaser or lessee is contractually bound to return the property should he or she fail to carry out the investments provided for in the first two years after purchase.

Thus, these later Treuhand privatization contracts have two types of teeth for their enforcement. As required by the Impediments Removal Law, the Treuhand has the contractual right to take companies back from the investors if those investors do not keep their commitments. The other type is a monetary penalty clause that operates like a liquidated damages clause in the common law system. The going rate for failure to keep job commitments is between DM 30,000 and 40,000 per job per year, while the liquidated penalty for failure to keep investment commitments is about 10 percent of the monetary amount of the commitment.

The Treuhand's second headache is deciding how strict to be in insisting that investors keep commitments or even whether to exercise its foreclosure prerogatives and take the company back. The scope of the problem of noncompliance has been generating increasing interest from the Finance Ministry and the parliamentary committees responsible for the oversight of the Treuhand. In 1993, the Bundestag's Treuhand Committee audited 2,840 privatized companies for compliance with their investment commitments. For 1991 some 17 percent of them did not fulfill their obligations.[17] According to a 1993 Treuhand study of 80 percent of all privatized companies, 15 percent of investors do not live up to their job guarantees.[13] On the average, however, this same study finds that investors exceed their job guarantees by a figure of 110 to 113 percent.[14]

Although the Treuhand possesses some heavy artillery in the form of these repossession prerogatives and monetary penalties, in practice, it does not insist on their strict enforcement except in special cases.[15] First, it does not want companies that it has already privatized coming back into its portfolio; second, it does not want to drive privatized companies out of business by insisting on its pound of flesh in very difficult economic times. This is a reflection of the Treuhand's ultimate status as an arm of the German government sensitive to the political problems caused by unemployment.[16]

How many of the already privatized companies will come back to the Treuhand's portfolio because of its foreclosure action is a matter of some speculation among Treuhand-watchers. It is thought to be unlikely that the Treuhand will take large numbers back before the 1994 legislative elections. How this problem is handled afterward will depend in large part on the next government coalition. If the Social Democratic Party is involved in the coalition, one might expect a greater willingness to take back companies and thus to continue to subsidize their existence.

Liquidation and Winding Up. The VAR is also responsible for the administration of liquidation proceedings. About 88 percent of Treuhand companies set for liquidation are managed according to a procedure that lasts three years from the time the Treuhand decides to send a company into liquidation. Because so many companies from the Treuhand's portfolio are being liquidated, one can therefore expect that the liquidation arm of the VAR will be busy well into 1997.

Reprivatization. Reprivatization is the term used by the Treuhand to refer to the return of industrial properties that were expropriated by the Nazis, principally from Jewish owners, by local authorities during the Soviet occupation from 1945 to 1949, or by the Communist government during the existence of the GDR, principally from persons who left the territory of the GDR up until June 1953 or in the framework of a 1972 reorganization of industrial conglomerates. The reprivatization of industrial properties is a small part of the larger problem of unjust confiscation of property in the eastern part of Germany discussed above. The operative principle of reprivatization is that a business shall be restored to its former owners if still comparable or substantially similar to its condition at the time of expropriation, taking into account technical advancements and general economic developments, unless restitution is impossible. The total number of claims affecting companies or other assets in the Treuhand's portfolio amounts to a little over fifteen thousand (of the more than 1.1 million total property claims filed in the general claim process), which means that practically every company in the Treuhand's portfolio is affected in one way or another by a restitution claim.[17]

As of the end of January 1994, 9,279 of the total reprivatization claims have been resolved by the Treuhand in one of the following ways.

Return of an entire enterprise	1,584
Return of a portion of an enterprise	2,787
Return of assets	1,832
Treuhand approval for claimant's sale of enterprise	1,264
Compensation of claimant	918
Denial of claim	934

Environmental Cleanup. A separate division of the VAR will monitor inherited environmental problems. In many Treuhand privatization contracts, the financial responsibility for environmental cleanup is divided between the Treuhand and the purchaser, frequently in such a way that the purchaser's annual and overall liability is capped at a specified amount. This means that the VAR will continue to need resources for environmental cleanup for years to come, not to mention the fact that because of the way privatization contracts operate, the Treuhand will in many cases be liable for cleaning up hazards that were not known when the contracts were entered into. Indeed, Frau Breuel has estimated that managing the ecological cleanup may take more than ten years.

Portfolio Management Gesellschaft (PMG)

The PMG will be a branch of the Ministry of Finance employing 50 to 80 persons. It will be responsible for all of the Treuhand's remaining company activity, which falls into two large categories: the large industrial enterprises that could not be sold and Management KGs.

Large Industrial Enterprises. The twenty largest companies left in the Treuhand's portfolio employed almost half the 170,00 persons working for unprivatized companies at the end of January 1994. These companies are the very large industrial enterprises that formed the core of the GDR's heavy industry. Today, many of them are dinosaurs, but they cannot be shut down because this would disrupt the regions where they operate and create a political outcry. These companies are particularly troublesome because many of them are in industries that are in recession worldwide owing to overcapacity, such as steel production,* shipbuilding, and vehicle construction. The mining industry is in particularly bad shape even in the western part of Germany. Chemical companies have their own special set of problems, not the least of which is the environmental damage caused by decades of neglect.

The Treuhand's strategy with regard to these companies has been to reduce gradually, but steadily, their number of employees either through layoffs or by selling off the divisions that are more competitive. In other cases, the Treuhand has invested substantial sums of money to upgrade their equipment and make them more palatable to private investors.

This being said, the only politically palatable choice for the German government in some cases is to allow the Treuhand to continue to operate them with state subsidies to cover their losses for the foreseeable future—it will be the PMG's task to manage this process.

Many of the mid-size companies that built relatively-high value added products and are traditionally important for the industrial core in certain regions of eastern Germany (but which were highly overstaffed and had ageing and inefficient plant and equipment) have been transferred to a Management KG.

Management KGs. A Management KG is a legal structure that allows the Treuhand to transfer the management and restructuring responsibili-

---

* See the following chapter.

ties of groupings of seven to fifteen selected Treuhand companies to an outside management company run by well-known private business persons who also contribute capital with the aim of restructuring and ultimately selling the companies. KG is the abbreviation for the German corporate form, the *Kommanditgesellschaft*, similar to the limited partnership under American principles.[18] A Management KG is set up by first incorporating a GmbH, which is designed to carry out the management functions of the KG. The private manager chosen for this task owns 96 percent of the shares of the corporation; the Treuhand owns only 4 percent. Thereafter, the limited partnership is formed with the management corporation as the general partner. The limited partner is, once again, the Treuhandanstalt, whose capital contribution is companies in its portfolio. The management corporation contributes cash and management expertise.[19]

The purpose of the KG is to restructure the companies in its portfolio and to privatize them within a limited time (usually three years) although it is permitted to sell them before the agreed-upon privatization period if a buyer is interested. Although transferring the ownership of the company to the KG, the Treuhand is still contractually responsible for making financial contributions to the operative companies in the KG and for providing agreed-upon restructuring financing to the management company.

What are the criteria for admitting companies into a Management KG? They must be recognized according to standards established by the Treuhand as being "fundamentally capable of being restructured," they must have a pressing need to be reorganized, they cannot have any foreseeable short-term chances of being privatized outright, and they must have at least 250 employees.[20]

Even though the Treuhand has only a small shareholder interest in the management GmbH and is only a limited partner in the KG, it has significant responsibilities. Its capital contributions to the KG include not only the companies themselves but also cash, which is used to finance losses and provide restructuring "supplements." The Treuhand also provides guarantees for the KG's other financing requirements.

The Management KGs are structured so that the private investors can cash out on the back end. In other words, they are entitled to a certain share of the sales proceeds when the companies in the portfolios are privatized. This gives them an incentive, of course, to do a good job in restructuring the companies and to try to sell them sooner rather than later.

At the end of 1993 there were six Management KGs. It is estimated that the PMG will be responsible for monitoring the activities of up to ten

Management KGs beginning in 1995. The KGs themselves could have up to 100 employees.

Treuhand Liegenschaft Gesellschaft (TLG)

The TLG, a subsidiary of the Treuhand, has been responsible for managing the significant real property assets of the Treuhand and for selling them off. The Treuhand's Phase II plan raises the possibility that the TLG could become a private enterprise, and it is expected to employ almost 950 persons.

From March 1991—when the TLG began selling off its holdings—through the end of January 1994, the TLG sold 19,956 individual pieces of real estate resulting in approximately DM 14.8 billion in sales revenue; 243,181 jobs created or preserved; and future investment commitments of DM 40.2 billion.

Selling off real estate will continue to be slow work compared with the industrial company privatization process, a fact that is confirmed by the relatively high number of employees foreseen for the TLG after January 1995. Part of the reason for this pace is that most properties are sold through an auction process that releases individual pieces of property piecemeal. The TLG does this deliberately to keep land values comparatively high. If everything were sold quickly, the worth of individual lots would be much lower.

Treuhand Osteuropa Beratungsgesellschaft (TOB)

In April 1992 the Treuhand founded this consulting subsidiary in order to offer the experience of the Treuhand privatizers and managers to the governments and privatization agencies of the former constituent republics of the Soviet Union and of Eastern Europe.

At present, the TOB is funded almost completely by a U.S. $30 million budget provided by the Ministry of Finance.[21] In other words, the TOB's consulting expertise is a sort of development aid from the German government. The TOB's services are offered to host governments, with the condition that only local currency expenses be paid by the governments.

The TOB is in the process of taking on staff and searching out projects. Although it has placed personnel in a number of central and Eastern European countries including the Czech Republic, Slovakia, Hungary, Romania, and Estonia, its most noticeable project has been advising the Russian Agency for the Promotion of Economic Reforms on a project to privatize retailers, wholesalers, hotels, restaurants, and transport companies in the Moscow region. There are approximately thirty German experts from the TOB and a German consulting company working closely with the Russian agency on this project.[22]

The TOB's basic financing is assured through the end of 1994. Its future activity depends on its ability to attract financial contributions from international development agencies such as the World Bank, the International Financial Corporation (IFC) and the European Bank for Reconstruction and Development (EBRD), as well as its ability to attract clients, so to speak, if its German government financing is not renewed, and it no longer represents development assistance for the host governments.

The First Phase of the Treuhand's Activity: An Assessment

This report has given a number of details about the privatization process. The numbers are indeed impressive. Within a very short period of time, the Treuhand has substantially succeeded in accomplishing what it set out to do—to privatize an entire economy. Yet the Treuhand remains highly controversial in Germany, and opinion is divided on the value of its work.

These opinions fall into certain broad categories. According to the "eastern view," the Treuhand has destroyed more than it has created, laying off thousands of workers from companies capable of producing perfectly acceptable goods. It has deliberately withheld cash to do anything more than limp along. No serious effort has been made at restructuring. The eastern view holds that the Treuhand has created mass unemployment and has not replaced the GDR industrial economy with anything viable. Instead, it has deindustrialized what had been the world's tenth-largest industrial economy. "Deceived and sold out" is the rallying cry of the disaffected.

Views about the Treuhand in western Germany can be broadly characterized according to political orientation. Those sympathetic to the CDU and the CSU might say that the main goal of the Treuhand was to privatize the economy of the GDR as quickly as possible. In this light, the Treuhand has accomplished 95 percent of its work. Although it has been expensive, no one has ever tried to privatize an entire economy before, and no one had any idea of what terrible shape the GDR companies were in until the Treuhand actually took over their management. Other factors contributing to the high cost of bailing out the eastern economy were the collapse of the COMECON trading system and the worldwide recession in certain key industries such as steel, shipbuilding, and coal mining.

Those whose political sympathies lie with the SPD (and also many easterners) seem to think that the quick privatization approach adopted by the Treuhand was fundamentally wrong. Many enterprises were hastily sold for prices well below their real value. The Treuhand should have made a much greater effort to restructure existing enterprises in order to preserve their value. Because the Treuhand's policies have contributed to the deindustrialization of the east, the federal and local governments should now attempt to help preserve the "industrial core" of certain regions.

The fast pace of privatization was based on a distinct policy decision. One of its initial results (whether warranted or not) was that many companies were sold to speculators who stripped them of their assets or to operators who did not have adequate resources to run them, resulting in bankruptcy or return to the Treuhand. In this context, it is amusing to note that there is increasing interest in the Bundestag Treuhand Committee in investigating how the privatization process was managed. A hue and cry has been raised as people suddenly realize, "My God, the Treuhand has been out of control the past three years and now we're going to get tough." In fact, the Treuhand was deliberately subject only to loose supervision so that it could accomplish its goal of selling off as many companies as possible by the end of 1994, the period coinciding with the Bundestag elections. Now that the lion's share of the work has been done, the government feels more comfortable in letting people engage in a little Treuhand bashing. It is good politics because it gives the CDU and the CSU someone else to blame for the widespread discontent in the east.

It is also true that the Treuhand has deliberately infused only enough cash into many companies in its portfolio to keep their heads above water. If the Treuhand had really tried to undertake the modernization necessary to "restructure" most eastern companies, the cost of privatizing the economy would have been much higher than it already has been. In this respect, the Treuhand has been much more clever than most people appreciate. The goal of this "short string" policy was to pass the cost of retooling and modernization on to private investors. In exchange, the Treuhand was willing to forgo sales proceeds.

It was stated earlier in this chapter that the DM 48.3 billion in sales proceeds realized by the Treuhand was paltry compared with to what some observers thought the GDR's industrial assets were worth in 1990. However, if one looks at the amount of money the Treuhand has pumped into companies in its portfolio to keep them afloat pending privatization and private investment in the near term (DM 188 billion as of the end of January 1994), this infusion of cash amounts to a powerful engine for economic growth, while its cost has been largely passed on to private investors.

The notion that the economy of the East has been deindustrialized is true in a literal sense. As stated above, 4 million persons were employed in the industrial sector at the time of unification. As of the end of 1993, this number had declined to 1 million. Laying the blame for deindustrialization on the Treuhand's lap is rather disingenuous. Most of the people counted as "industrial" workers in the GDR had nothing to do with producing goods. Merely eliminating the people employed in ancillary social activities has dramatically reduced the industrial workforce. If one then counts the number of job commitments made pursuant to privatization contracts with the Treuhand (1,494,430 at the end of January 1994), and if one assumes that these commitments will be kept and counts the net number of jobs created by investment unrelated to Treuhand companies, the industrial employment picture does not seem so skewed.

Indeed, the bitter truth is that the economy of eastern Germany would have completely collapsed if the Bundesrepublik had not bailed it out, particularly with the collapse of the Soviet Union and its trading system. Few companies in the Treuhand's initial portfolio would have been capable of competing in an open, capitalist economy, especially Germany's, which is subject to intense competition from the other countries in the European Union.

In the end, the so-called deindustrialization is symptomatic of a much deeper trend in the industrial economies of the West. There is less and less heavy industrial production. Those companies that survive must do so on the basis of highly skilled labor, high productivity, and efficient use of technology. Of these factors, eastern Germany boasts only the first. If its economy is to do more than sputter along, productivity in an aggregate sense must increase, equipment must be replaced, and there must be a relatively rapid transition to a more service-based economy.

The cost of bailing out the eastern economy has been onerous, but western politicians were aware of its approximate extent when they started (their continual indignant protestations to the contrary). It remains to be seen whether the cost of bailing out the East is going to drag down the West. Most informed Germans think that the size of the eastern German market and the money spent to revive it is really a drop in the bucket. After all, there are more people in Nordrhein-Westphalen than in all five new eastern states. The real problems with German public finances are the rapidly increasing cost of the social welfare state, a population that is aging too rapidly to bear its cost, and Germany's inability so far to adopt a sensible immigration policy that would infuse working-age individuals into the economy.

At the end of the day, the Treuhand's work will have to be assessed by how well the transformation to a market economy has been achieved. Criteria include the number of companies that will come back to the Treuhand's portfolio, the extent to which privatized companies keep their investment and employment commitments, the number of privatized firms that go bankrupt and, in a more macroeconomic sense, how well the economy of the five new federal states performs, and the length of time it takes to reduce unemployment and correct labor imbalances in the East.

There is no evidence so far to suggest that the doomsday scenarios about the return of large numbers of companies to the Treuhand's portfolio and waves of bankruptcies will be played out. As mentioned above, there is also some reason to believe that the investment commitments and job guarantees made in the privatization contracts will by and large be kept. Even as the economy of the western part of Germany is mired in recession, there was growth of almost 6 percent in the eastern part in 1993 and 8.5 percent is projected in 1994. The real challenge will be increasing the productivity of eastern workers. In the aggregate, productivity in the East is only about 50 percent of what it is in the West, but the wage level is rising almost to the western level. One should not be misled by this statistic, however. On an individual basis, eastern workers are just as skilled and productive as their western counterparts and perhaps even more motivated due to their relief at having a job in an economy that has 30 percent unemployment. The aggregate productivity imbalances in the East during the first phase of the Treuhand's activity have been largely the result of too many people working for companies in the Treuhand's portfolio, particularly the largest ones.

Observers will be watching closely to see how the government that comes to power at the end of 1994 balances the competing concerns of reducing subsidies to inefficient companies, increasing employment and productivity, and giving easterners the conviction that they have a stake in their transformed economy. The jury is still out. Much depends on whether investment commitments made by the buyers of Treuhand companies for the periods ending in 1995 and 1996 will provide the basis for the sustained growth of the privatized companies and the economy of Germany's five new states.

Notes

1. *Gesetz zur Privatisierung und Reorganisation des volkseigenen Vermögens vom 17 Juni 1990:* text in *Codex Iuris, Wiedervereinigungsrecht II—Eigentum, Investition, Vermögen,* ed. by Helmut Grieger, 2d. ed. Aug. 1992 (hereafter *Codex Iuris*).

2. The building itself has a more notorious history. Although designed before the Nazis came to power, it was completed in great haste between 1933 and 1935 in order to house Hermann Göring's Luftfahrtministerium, the Luftwaffe headquarters. It was also the headquarters of the Soviet occupation forces in East Berlin between 1945 and 1949.

3. *Gesetz zur Regelung offener Vermögensfragen vom 23 September 1990* (hereafter, the "Property Law"); as amended, in *Codex Iuris*. For an excellent description of how the Treuhand Law and the Property Law arose in the context of German unification and how they dealt with outstanding property claims, see Martin Elling, *Privatization in Germany: A Model for Legal and Functional Analysis,* 25 *Vanderbilt J. Transnational Law* 581-642 (Nov. 1992).

4. *Gesetz zur Regelung offener Vermögensfragen vom 23 September 1990,* text, as amended, in *Codex Iuris.*

5. *Gesetz zur Beseitigung von Hemmnissen bei der Privatisierung von Unternehmen und zur Förderung von Investitionen vom 22 März 1991,* text in *Codex Iuris.*

6. Unless otherwise noted, the source of all data in this report concerning the privatization activity of the Treuhand and the status of its portfolio comes from the *Monatsinformation der THA* dated as of 31 January 1994. This is a monthly summary of the Treuhand's activity prepared by the Central Auditing Department.

7. Although many potential investors inquire as to whether they can purchase only a majority stake in a Treuhand company, this solution has been looked upon with disfavor by the Treuhand for the same reason that investors are eager to have it; namely, that the German federal government would continue to have an equity interest in a private company. This explains the relatively low number of this type of transaction, most of which were completed in the early stages of the Treuhand.

8. Some 88 percent of the companies that the Treuhand liquidates are wound up according to this three year procedure. Approximately 12 percent are liquidated according to a procedure called *Gesamtvollstreckung* under German law, which means that the companies close their doors and cease operating as soon as the Treuhand decides to subject them to this procedure.

9. For a description of the first incarnation of the "Phase II" plan, see SZ Gespräch mit Treuhand-Chefin Birgit Breuel, *Süddeutsche Zeitung,* 19 February 1993, 26; and Treuhandanstalt / Pläne für die Phase II ab 1995–Auf die Nachfolgerin warten viele Aufgaben, *Handelsblatt,* 6 April 1993, 1. The successive steps for consolidating the Treuhand's operating divisions in the course of 1994 and the structure of Phase II successor entities are discussed in further detail in a letter dated 10 November 1993 from Frau Breul to Treuhand employees.

10. In addition to the entities described in the text, a company will provide various services (principally data processing and computer manaement) to the Treuhand and an entity known as the Verwaltungs und Verwertungs Gesellschaft vom Land- und forstwirtschaft Vermögen (BVVG), which will be responsible for the management and ultimate sale of agricultural land and forests within the territory of the former GDR. Through the end of January 1994, this agency had entered into 2,170 sales contracts resulting in DM 94 million in proceeds, and DM 1.162 billion in investment commitments. After 1995 the BVG is expected to employ between 300 and 470 workers. Both agriculture and forestry pose special problems, requiring the continued operation of the BVVG well into the future. On the agricultural end, most of the Treuhand's holdings are former agricultural production communes—huge groupings of farmland that have the potential to greatly increase Germany's agricultural production if fully exploited. This is problematic in the context of the European Union's general effort to reduce agricultural production and subsidies. As for the forests, the government in Bonn decided in 1993 that sales of wooded areas should be suspended pending a review of the environmental consequences of their sale to individuals.

11. For a general discussion of the legal issues relating to Treuhand privatization contracts, see Paul Dodds and Gerd Wächter, "Privatization Contracts with the German Treuhandanstalt: An Insider's Guide," *International Lawyer* (Spring

1993); and Thomas Kaiser, "Rechtsprobleme ausländischer Investoren in Ostdeutschland und wie wir sie lösen," (A presentation to the Treuhandanstalt Investment Fair Saxony, 6 May 1993, Leipzig).

12. "Treuhandanstalt / Die Einhaltung von Investitionszusagen und Beschäftingungsgarantie," *Handelsblatt*, 17 May 1993, 13.

13. "Breuel: 15 Prozent der Firmen halten Zusagen nicht ein," *Die Welt*, 14 June 1993, 15.

14. Ibid.

15. See Michael Muth, "Taking a Whole Economy Private: An Interview with Birgit Breuel, President of the Treuhandanstalt," *McKinsey Quarterly*, No. 1, (1993): 3–12.

16. See "Der Konjunktureinbruch hinterläßt auch bei der Treuhand seine Spüren," *Frankfurter Allgemeine Zeitung*, 14 June 1993, 13.

17. "Fast Alle Treuhandunternehmen durch Alteigentümer beansprucht," *Frankfurter Allgemeine Zeitung*, 25 February 1992, 17.

18. Ulrich Koch and Thomas Meyding, "GmbH & Co. KG: The German Peculiarity," in *International Financial Law Review*, (Special Supp April 1992).

19. For a fuller description of how the Management KGs are structured and operated, see "Die Management KG, Treuhandanstalt," Press Release from 17 February 1993.

20. Ibid.

21. "Die Treuhandanstalt bietet ihre Erfahrungen international an," *Frankfurter Allgemeine Zeitung*, 18 May 1993, 15.

22. "Privatisierung in der Moskauer Region mit deutscher Hilfe," *Frankfurter Allgemeine Zeitung*, 2 March 1993, 14.

2

The Politics of Restructuring Business Enterprises in the Former GDR: The Case of EKO Stahl

Mark J. Jrolf

As of 31 March 1993, almost three years after the economic and monetary union between East and West Germany, underemployment in the east was approaching 35 percent; state fiscal transfers from West to East had reached DM 220 billion per year; and over two thousand companies with 357,000 employees remained in the possession of the Treuhandanstalt (THA), the state privatization agency.[1] One hundred fifteen of these firms employed more than five hundred people each and, in many cases, supported entire communities. As the years passed, without private investors, the chances of these firms surviving in the market economy diminished. The threat of their closing, which would destroy the communities that depend on them, alarmed Germany's political leaders. The German government came to realize it could not wait for private investors to rescue the East. The government, through the THA, would have to initiate the restructuring itself.

The challenge of transforming companies into self-sustaining employers would surely be formidable. The experience in the new federal states has shown that large, unprivatized firms of the former German Democratic Republic (GDR) require a three-stage transformation process that consists of stabilization, adaptation, and a radical new product or production development to establish a competitive position in the new market economy. Managers can stem the losses by cutting costs and improving processes. They can make their firms look and act like western rivals by redesigning the organization and cultivating a capitalistic culture. Once they have overcome these formidable challenges, however, they are still left with a company lacking the critical elements of any successful business enterprise: customers and competitive advantage.

In a slowly growing market such as Europe's, opportunities for new firms come only with a major product or process innovation. Recognizing the need for innovation, the Treuhand officially supported the use of its funds for major investments in new technologies and facilities. In practice, however, using state funds to build potential competitors against powerful western firms proved politically difficult. The experience in the former GDR has revealed the inherent conflict in Bonn and Brussels between the need to foster the interests of the European Union's established institutions and the need to aid those states struggling to become freemarket democracies.

This chapter will examine the restructuring efforts of the EKO Stahl Company. As one of the GDR's largest flat-rolled steel producers, EKO supported the entire city of Eisenhüttenstadt, which was founded along with the steel mill in 1951. At the time of unification, EKO directly employed 11,500 of the city's 50,000 inhabitants and comprised 92 percent of its industrial revenues. After unification, the company lost its markets as the COMECON economies collapsed and western competitors arrived. Unable to privatize the company and unable to close it down, the Treuhandanstalt began the process of restructuring. EKO managers were able to stabilize the company and make significant progress adapting it to the demands of the market economy. They also developed a four-year investment plan that would revolutionize steel making in Germany and establish the company as a long-term competitor in the European market. Although the company surmounted many of the economic challenges, it took significant political power to overcome the influence of established western competitors in Bonn and Brussels.

The case of EKO Stahl demonstrates that the greatest obstacles to restructuring are not unskilled eastern managers, inefficient cost structures, or lack of market knowledge. Instead, eastern firms must overcome the lack of political will to allow them a realistic chance of survival at the possible expense of western competitors.

The purpose of this chapter is not to argue against the efforts to restructure eastern companies. Rather, it is to illustrate the steps being taken and to underscore the economic and political difficulty of creating the new economy. If officials are serious about saving jobs in the East, they must be prepared to accept the costs.

Restructuring Needs in the New Federal States

As in all other former centrally planned economies, most of the industrial enterprises of the GDR proved incapable of surviving in the new market economy without significant restructuring. Companies suffered a collapse in their traditional markets as former state-owned customers went bankrupt or reduced their inefficient production levels. The remaining demand has been diverted to higher-quality western suppliers. To recover from the dramatic dissolution of their customer base, firms must penetrate new western markets.

The loss of traditional markets has been particularly severe for industry. The economic and monetary union intensified western competition, making eastern exports more expensive.

The deficiencies of the state-owned firms led to inefficient structures, high costs, and a mix of poor-quality products that did not adequately serve customers' needs. To compete in the free market economy, firms must control costs, develop new products, enter new markets, and produce high-quality goods—all of this requires a massive restructuring and reeducation effort. "What is needed is nothing short," observe some economists, "of the orderly closing of most of the production structure and the creation of a whole new economy."[2]

Germany's initial policy was to let the market decide which elements of the old structure were worth saving and to close the remaining firms. It supported this policy with subsidies and tax incentives encouraging new investment. Private investors, however, bought too little of the old structure, and new investment was insufficient to fill the gap. Consequently, the Treuhand had to choose between liquidating much of eastern Germany's industrial base or leading the restructuring process itself.

The restructuring of EKO Stahl will be discussed below. While EKO was still a THA property, its eastern management team took responsibility for stabilizing the company and adapting it to the market economy. The company's long-term success, however, depended on its ability to muster the necessary capital and political clout to support investment in the most efficient steel production processes. Given Europe's steel overproduction, this would be a difficult task.

A Brief History

EKO Stahl and Eisenhüttenstadt ("city of iron melting") came into existence in 1951 when GDR planners sought to create jobs for the thousands of Germans returning from Germany's prewar possessions in the east. Located on the Oder River near the village of Fürstenberg, Eisenhüttenstadt grew with the steel mill into a city of fifty thousand. Since the EKO Stahl plant is the only major business in the area, the town depends wholly on the fortunes of the company.

Initially, planners envisioned developing EKO into a fully integrated steel mill. The mill would have the complete capacity to take the basic raw materials for steel—iron pellets, sinter, limestone and coke—and process them in a blast furnace, producing pig iron. The pig iron would then be processed in a basic oxygen furnace producing molten steel; further processed through a continuous caster, producing semi-finished steel products; and then run through hot-rolling and cold-rolling mills to produce slabs and sheets of flat-rolled steel.

The GDR's financial difficulties in the mid-1950s, however, meant plans had to be scaled back to simply a mill producing pig iron to be finished by other mills throughout the Eastern Block. In 1968 EKO was caught up in the move toward industrial centralization and at that time the company became the seat of an integrated group of steel industry companies: Bandstahlkombinat Eisenhüttenstadt Hermann Matern.

Throughout the 1960s and 1970s, EKO grew with the GDR economy. To support the Company's expansion, the GDR actively recruited citizens to move to Eisenhüttenstadt. Young workers were given higher salaries and larger apartments than those available elsewhere in the country. The region became an attractive destination for young families trying to improve their standard of living.

In 1984 EKO finally opened its flat-rolled steel mill. Built with the world's most modern technologies, the mill today remains one of Europe's most efficient. Its opening fulfilled every aspect of the company's original plan to become an integrated facility, except for the crucial hot-rolling capacity. The lack of such capacity meant that the EKO's production process continued to be hampered by inefficiency: EKO had to find customers for its semi-finished steel or transport it to firms with hot-rolling capacity and then bring it back again for cold rolling. To feed its cold-rolling mill, EKO therefore had its steel hot rolled by another firm or bought it directly from other companies. This meant that EKO faced not only an unreliable supply of steel but also additional costs for transport and for its suppliers' profit margins. This was the company's structure as unification approached.

On the eve of unification, the *Banstahlkombinat* Hermann Matern employed 17,000 workers and comprised steel-rolling and treatment plants in the towns of Finow, Oranienburg, Bad Salzungen, Burg, Olbernhau, and Aken, in addition to the EKO Stahl plant in Eisenhüttenstadt. EKO employed 11,510 people with a total annual output of more than 6.5 million tons of steel.

Prior to unification, EKO appeared to be one of the healthier companies in the GDR. The company operated at 90 percent of capacity and sold roughly 90 percent of its production domestically. EKO's pig iron production primarily supplied its own molten steel facility. It sold two-thirds of the semi-finished steel production to other GDR steel firms. The other third traveled west for hot-rolling and then back to Eisenhüttenstadt. The company's cold-rolling facility supplied flat-rolled product to the GDR auto industry and manufacturers of home products, such as washing machines and refrigerators. The firm also successfully sold 500,000 tons of flat-rolled steel to the West.

The Treuhand Takes Over EKO

On 17 June 1990 with a treaty for economic and monetary union already signed and political union clearly in sight, the GDR's first democratically elected government legally transferred all state-owned enterprises to the THA. The government commissioned the Treuhand to: (1) privatize wherever possible, (2) restructure companies with a view to later privatization, and (3) close companies with no chance of surviving in a market economy. Restructuring meant breaking up the *Kombinate*, selling or closing unnecessary divisions, and reducing over employment. Accordingly, the THA dissolved the strip steel *Kombinat* (Bandstahlkombinant) and reincorporated the operations in Eisenhüttenstadt as EKO Stahl AG.

In constructing EKO's managing board, or *Vorstand*, the Treuhand took the unusual step of naming three executives who were with the company prior to unification, and only one from western Germany.

Dr. Karl Doring, former general director of the Bandstahlkombinat Eisenhüttenstadt, is chairman of the *Vorstand* and chiefly responsible for the manufacturing function. He studied in the Soviet Union and served previously as the deputy minister for metallurgy in the GDR. Mr. Conrad, a forty-year veteran of EKO and formerly responsible for information and statistics at the company, leads finance and controlling. The chief of marketing, Mr. Hoppe, has been with the company for over twenty years and ran distribution prior to unification. The fourth member of the *Vorstand*, Mr. Neumann, is the only senior manager from western Germany. He is the director of personnel and human resources. Mr. Neumann previously headed the division of personnel at a subsidiary of the German steel giant, Thyssen, in Essen.

One would think such a management team dominated by easterners might lack the skills needed to lead the transition to a market economy. On the contrary, EKO's managers rose to the challenge of saving their company and skillfully reduced the firm's losses, improved its efficiency, and began to adapt to western market demands.

EKO Management Reacts to Crisis

With unification came the collapse in EKO's markets. Total sales fell by 50 percent between 1989 and 1991. With the invasion of western goods, eastern auto and white goods industries virtually ceased to exist. Consequently, sales of flat-rolled products from the cold-rolling mill fell by 46 percent. A 73 percent drop in steel production throughout the GDR from 1989 to 1990 led to the loss of the company's key customers for semi-finished steel and pig iron.[3] Outside sales for these two products fell by 31 percent and 95 percent, respectively, from 1989 to 1991. In many cases, customers who managed to maintain their production levels switched their orders from EKO to higher-quality western suppliers. The company also lost sales because some of EKO's steel-manufacturing customers were sold to German steel firms in the West. The new owners substituted steel from their own facilities for supply from EKO.

As the company's markets began evaporating, it faced severe financial difficulties. Falling sales meant falling production. EKO's capacity utilization rate fell from 90 percent in 1989 to 41 percent in 1992, making it impossible for the company to cover its fixed costs. In addition, the company's per-person labor costs rose to west German levels by April 1994, and the market price of steel was falling precipitously. EKO's new owner, the Treuhand, had three options: rely on the Finance Ministry to cover the enormous losses until a private investor could be found, liquidate the firm, or start the restructuring process at once. The Treuhand directed the company to begin the stabilization phase of a restructuring program.

In reaction to plummeting sales, EKO management immediately acted to contain costs by cutting back production, eliminating the multiple layers of management, reducing the number of production workers, and breaking down vertical integration. Production was cut back to correspond to falling sales, rather than build unwanted inventories. By 1992 production had fallen by 55 percent from 6.5 million tons in 1989, leaving approximately 60 percent excess capacity at the company. Although the company did not immediately dismantle its unused capacity, it acted quickly to eliminate the redundant jobs. Between 1989 and 1992 EKO reduced the workforce by 70 percent, cutting not only those jobs associated with the decline in production, but also those representing the over-employment that existed prior to unification. By the rough measure of the number of tons produced per employee, productivity increased 50 percent, from 566 tons per employee in 1989 to 846 tons in 1992.

The management structure of the EKO *Kombinat* under the GDR had evolved into a complex bureaucracy, much of which was irrelevant to the production of steel. For example, it was responsible for meeting the planning and security control needs of the central ministries. For this purpose it created a *Stabs- und Funktionalorgane des Generaldirektors*. The technical staff of the *Organe* oversaw the activities of the entire company, duplicating many functions carried out elsewhere in the firm. Management layers were also created to provide positions and titles for Party members in good standing.

By 1993 EKO management had cut the numbers of managers to 235 (in 1989 the company had 500 managers). It also halved the layers between a production worker and the executive board from eight to four.

EKO's top executives focused on the company's core business by divesting many tangential operations. The firm privatized, or reincorporated as separate businesses, operations such as transport, hydraulic maintenance, industrial gases, and office supplies. In total, EKO resettled 36 companies and 1,574 jobs. Other layoffs were concentrated around activities that had lost their market or could be performed more efficiently outside the company. Such areas included equipment building and the manufacture of spare parts.

The company's managers alone determined how many and who would be laid off. They made the staff reductions systematically and as constructively as possible. Between 1989 and 1993 approximately eight thousand employees left EKO. In the initial uncertainty of 1990 and 1991 more than a thousand workers resigned and moved to the west, at times at a rate of one hundred per month. Fifteen hundred workers were resettled in the operations spun off from EKO. Another seventeen hundred workers over the age of 55 took early retirement, and approximately one thousand workers accepted a severance package available to employees over the age of 50 and/or were permanently assigned to the part-time work program. The remainder were put into part-time jobs or state-financed work programs.

EKO rebuilt its organization to take on the challenges of the free market. Managers and employees went to classes and seminars; the company developed an advanced cost-control system, built a marketing organization, and began revamping its manufacturing operations with a customer-oriented "total quality management (TQM)" program.

EKO Identifies and Controls Costs

Immediately after economic and monetary union, EKO began working with retired executives from western German steel companies to design a cost-control and information system. EKO hoped the system would accurately measure the cost of producing particular products and running certain processes. With this information, managers could make cost-benefit decisions, design restructuring plans, manage cost-cutting programs, make pricing decisions, and more. The system could also help develop a profit-oriented mentality in the company.

EKO's controlling function had been fairly well developed prior to unification because of the central planners' appetite for information. The information, however, was not always useful for management decision making. Costs were tracked closely, but only in the aggregate. The system did not indicate, for example, how much labor or energy was consumed producing a particular product or running a particular process. In 1987 and 1988 the company's managers—feeling overburdened by the central planners' ever-increasing production requirements—undertook a project to measure profits and losses based on Western market prices. By demonstrating that some types of production were profitable and others were not, EKO hoped it could convince the state to allocate its capacity to the profitable lines and stop requesting the unprofitable production. Although the plan ultimately did not interest the state, it did force EKO to develop a more detailed knowledge of its costs.

Thanks to those previous efforts, EKO was able to develop a fully automated system in conjunction with the management consulting firm, Roland Berger. The new system enabled the company to allocate direct and indirect costs to specific products. With this information EKO can calculate, for example, the additional cost of specifically producing for auto manufacturers. Companies use this cost information to set prices and develop budgets. At firms transforming from a planned economy, however, the exercise can be made more difficult by unstable markets and excessive overcapacity.

Collapsing markets or, in the case of EKO, a European steel crisis, can make forecasts unreliable. If the company expected to sell a thousand tons of steel in 1993 and has fixed costs of DM 10,000, it would need to charge DM 10 per ton to cover its fixed costs. The company would base its pricing decision on the notion that its costs per ton are its variable costs plus DM 10. If the market collapses mid-year and the company only sells five hundred tons, its fixed costs will be DM 20 per ton. EKO, like many western companies, began recalculating its standard costs every six months in order to diminish the risk of inaccurate pricing in unstable markets.

Whereas unstable markets lead to incorrect forecasts, overcapacity can lead managers to make the wrong decisions with a technically correct forecast. The types of fixed costs associated with capacity include depreciation, energy, and maintenance. Firms like EKO, which utilize only 40 percent of total capacity, have excessive unused capacity and, therefore, high fixed costs relative to what they produce. If EKO were to divide its expected production by total fixed costs, including the depreciation of unused capacity, it would calculate an extremely high fixed cost per ton of production. Using this information for pricing decisions, or to decide whether or not to produce a product, would lead the company to either price far above the market or decide not to produce anything. EKO chose to account for this by including only 75 percent of its fixed costs in standard costs. Furthermore, it began using a pure variable cost estimate to know the point below which it should not produce in the short term. By adapting its cost system to account for these variables, the company is making decisions now to secure its market position in the future.

EKO uses its cost system to manage the transformation from a production-oriented system to a profit-oriented one. Each month managers receive a cost report for their area and must explain all deviations from their budget. EKO is implementing a cost reduction program in the same way. Managers set cost reduction targets and then measure their actual performance on a monthly basis. Any failure to meet the targets must be explained to the *Vorstund*. With the new cost system, the company also tracks other costs for the first time, such as the capital cost of holding excessive inventories.

The information is also useful to other departments. Marketing can estimate the cost of large, special projects. Quality control uses it to measure the cost of poor quality. The system is not yet used to determine goal-oriented incentive pay. Nonetheless, EKO's cost control system has oriented the whole company toward thinking of costs—just as the consultants would have designed it.

EKO Builds a Marketing Organization

EKO management set out a marketing strategy that stressed three objectives: (1) to sell high-quality flat-rolled steel to key west German steel customers, (2) to strengthen ties with remaining customers in the new federal states, and (3) to strengthen ties with the former Soviet republics. To pursue its strategy, the company immediately organized a sales force and marketing team of former engineers, technicians, and production workers. The new team knew a great deal about the product and its performance. They knew nothing, however, about catering to customers or setting prices. The company and its new marketing team had no experience analyzing potential markets, evaluating competitors, or identifying customers and their product needs.

The new team tried to develop its marketing skills as quickly as possible through both formal, consultant-led courses and extensive experience sharing. Consultants taught market analysis, pricing, and sales force organization, while effective sales representatives were devloped in a series of conferences within the company.

Consistent with its three marketing objectives, the company organized the sales department into three divisions focusing on western Germany, the new federal states, and Russian–Eastern Europe markets. The company's market strategy for western Germany focused on developing closer ties with western customers and establishing a reputation as a quality producer. It opened a sales office in the city of Essen immediately after unification and implemented the following four goals to overcome its image as a supplier of low-cost, low-quality products:

1. to improve the quality of production;
2. to offer more sophisticated products;
3. to reintroduce the company to the customer through customer conferences and trade shows; and
4. to working directly with major customers to build a "quality/ service" partnership.

Although the market in the new federal states had collapsed, EKO saw long-term value in maintaining its relationships with its traditional customers there. The company chose to serve the region out of both its headquarters in Eisenhüttenstadt, and a new subsidiary formed with west German Krupp Stahl. Called EKO Krupp Stahl Handel (EKS), the new subsidiary supplies small customers in the new federal states. Although EKS would seem to be a good place for EKO to learn western marketing techniques, it is staffed primarily by EKO employees and, therefore, transfers very few of Krupp's skills.

EKO manages its Russian–Eastern Europe market from a newly established export office in Berlin (called EKO Stahl Handel) and the main office in Eisenhüttenstadt. Shortly after unification, the German steel giant, Thyssen, bought a 51 percent stake in EKO Stahl Handel. The subsidiary sells primarily to smaller customers throughout Western and Eastern Europe.

Surprisingly, the partnership with Thyssen has yielded few strategic benefits. Like at EKS, most of the employees are from EKO, providing little opportunity for learning. Furthermore, Thyssen does not serve any of its own customers through EKO Stahl Handel, eliminating any opportunity for EKO to open new markets through Thyssen.

Eisenhüttenstadt handles the company's larger customers in the Russian—Eastern Europe market. Early on, EKO identified its relationship with Russia as a unique competitive advantage. Although the Russian market has had been difficult since the fall of communism, EKO believes the relationship will eventually pay off. The company is one of the very few in western Europe that have successfully conducted business with the former Soviet Union. In 1992 EKO was selling more than 250,000 tons, or 35 percent of its flat-rolled steel production, to Russia through a direct barter agreement: Russia takes the cold-rolled flat steel in exchange for the hot-rolled steel EKO needs to make its cold-rolled sheet. Although the quality of Russian hot-rolled is not always sufficient for the company's western customers, the barter arrangement allows EKO to continue nurturing this valuable relationship. In contrast, many other companies have lost their ties to the Russian market.

EKO Becomes a "Total Quality" Organization

The company's chances of penetrating western markets and competing with established western producers depend heavily on its ability to become a quality-oriented organization. High-quality production is critical to delivering more sophisticated products, satisfying customers, and lowering costs. To achieve it, however, the "total quality" mentality must permeate the entire company.

Prior to unification, EKO managers knew of the need to focus on quality. Each company in the GDR was responsible for the quality of the goods it delivered. If a customer could not use the goods available, the supplier had to import replacements. For this reason, delivering unusable goods added a great deal to companies' costs. Unfortunately, this regulation did not enforce widespread quality discipline, because "unusable" still permitted significant imperfections. EKO's small export trade also made the firm familiar with quality standards in the West. Under the monopolistic conditions of the planned economy, however, there was no incentive to adopt these standards.

Following unification, EKO made total quality management (TQM) a top priority. The company began to implement its quality program through extensive training courses for all employees. It listed quality measures in the job descriptions of each employee and enforced quality assurance methods throughout the company.

EKO's TQM plan included a twenty-day training program for every employee that emphasizes the value individual workers can add to the company and encourages employees to become decision makers. In addition, participants learn specific techniques for measuring their own performance, such as statistical process control, and exercising their problem-solving abilities. Other courses include customer service for production workers and technical steel performance measures for salesmen. At the end of the twenty days, participants lead a group of colleagues through the investigation of a particular company problem. The company hopes its employees will use this training to take on a greater role in ensuring high-quality work.

EKO also redesigned its business process to give the quality department some control over production. Under the new structure, customer orders proceed from sales to quality assurance, rather than directly to manufacturing. Quality assurance then determines the production specifications for each product and follows the product through its manufacture. With this mechanism, the customer's needs drive the entire production process.

The company estimated in early 1993 that it had implemented 60 percent of its quality program. Outdated equipment and the lack of hot-rolling capacity, however, continue to hamper the company's efforts. EKO works closely with its equipment suppliers to improve the performance of the equipment it has, but real progress requires significant new investment.

Successful Adaptation?

EKO quickly took great strides toward becoming a competitive producer and was able to succeed in some important markets. By 1992 sales to western Germany quadrupled to 425,000 tons. EKO had landed contracts with Mercedes Benz, BMW, VW, and Opel. It introduced a number of new products and improved quality in many areas. The transformation, however, was not yet complete.

According to company estimates, only the west German market, where EKO provided a higher value-added product, was profitable. Its business with Russia covered costs, while business outside of Germany and in the former Eastern Bloc was not profitable. One cannot easily judge this lack of profitability. The entire flat-rolled steel industry was suffering through a difficult price competition, with the market price of some of the company's traditional cold-rolled steel product falling by 40 percent since 1990.

Excess capacity, the lack of hot-rolling capacity, and the difficulty of breaking into new markets all slowed EKO's transformation. The company's managers realized that becoming as good as its western competitors would not be sufficient to take sales away from them. EKO must be better. Making this jump would require either a great deal of time and luck, or significant investment in new product development and production processes. The EKO team of eastern managers again demonstrated its ability in this final component of the restructuring. It designed a sweeping investment plan to transform itself into a modern "minimill" steel producer fashioned after the Nucor example in the United States.

EKO's Long-Term Investment Plan

In late 1992 EKO's management proposed a long-term business plan to transform the company into a self-sustaining competitor in western markets. The plan called for the following three developments:

1. It would modernize the cold-rolling mill at a cost of DM 310 million.
2. It would close the company's 2.40 million-ton annual capacity pig iron and 2.12 million-ton annual capacity molten steel facilities and replace them with a 900,000 annual capacity ton electric furnace. The electric furnace would make steel from 100 percent scrap rather than the more expensive process of making pig iron from ore and coke and molten steel in a basic oxygen furnace. The electric furnace would cost DM 200 million.
3. The electric furnace would pour hot steel directly into a newly developed thin-slab caster that automatically produces slabs of hot-rolled thickness. The thin-slab caster would require an investment of DM 550 million.

For a total investment of DM 1.06 billion, EKO would likely become one of Europe's most efficient steel producers. The electric furnace technology has enabled many new firms to enter the stagnant U.S. steel industry. These new minimills have successfully taken market share away from the established integrated producers by beating them on flexibility and price. In their 1986 study, Donald Barnett and Robert Crandall estimated that an efficient minimill could produce one ton of steel rod at approximately 66 percent of the operating cost of an integrated firm.[4] U.S. minimills are now beginning to employ the thin-slab casting technology to compete with the integrated producers in the large market for flat-rolled steel. Nucor Corporation entered the market in 1989 and has already captured 1 million tons of business. With a cost advantage of at least $45 per ton over every other producer, Nucor is confident it can continue to make gains in this last stronghold of the integrated producers.

Following the Nucor model, EKO's business plan would make it a more profitable, albeit smaller, company by 1997. The company has estimated that the new structure would enable it to reduce per-ton material costs by one third and personnel costs by half. After taking increased energy usage into account, EKO expected to decrease total costs by 18 percent as a percentage of sales, allowing the company to become profitable for perhaps the first time in its existence.

EKO was fortunate to have arrived at a business concept that would give it a competitive advantage in its existing area of expertise. Enriched with a management team that proved its ability to adapt to the market economy and with a viable plan for the future, EKO seemed to be one of the best candidates for state-led restructuring. Unfortunately, the strength of EKO's plan pitted it directly against the interests of west European steel producers, eager to protect their hard-won markets. In this environment, the imperative of rescuing the East was eclipsed by self-interest.

European Commission Blocks Restructuring Plan

In many ways, EKO Stahl has been a model for transforming businesses of the former Eastern Bloc into capitalist competitors. Its management made great strides in cutting costs and creating a culture focused on the customer and overall quality. To succeed in the stagnant western market, however, requires a better product or process than that offered by established firms. Developing a better product or process requires significant investment. In the case of most of the Treuhand's unprivatized businesses, this investment must come from the state. By definition, if the restructuring succeeds, the state's investment will have created not only sustainable employer in the East but also competition for the West's established firms. Failure to sort out this political dilemma at the outset threatens to send the European Union and the German government down a costly path of investing considerable sums in the stabilization and mainstreaming of firms, only to see the rescue foiled by political realities. If state funds cannot be invested in the task of creating eastern competitors, then the companies ought to be closed immediately. Perhaps the money could be spent more productively on attracting new businesses to the area.

The European Commission recommended that the Council of Ministers vote against the EKO plan. Because EKO falls under the jurisdiction of the European Coal and Steel Community, Brussels can block any program requiring state aid. It chose not to consider the restructuring needs of the new federal states as a special case, deciding instead to lump EKO together with long-established firms in Spain and Italy making similar requests.

Brussels argued against the EKO plan on the following three grounds:

1. The prospects of the planned technologies at EKO were more dubious than presented.
2. The absence of a private investor characterized the EKO plan as 100 percent state aid and called into question the plan's basic soundness.
3. The EKO plan called for massive state subsidies to increase steel capacity at a time when the EU needed to reduce overcapacity.

None of these three arguments was valid given the special situation in the new federal states. First, the electric furnace and thin-slab casting technologies included in the EKO plan have yielded great success in the United States. These technologies are very well suited to smaller firms less capable of making large capital investments. Second, private investors—in this case large, foreign steel firms—did not pursue EKO because of the limitations of operating within the European Coal and Steel Community. While the Union's restrictions on capacity and production discourage foreign investors, they provide enough flexibility to allow EKO to earn sufficient returns to maintain a satisfactory base of employment in Eisenhüttenstadt. Finally, EKO's plan would significantly contribute to the reduction of Europe wide steel capacity. According to EKO's plan, the company would eliminate its pig iron capacity, its raw steel capacity would be reduced from 2.1 million tons to 900,000 tons, and its cold-rolling capacity would drop from 1.8 million tons to 1.2 million tons.

The Commission countered by claiming that the introduction of the thin-slab caster (which effectively would have added 900,000 tons of hot-rolled capacity annually) would have offset the 58 percent reduction in capacity. However, in addition to being much smaller than this reduction, the 900,000-ton addition of hot-rolled capacity would not have represented a loss of production to any of the existing hot-rolled producers. With 75 percent of EKO's hot-rolled steel coming from Russia, European suppliers would not lose sales if EKO produced for its own needs. The Russian capacity is not likely to otherwise enter the European market because of the complicated barter arrangement required and because of its poor quality. Nor would refusing EKO permission to build the thin-slab caster with state funds create hot-rolled business for the established competitors. Without this technology, EKO would likely close.

The EKO plan offered the company and the city of Eisenhüttenstadt a realistic chance of surviving. The anxiety in Brussels was understandable: Investing DM 1 billion of state money in a steel company in the new federal states is a risky move, especially when other steel industry firms throughout Europe were closing their doors. Politicians are nevertheless paid to make these difficult decisions. If they believed the companies of the former GDR did not deserve special treatment, then the original Treuhand privatize-or-liquidate policy should be pursued. Companies not yet privatized should be closed so that those funds can be redeployed toward a more productive venture. If on the other hand they believe that these companies deserve a chance to compete in a market economy, then state-supported restructuring should proceed, and privatization should be completed.

Epilogue

As of June 1994 the fate of EKO remained undecided. The business plan had not been implemented and privatization had not been completed. During the spring of 1994 it appeared that a successful sale had been negotiated among Riva, an Italian steel group, EKO, and the Treu-hand. Riva's plans included the development of the 900,000-ton-per-year hot-rolling mill. It was accepted by German and EU authorities only on the condition that EKO's capacity elsewhere be cut back. Apparently, however, disputes regarding the timing of layoffs and the composition of the advisory board ultimately caused Riva to walk away from the deal.

The failure of the Riva bid prompted a previous consortium, whose members include the western German companies Thyssen and Preussag, to reconsider their interest. However, it appears that the political issue of whether or not to continue support of EKO remains at the center of dis-cussions, resulting in ongoing difficulties in reaching a sales agreement acceptable to bidders, company management, the Treuhand and EU officials.

Notes

1. The number of underemployed includes the unemployed, and people in reduced work-time programs (*Kurzarbeit*) or temporary work programs (*arbeitsbe-schäftigung Maßnahme*). *Ausgewahlte Wirtshaftsdaten zur Lage in den neuen Bun-desländern*, Bundesministerium für Wirtschaft, 12 March 1993. Transfers between East and West: Herbert Henzler and H.C. Lothar Späth, "Zur wirtschaftlichen Entwicklung der neuen Bundesländer, Ein Playdöyer für neue Wege und Strate-gien," 19 October 1992. Number of Treuhand firms and employees: *Monatsinfor-mation der THA*, Treuhandanstalt, 31 March 1993.

2. Olivier Blanchard, Rudiger Dornbusch, Paul Krugman, Richard Layard, Lawrence Summers, *Reform in Eastern Europe*, 1991, xvi.

3. Bertold Huber, "Work and the Unions," *German Politics and Society*, (Summer 1991) 41.

4. Donald F. Barnett and Robert W. Crandall, *Up From the Ashes: The Rise of the Steel Minimill in the United States*, August 1986.

3

Less than a Universe of Difference:
Evaluating the Reality
of German Finance

Adam S. Posen

On 24 March 1993 Daimler-Benz AG announced that it had reached an agreement about accounting practices with the United States Securities and Exchange Commission (SEC). This agreement enabled the corporation to be the first German firm to directly list its shares on the New York Stock Exchange, beginning 5 October 1993.[1] Daimler's decision represents more than the groundwork for a single, albeit large, financial transaction. It is also the choice of one financial system, the Anglo-American arm's-length transactions model, over another, the Germanic model of relationship banking. The firm choosing in this case was the very one whose close, long-term, relationship with Germany's largest bank has long exemplified the German system.

Moreover, Daimler's announcement coincided with the emergence of an opposing consensus in the United States. After fifteen years of study and hand-wringing over the United States' failure to invest for the long-term, a wide range of business leaders, policymakers, and academics finally agreed that the U.S. system of allocating capital investment was failing. They further agreed to advocate a change to something resem-

Initial research for this chapter was carried out while the author was a Robert Bosch Foundation Fellow in the Federal Republic of Germany, 1992–1993. The author is grateful to the Bosch Foundation and the Brookings Institution for financial support, and to his two host institutions in Germany—Deutsche Bank's Berlin Region and the Deutsche Bundesbank—as well as to numerous individual German bankers and economists for their help and advice. The contents of the chapter remain solely the author's responsibility.

bling the German system, which deemphasizes short-run stock performance and encourages equity stakes by banks in industrial firms.[2]

How can Daimler-Benz's decision—and similar choices taken by an increasing number of other German firms—be reconciled with the widely perceived advantages of relationship banking with one of Germany's *Grossbanken?* Furthermore, why have innovative startup firms consistently been denied access to such banking relationships, or even domestic venture capital, throughout the postwar era in Germany, if German lending takes such a long-term perspective? What explains the failure of the German banks to take equity stakes in, and provide long-term loans to, many of the most viable firms in the *neuen Bundesländer* (the new federal states of the former German Democratic Republic) as they already did in analogous situations during the late nineteenth century and in two postwar reconstructions in this century? The answers lie in understanding German investment.

The Idealized Picture of German Industrial Finance

German relationship banking has long been a strong alternative to the Walrasian, transactions-based capital markets of the Anglo-American countries. For some historians,[3] bank-firm ties were the common thread of German industrial development. German bankers themselves sharply contrast their practices to the impersonal and short-term finance in the United States, the United Kingdom, and other liberal economies.[4] The widespread impression of dense overlapping ties between German banks and German industry gave rise to the *Macht der Banken* debate in 1970s. During the debate, a number of members of both the Free Democratic Party (FDP) and Social Democratic Party (SPD) lent support to the curtailing of bank power, the lasting effects of which persist to this day.

Nonetheless, closer examination of the record indicates that the differences between German and Anglo-American banking, as well as the power of banks over German industry, are exaggerated. What we can term the "idealized model" of German finance, which is explicitly or implicitly behind most discussions of the German investment time-horizon,[5] misrepresents the actual practices of German banks with respect to the processing and offering of information, and the extent of the banks' coincidence of interests with their industrial clients.

The idealized model of German finance has nine elements, each one of which distinguishes German finance from post-1930s American finance. First, every German firm has a single *Hausbank* which is the source of all financial services for the firm.[6] Second, the bank providing the services is a universal bank, so it is legally capable of meeting any customer need. Third, the major form of investment finance for firms is long-term bank lending. Fourth, the criteria German banks employ for deciding on loan projects go beyond the financial numbers to future prospects of the firm. Fifth, when a firm runs into short-run difficulties, the bank tides it over or restructures it without foreclosing.

Sixth, the bank takes an equity stake in the firm as an investment. Seventh, the bank votes most of the firm's shares, between its own holdings, shares lent by other banks, and proxies given by small shareholders.[7] Eighth, senior bank officials serve on the *Aufsichtsrat* (supervisory board) of the firm. And finally, the bank provides industry-specific advising on strategic and technical matters.

If all nine aspects of the German financial relationship were indeed the case, it would be easy to explain long investment time-horizons. The bank would have all the corporate customer's financial business; it could provide the necessary services; and it would not alter its lending precipitously in response to short-run deviations in earnings. Moreover, the idealized German bank would have the incentive to see the company perform well, the information necessary not only to monitor but also to improve company performance, and the power to implement its recommendations. In the idealized view, the German bank is the all-knowing, all-powerful principal, and the German firm is its "constrained-to-flourish" agent. Yet each one of these aspects is weaker than is generally assumed, and a couple of them are simply false.

The Actual Borrowers and Lenders

Foremost in the idealized picture is that every German bank envisions itself as though it were Deutsche Bank, Germany's largest bank. The average German lender is in fact a local *Sparkasse* (state government-owned savings bank) or *Volks/Raiffsenbank* (credit cooperative, rural, or union tied). These two bank groups (as defined by the Deutsche Bundesbank) provided 32.4 percent of all long-term lending to German nonfinancial firms in 1990, and consistently over 30 percent of such lending since 1970. In contrast, the share of German long-term lending to industry provided by the *Grossbanken* has more than doubled since 1960,[8] but from a starting base of only 4 percent. All privately owned banks, including the big three, only provided 22.4 percent of long-term lending in 1990, up from 12.0 percent in 1970, but most of this growth in the lending business has come at the expense of government programs.[9]

Sparkassen and *Kreditgenossenschaften* do not have the capabilities of the idealized model described above. They must farm out to their group clearing banks (the *Landesbanken*, the *Deutsche Girozentrale*, or the *Bank für Gemeinwirtschaft*) almost all financial services beyond simple lending, despite their legal status as universal banks.[10] Constrained by charter to take fewer risks with their assets than private banks, they also have additional limits on their ability to take equity positions in their clients, and are legally confined to serving the needs of particular (often small) regions. Finally, these savings banks and credit unions do not have the research teams or consulting expertise necessary to advise firms on strategic or industry-specific planning.[11] In short, the large share of German industry that borrows from this sector receives few of the touted benefits of German banking.

A similar point may be made with regard to the borrowers in the German economy; if all banks are thought to be Deutsche Bank in the model, all firms are discussed as though they are AEG, Daimler-Benz, or Mannesmann. In fact, the bulk of German industry is composed of thousands of small- and medium-sized companies of the *Mittelstand*. These companies usually do not have publicly traded stock, and they often have *Beiräte* (advisory boards), if anything, rather than *Aufsichtsräte* (supervisory boards). Banks have far fewer formalized channels of access and control to these smaller firms.

Sources and Forms of Financing

The idealized German banking model does not even hold up when one considers those firms that *do* borrow from private universal banks. Small firms usually deal with two to three banks, while large firms will often have more than one *Grossbank* as part of a syndicate.[12] In recent years, the largest German firms have gone directly to capital markets themselves, as in most of the industrial world. Moreover, the array of financial services offered by any of the larger private German banks except the *Grossbanken* has been shrinking in recent years as part of a widespread strategy of niche marketing through specialization.[13] Meanwhile, the big three have acquired consulting firms, insurance companies, and mortgage banks, among other things, as they seek to become truly one-stop financial supermarkets *(Allfinanz)*. Nonetheless, they have largely failed to integrate the activities within the firm or to capture many economies of scale.

Deutsche Bank, for example, acquired Roland Berger and the Deutsche Gesellschaft für Mittelstandsberatung (a consulting firm focused on the *Mittelstand* market) to offer strategic advice, Morgan Grenfell in London to offer investment banking, and a number of insurance firms. Yet they have offered neither significant competition for (the often foreign) specialist firms in these expanding market areas, nor have these acquisitions been sufficiently integrated into the main holding company to gain any real benefits from economies of scale. In fact, under the current *Vorstand*, Deutsche Bank policy has emphasized leaving these and further acquisitions to their own devices and identities.

Furthermore, while long-term bank loans remain the most important source of external finance for German firms, retained earnings are and have always been the greatest source of investment finance overall. From 1980 to 1989, the share of German industrial firms' investment financing contributed by retained earnings was 67.2 percent, similar to the shares of 61.8 percent from 1970 to 1979 and 65.9 percent from 1960 to 1969. Studies confirm that the bank-lending share of long-term investment finance in Germany (11.1 percent from 1980 to 1989, 13.6 percent from 1970 to 1979, and 11.2 percent from 1960 to 1969) is in line with that of the United Kingdom and the United States, among others.[14] They also show that around 20 percent of total (both short- and long-term) external funds for industry come from banks in most major economies, including Germany. Although German firms may have a capital base tied more to debt than to stock than the typical Anglo-American firm, at the margin they rely on bank lending to the same degree.

Lending Criteria and Project Appraisal

In appraising creditworthiness, the German banks do not differ as much from their Anglo-American counterparts as is often held to be the case. A sampling of various banks' training materials and of actual *Risikoraster*, i.e., risk rating forms (the scoring sheets used by banks' corporate department loan officers to evaluate loan applications), reveal no instance where a weight of less than 20 percent was placed on either the applicant firm's current balance sheet or their provision of collateral;[15] cashflow might be weighted a little low by U.S. banking standards, while the weight on collateral is at least as high. Discussions with German bankers show collateral tends to play a larger role than in the United States.

Unlike American bankers, German bankers also took into account (between 10 and 20 percent of the point score) the personal qualities of the prospective borrower, i.e. management skill, trustworthiness, commitment to the firm. Like collateral, these personal issues loomed large in discussions held by German loan officers. These impressions of the loan criteria used by German banks are supported by research into a representative sample of textbooks used for training German bankers:[16] the texts offered instructions in the number crunching aspects of loan appraisal that would be familiar to any reader of analogous American textbooks, but they also featured sections stressing the importance of personal factors and collateral.

German bankers also appear more patient with firms' short-term difficulties once a loan has been made, although it still does not reach the levels ascribed to the bankers in the idealized model. Putting aside the famous case of the AEG rescue in 1983, which was based on government pressure and funding, German banks do bail out and restructure troubled firms far more frequently than U.S. or U.K. investors do, but this appears to be the exception rather than the rule.[17] The question of collateral is pivotal in banks' decisions on whether to intervene on a client's behalf or to simply foreclose; where banks have enough collateral, they can afford to let firms go under, whereas "banks are more inclined to participate in rescues the more they stand to lose because a smaller proportion of their loans are secured by collateral."[18] The tendency toward caution is compounded by the legal liability to other stakeholders which German banks assume if they take charge of a rescue effort. In short, German banks do engage in rescues, but usually only where they are the major exposed stakeholder.

Participation and Board Representation

These rescues, however, are the main source of equity stakes by banks in nonfinancial firms. It is rare for a German bank to acquire a *Beteiligung* (participation) solely for investment purposes. The bulk of bank holdings even now represents shares given in lieu of other collateral by nonbank firms during the postwar reconstruction. The size of the holdings in relation to the limited liquidity of the German stock markets, and the need to declare capital gains on stocks that are listed in company books at their original purchase price, deter their sale. The enormous share of Daimler-Benz held by Deutsche Bank (25.4 percent in 1992), for example, only reached such heights as part of an effort to block the takeover of a controlling interest in the firm by Kuwaiti buyers after the Flick Trust sold its shares in the 1960s. Deutsche Bank has nevertheless managed to reduce its Daimler holdings from a high of 31 percent, and all the banks have been slowly reducing their portfolios of unrelated businesses.

This does not preclude beneficial effects of share ownership on the banks' part for those firms in which the participation is significant. These effects are indeed amplified by the voting of small shareholder proxies, as outlined in the idealized vision of German banking. Because the shareholdings by the banks are taken reluctantly, however, and are usually the result of accident rather than of strategic investment, the effect on German industry is quite limited and haphazard. Furthermore, the amassing of share voting power has usually been used to block shareholder initiatives, often of a political nature, rather than to set business policy. As in U.S. companies, corporate decisions are generally taken elsewhere than at annual meetings.

The *Aufsichtsrat* is often supposed to be the "elsewhere" where decisions are made. Yet the notion that German bankers parlay their board seats into advising and monitoring of German firms' activities is exaggerated, even for those firms structured with the two tier board system. The supervisory boards meet two to four times a year, working on an agenda set by the management board, which is composed solely of firm insiders. It is exceedingly rare for even the chairman of the supervisory board to take an active rather than reactive stance. Meanwhile, the supervisory board has about a 50 percent chance of being chaired by the firm's former CEO *(Vorstand Sprecher)*, hardly an outside force. Only major decisions, such as plant closings or takeovers, are required by law to be discussed by the board; and given that union representation on the supervisory board is legally required, management is often unwilling to expand the realm of issues discussed.

When banks send representatives to supervisory boards, they usually send those who, commensurate with the prestige of being on the board, are senior executives or bank management board members who have multiple board memberships, limited technical knowledge outside of banking, and significant time responsibilities within the bank. Although the banks claim to provide in-house counsel on financial matters to those firms on whose boards they sit, it is unclear how this advice differs from that which they normally provide their clients. The biggest difference between German supervisory boards and U.S. boards of directors is their greater willingness to remove CEOs, or more commonly, not to renew the *Vorstand* members' five-year contracts. While this does catch problems before they get out of hand, the boards are not "activist" in a broad sense.

The recent near bankruptcy of Metallgesellschaft,[19] Germany's fourteenth largest company, perfectly illustrates the limits of board monitoring and underscores the argument that the supposed advantages of German-style finance are largely a myth. Despite concentrated ownership (65 percent of the firm's stock is held by institutional investors, including 35.8 percent held by Dresdner Bank, Deutsche Bank, Allianz Insurance, and Daimler-Benz), and a distinguished *Aufsichtsrat* headed by leading Deutsche Bank *Vorstand* member Ronaldo Schmitz, the firm has encountered a crisis caused by one large project. The project itself was exactly the sort of major investment decision subject to board oversight (rather than just general poor management), yet despite all precautions, it nearly wiped out the giant firm's equity capital and more than halved its stock price. The nearly $1.5 billion (and climbing) losses suffered by Metallgesellschaft were the result of oil futures speculation, exactly within the putative expert advising capacity of the financial firms already mentioned, as well as that of co-owner the Emir of Kuwait (20 percent stake).

This leads us to the final aspect of the idealized model to be cut down to size: the information provided to the firm by the lending banks. Shonfield, among others, mentions technical departments said to be attached to German banks that allowed for close consulting and evaluation of investment projects. Such departments do not exist. A few banks that have acquired business consulting firms can claim such expertise, but this is a recent development. In addition, German banks have no sources of information about prospects in industries beyond that available to U.S. banks. Deutsche Bank Research preceded the *Sparkassen* organization only by about five years in creating *Bereich* (industrial sector) reports; since the subsidiary makes a tidy profit selling these reports to other financial firms, it stands to reason that this research represents a capability most other banks do not yet have. And as with the *Sparkassen* reports, these are as external and standardized as those offered by Standard and Poor's, for example, in the United States.

The Limited Distinctiveness of German Industrial Finance

Table 3.1 presents the realities of the current German financial system in contrast to both the model of German finance and the free-market baseline of the UK and US systems. What remains that is distinctive about the practice of German relationship banking is:

1. the significant nuancing of financial criteria by personal factors of the prospective borrower;
2. the occasional private bailout or restructuring of firms in trouble, but usually where there is low collateral on outstanding loans;
3. the reluctant holding of equity stakes in firms in cases where the firm is in need of financial support and considered strategically important to the national economy; and
4. supervisory board membership allowing basic monitoring of management's intents and competency.

Legal differences about universal banking and proxy votes, as well as historic reliance by firms on debt rather than equity have little effect on the practice of German finance, and thus cannot be invoked to explain the differences in German attitudes toward investment time-horizons or patterns. Moreover, because German banks do not have the information or the capabilities to constrain firms into becoming ideal agents of the

-

TABLE 3.1 The Ideal and the Reality of German Finance

Aspect	Model	Reality	Contrast to U.S./U.K. Practice
Services offered by bank to firm	Universal	Specialized—except for Grossbanken	Minimal, given recent growth of bank capabilities
Major form of firm investment finance	Long-term bank loans	Primarily Retained funds	None in bank share of external funds
Funding criteria used by bank	Future prospects—not just cash-flow	Standard financial and personal trust	Raw numbers are nuanced—but by person, not future
Equity stake of bank in firm	Acquired willingly, large (often >10 percent), retained	Acquired because of prior problems, sold if possible	Significant—even undesired stakes alter incentives
Reaction to firm's short-run problems	Bank is patient / leads in efforts to restructure	Early foreclosure option or team restructuring	Can be significant—varies greatly from case to case
Bankers as members of firm's board	Almost always—with large role in firm's decisions	Often—but small and reactive role in most decisions	Minimal—role of Aufsichtsräte is exaggerated
Advising provided by bank to firm	Strategic and industry specific	Financial and rarely technical	None

shareholders, we must turn to the effect of firms on the banks to reconcile the results with the practice of German investment.

The Members of the German Investment Club

Germany can be seen as the prototype of what may be called a "members only" financial system.[20] In such a system, borrowing firms have some market power over lenders because of turnover costs to lenders in switching from old to new clients. The firms who have already borrowed take advantage of these costs in negotiating loan terms with lenders, extracting benefits up to just below the point that it would be cheaper for lenders to replace the incumbent, or "member," firms. As a result of these below market prices, lenders offer fewer loans than those demanded by all firms in the economy, with member firms getting funding first. In fact, the members have extremely stable, long-term investment funds, while the nonmember firms have difficulty getting capital. Lenders are patient with borrowers to the extent that the turn-over costs are high, and remain so. As costs change, so should lending relationships.

The distinctive aspects of German finance offer numerous opportunities for turnover costs (equity stakes, personal and board ties amongst firms, bank reputation at stake through board membership) as well as the sense that these have been to some extent exploited by the borrowing firms. In addition, Germany has clear evidence of credit rationing as seen by the personal criteria used to allocate loans and the sharp effectiveness of monetary policy. These "members only" aspects result in the pattern of investment that we see in Germany today.

Large German firms, such as Daimler-Benz, Krupp, Siemens, and Grundig, all needed to rebuild after World War II. But they had no assets to offer, only future profits. The German banks had no other place to put their funds—most of which were Marshall Plan or Federal Republic monies and were thus earmarked for domestic investment—and so took equity stakes in the old heavy industries in return for credit. Moreover, the banks were cajoled and begged by various firms to come onto their *Aufsichtsräte* to legitimize their business. Obviously, when Hermann Abs of Deutsche Bank sat on more than thirty boards personally, he was not engaging in detailed technical or strategic advising to each firm; rather, he was staking his reputation on their success.

This meant that the large customers of the German banks were able to impose significant turnover costs on the banks. German stock markets were even more illiquid then than they are now and so the banks were stuck with their equity stakes in industry if they wished to avoid a penalizing sale price; German firms supported the government recognition of

Verbände (business associations) in the policy process, which facilitated coordination among borrowing firms. German private banks found their ability to attract savings as well as customers away from the public sector financial institutions (or the mattresses at home) was tied to the fortunes of German industry. As a result, these original "member" firms of the postwar German economy have received credit with a great deal of stability, and have thus been allowed long time-horizons for investment.

Second, Germany continues to have a dearth of high-technology start-up firms despite its widely touted patient capital. That capital is patient only for members, not strangers. New firms are unable to pay the cost of credit necessary to make it worthwhile for the banks to drop their old borrowers and pay the requisite turnover costs, and so no credit is made available to them. Porter summarizes extensively and well the reasons why technological innovation is more likely to occur in small, new firms than in old, larger ones.[21] In Germany, the exclusion of new firms has resulted in an absence of internationally competitive companies in areas such as telecommunications, biotechnology, pharmaceuticals, and computing, despite German success in related but lower-tech sectors such as industrial chemicals and machine tools.[22]

Third, the current shortfall of private lending to and investment in the privatized firms of the states of the former GDR can also be seen as the result of a "members only" financial system. At first glance, the best of these firms—e.g., Zeiss Optics, KWO Kabel, numerous local service businesses—present the same opportunities for future growth as west German firms offered in the late 1940s, or German firms in the 1920s, but at lower risk, given their affiliation with the mostly prosperous Federal Republic.[23] But banks are passing up these opportunities. Why is this so? Basic funding for infrastructure and loan subsidies are even being provided by the public sector (the federal government, the union, and *Länder*) at levels exceeding the proportions seen during the Marshall Plan.

These potentially successful firms in the East are denied credit because the German banks now have other places to put their money, and those places lock the money in with turnover costs, in contrast to the days of postwar reconstruction. When every firm is starting from ground zero, there are no membership differences between firms, but when some firms are already long-standing members, other firms can be excluded as strangers. Stories abound of western German industrial firms discouraging investment in eastern German firms, such as the steel industry's opposition to Brandenburg's effort to convert to minimills near the Polish border, or buying firms from the Treuhand only to shut them down. Tellingly, the large east German firms in the industries in which western Germany is most competitive—like steel, mining, and chemicals—are the ones that the Treuhandanstalt has generally failed to sell.[24]

Perhaps this is understandable for the competing western German firms. Yet few German universal banks are trading loans for equity stakes in the new firms of the *neuen Bundesländer* either, especially in comparison to their eagerness to lend during the reconstruction of postwar West Germany. Chancellor Kohl had to intervene personally in the various finance *Verbände* in the spring of 1993 to get a commitment of DM 1 billion of private bankers' funds. Without his involvement, the banks would simply have processed government loans and others' investments. Whereas in the 1940s, German firms could compete for bank funding only on the basis of what price they would offer banks for capital, or what quality of investment project they could present, in the 1990s, German firms of long-standing can compete on the basis of market power due to prior borrowing, while new firms cannot overcome the wedge in prices provided by turnover costs to banks. This leaves the companies of the *neuen Bundesländer* out in the cold.

Finally, what about the decisions of Daimler-Benz and other firms to leave their long-term borrowing relationships with their banks? If bank monitoring, board membership, and debt financing inherently provide advantages to industrial firms, then the move is difficult to explain. Yet if these firms engage in their borrowing relationships to the extent they can extract rents, we would expect them to exit the relationships when the level of turnover costs decreases—and this is what has happened in the financial world in the last decade.

While Deutsche Bank still cannot dump its 25 percent of Daimler-Benz shares on the market, it can now limit its exposure through various hedging strategies,[25] play down its ties to the fortunes of the firm by scapegoating the labor representation that makes up half the supervisory board,[26] and cut the cost of bringing new clients on board through the investments already made in electronic banking and in the information sources of DB Research. Simultaneously, the size of the bonus extracted from Deutsche Bank in the form of rents has shrunk relative to the cost advantages to Daimler-Benz of dealing with British or American financial specialists, or going to the markets directly, in today's deregulated, internationally integrated financial market. And as the Metallgesellschaft incident demonstrates, the direct benefits to industry of banker stakes and monitoring, outside of the leverage they grant the member borrowing firms, are less than overwhelming.

The long time-frame of investment for old German companies, the absence of funding for high-tech start-ups, the foregoing of a seemingly repeated historic opportunity in the former East Germany, and the current departures of top German firms from their "relationship banking" ties all can be traced to the contemporary reality of the German financial system, which belies the model of "universal banking" commonly used to describe it. Its weaknesses are too apparent for it to be held up as an example for American banks to emulate.

Notes

1. "Daimler Plays Ball," *Economist*, 27 March 1993, 90; "Financing Boom: Foreign Firms Raise More and More Money in the U.S. Markets," *The Wall Street Journal*, 5 October 1993, A1.

2. Michael E. Porter, "Capital Disadvantage: America's Failing Capital Investment System," *Harvard Business Review* (September–October 1992) 65–82; Michael T. Jacobs, *Short-Term America*, (Boston: Harvard Business School Press, 1991).

3. Alexander Gerschenkron, *Economic Backwardness in Historical Perspective*, (Cambridge: Harvard University Press, 1962); Andrew Shonfield, *Modern Capitalism: The Changing Balance of Public and Private Power*, (Oxford: Oxford University Press, 1969).

4. See, for example, Ulrich Cartellieri, "Statement to the U.S. Senate Committee on Banking, Housing, and Urban Affairs," 13 June 1990, or Hans-Helmut Kotz, "Germany's Banking on Relations: On Selling a Dull Product," *Revue d'Economie Financiere* (Winter 1992).

5. My "idealized model" summarizes the relevant writings of Shonfield, *Modern Capitalism*; John Zysman, *Governments, Markets, and Growth: Financial Systems and the Politics of Industrial Change*, (Ithaca: Cornell University Press, 1983); Peter A. Hall, *Governing the Economy* (Oxford: Oxford University Press, 1986); and Jacobs, *Short-Term America*. They give extremely similar pictures of the German financial institutions and are frequently cited by other authors. Their depiction stems in large part from Gerschenkron's description of the *Kredietbanken's* role in Germany's late industrialization (in *Economic Backwardness*.) These authors base their argument on the idea that the main aspects of those aggressive nineteenth century bank practices persist in tempered fashion in the *Grossbanken* of the postwar era.

6. The *Hausbank* also arranges and leads syndicated lending or services when the firm's project is too big for it to handle alone.

7. This is the result of the *Depotstimmrecht*, a law that encourages small investors to leave their shares on deposit at a bank and then sign over their proxy rights to the shares for a fifteen month period.

8. The three *Grossbanken* are Deutsche Bank, Dresdner Bank, and Commerzbank.

9. The growth of market share of private banks beyond the big three is largely attributable to specialized services offered by lenders after the worldwide financial deregulation of the 1980s stimulated demand for advanced products.

10. These clearing banks do have a full range of capabilities but have no depositor or branch base of their own. Only very recently have they begun to attract customers in their own right (largely following the example of WestLB).

11. In January 1993, I visited the *Deutsche Giro- und Sparkassen Verband*

(DGSV—the German Association of Savings Banks) in Bonn. The DGSV was then in the beginnings of a program of offering to member banks on a subscription basis *Bereich* (industrial sector) Reports. While these reports did make some use of data compiled from subscribing banks, they were fundamentally the work of an outside consulting firm. Some sample copies were extremely similar to the reports contracted out for from the various research agencies by American financial firms.

12. P. A. Braun, "Das Firmenkundengeschaeft der Banken im Wandel" (Ph.D. diss., Department of Economics, University of Augsburg, 1981).

13. Alfred Steinherr and Christian Huveneers, "Universal Banks: The Prototype of Successful Banks in the Integrated European Market? A View Inspired by the German Experience," CEPS Financial Markets Research Unit, *Research Report #2*, 1989.

14. Colin Mayer, "Financial Systems, Corporate Finance, and Economic Development," in *Asymmetric Information, Corporate Finance, and Investment*, ed. R. Glenn Hubbard (Chicago: University of Chicago Press, 1990).

15. The exact weightings of the various factors, and which factors are considered, are confidential property of the banks themselves and cannot be further identified.

16. The survey included the principal books used in the internal training programs of the Bundesbank and Deutsche Bank, and the university courses in banking at the Goethe Universität (Frankfurt am Main), Köln Universität, the Technische Universität Berlin, and the Free University of Berlin.

17. Jeremy Edwards and Klaus Fischer, *Banks, Finance, and Investment in Germany*, (Cambridge: Cambridge University Press, 1994).

18. Ibid., 15.

19. See Ferdinand Protzman, "When German Safeguards Fail," *New York Times*, 28 February 1994, D1.

20. For a more detailed exposition of the theory behind this approach, and application of it to a range of countries, see Adam S. Posen, "Why Did the German Bonds Bind? A Members-Only Model of Investment Relationships and Time-Horizons" (presented at the annual meeting of the American Political Science Association, 4 September 1993).

21. Michael E. Porter, *The Competitive Advantage of Nations*, (New York: Free Press, 1990), chap. 2.

22. Ibid., chap. 7.

23. Which, granted, comprise only about 20 percent of the former businesses and employment of the GDR, but do still exist.

24. Roger Cohen, "The Growing Burden of Germany's Unification," *New York Times*, 8 March 1993, D1.

25. One might even argue that the diversifications in aerospace, armaments, and electronics urged on Daimler by the late Deutsche Bank chairman Albert Herrhausen in the 1980s (and since completed) was an effort by the bank to get more security for its investment because the bank could not opt out of its investment.

26. Whose representation has been in effect only for large companies outside the steel and coal industry since 1976.

4

Germany at Maastricht: Diplomacy and Domestic Politics

Colette Mazzucelli

Die Einheit der Nation ist für uns nicht wie in früheren Zeiten das höchste Ziel, sondern es gibt Werte, die höher sind, vor allem Frieden und Freiheit. Auch steht nach unserer Vorstellung ein geeintes Europa über der Nation.
　　　　　　　　　　　　　—President Karl Carstens, 26 October 1986

On 12 October 1993 the German Federal Constitutional Court rejected an appeal that the Maastricht Treaty violated sovereign rights laid down in the Basic Law. This was the last hurdle to clear in the process of ratifying the treaty at the national level. The Treaty on European Union entered into effect on 1 November 1993.[1] The Karlsruhe decision came almost a year after the Bundesrat had concluded its ratification of the Treaty on European Union. Treaty negotiations, which took place from January to December 1991, involved two intergovernmental conferences (IGCs) to amend the Treaty of Rome. The IGCs on Economic and Monetary Union (EMU) and Political Union came to a close on 9–10 December 1991 at the European Council in Maastricht. By analyzing German diplomacy during the negotiations, this chapter assesses the role of Germany in the new Europe. The changes can be viewed in the context of two processes. The first process, European integration, underwent significant changes in the mid-1980s. As a result of the program to complete the internal market, known as "1992," the European Community (EC) began a new phase in its evolution. The second process, German unification, set off with lightning speed in 1989.

The chapter epigraph is quoted from "Signatur der Zeit," *Handelsblatt*, 30–31 October 1986, p. 1.

The unification of Germany on 3 October 1990, coupled with the fall of Communist regimes in Eastern Europe and the former Soviet Union, marked a transition in East-West relations. The Federal Republic of Germany, conscious of both its geographical position at the heart of the Continent and the weight of history in European affairs, consistently seeks to assert its influence in multilateral fora. In coming years, the role of Germany on the world scene will manifest itself less "in the form of a classically sovereign state and more as an influential member of international communities, notably, the EC and NATO."[2] The Federal Republic's active participation in the Maastricht negotiations illustrates a firm commitment and contribution to stability on the Continent.

Germany in the New Europe

Since World War II German foreign policy has consistently sought expression in the context of two multilateral fora—NATO and the EC. In the mid-1980s, Chancellor Helmut Kohl and Foreign Minister Hans-Dietrich Genscher saw an opportunity to foster economic growth and further the aim of political unification by revitalizing the European integration process. In tandem with French president François Mitterrand, the German leaders capitalized on the arrival of Jacques Delors as president of the European Commission in 1985. Key decisions taken at the European Council in Milan led to the first major amendments to the Treaty of Rome, taken at the Luxembourg European Council in December 1985. The amendments, otherwise known as the Single European Act, launched the process to complete the internal market by 31 December 1992.

The Federal Republic's active participation in the integration process has enabled the country to translate its economic power into political influence. The Federal Republic views the European Union (EU) as an open and outward-looking community firmly based on the rule of law.[3] Difficulties remain, nonetheless, in the transposition of EU directives into German legislation because member states have been given very precise directives from Brussels.[4] In Germany, it is also due to the complexity of federal-state relations in those areas where the states retain sole jurisdiction. The transposition process, however, remains essential to complete the market in areas where agreement to harmonize laws is sensitive, i.e., health issues. The implementation of directives in national legal systems will greatly affect the domestic structures of all member states.[5] It is part of an integration dynamic that gains its own momentum via "a series of creative contradictions with national policies that can be resolved only by further steps down the European and presumably federal road."[6] As

Foreign Minister Klaus Kinkel stated, this dynamic is clearly in the tradition of Jean Monnet's approach.[7]

The same integration dynamic that pushed "1992" forward prompted the Genscher Memorandum in 1988, which advocated plans for EMU. During the first half of that year, the Federal Republic held the rotating presidency of the Council of Ministers. The German presidency achieved an agreement known as the Brussels package, a financial reform that enabled the EC to carry out the plans outlined in the Single European Act.[8] The negotiations during the Brussels European Council in February 1988 required a series of delicate compromises on complex dossiers. Kohl provided the leadership of a strong member state to resolve what was essentially the same set of issues before the Danish presidency only a few weeks before.[9] At the European Council in Hannover, the heads of state and government asked a committee under the chairmanship of Jacques Delors to prepare a report on Economic and Monetary Union. The Delors Report was presented at the Madrid European Council in June 1989. The heads of state and government agreed that the first stage of EMU should start in July 1990 and that an intergovernmental conference should map out its later stages.

During the French presidency in the second half of 1989, the process of German unification gathered momentum. France, caught off guard by the rhythm of events on the other side of the Rhine, made EMU the cornerstone of its European policy. French logic was clear and simple. Increased integration was necessary in order to anchor Germany to the West and to avoid the Bundesbank's dominance in the monetary field.[10] Pooling sovereignty would increase French leverage by giving it a seat on the board of directors of the future European Central Bank. At the Strasbourg European Council in December 1989, the decision was taken that the IGC on Economic and Monetary Union should begin at the end of 1990. Those member states within the EC who advocated a federal Europe, notably Belgium, Italy, and Germany, followed the initiative of Delors who suggested in a speech to the European Parliament that two conferences, one on EMU and one on Political Union, should be held in parallel. Seizing the initiative once again as the "motor for Europe," Kohl and Mitterrand issued a joint letter in April 1990 which called for the opening of a second IGC on political union in December 1990.

German Diplomacy and Negotiations on EMU

The negotiations on EMU proceeded on the basis of a consensus among eleven of the twelve member states, with the exception of the United Kingdom. Agreement among the eleven, as outlined in the conclusions of the European Council in Rome during October 1990,[11] included a common understanding of the basic characteristics of the economic union and on the principal features of the monetary union. The former would be "an open market system that combines price stability with growth, employment, and environmental protection and is dedicated to sound and sustainable financial and budgetary conditions and to economic and social cohesion." The latter would introduce a new monetary institution comprising member states' central banks and a central organ. It would exercise full responsibility for monetary policy with the essential task of maintaining price stability. The monetary institution would also be "independent of instructions" from member state governments and would most likely issue a single currency. [12]

The French delegation at the intergovernmental conference on EMU seized the initiative by submitting a complete draft treaty on Economic and Monetary Union dated 25 January 1991. This text had stimulated discussion among the member states and the Commission and prompted the German delegation to table its own draft text on 26 February 1991.[13] In this text, the Federal Republic's position on EMU, influenced strongly by the Finance Ministry and the Bundesbank, is clearly stated. Three issues of contention were evident throughout the negotiations: political control, (including the institutional balance in the Community), economic discipline, and rules governing the transition phases to EMU.[14]

Undoubtedly, one of the Federal Republic of Germany's (FRG) cardinal principles on the road to EMU is the independence of the proposed European Central Bank (ECB) as the guarantor of price stability. According to one German participant at the IGC, the Germans do consider that the notion of autonomy (by which the Bundesbank is at times subject to some degree, however limited, of political influence) as relevant here.[15] What remains essential for Germany is that the ECB has some say in determining the exchange rate policy. The French proposal for a "gouvernement économique" tried to limit the ECB's autonomy in two ways.[16] First, according to the French, the European Council, as the highest political authority, would have the power to determine the general policy orientations with which the Central Bank should also comply. Here, as in the negotiations on political union, the suggested predominance of the European Council, an extra-Community body, introduced a degree of intergovernmentalism contrary to the institutional balance in the Community.

Second, limiting the ECB's decision-making authority to domestic monetary policy, and granting the authority to pursue exchange rate policies to the Council, would infringe on the autonomy of the ECB. From the German point of view, the question of whether political authorities, notably the Council, should have the authority to lay down guidelines for the Community's exchange rate policy—requiring the European Central Bank to carry out its transactions within those guidelines—would create an ambiguity regarding the ECB's autonomy. This ambiguity would be far more serious at the European level given both the absence of a tradition of central bank autonomy in the European Community as a whole and the uncertainty regarding the content of economic union. The resulting compromise, stated in Article 109 of the Maastricht Treaty, aims to achieve an autonomous policy, narrowly focused on price stability, with a minimum of external controls, whether from the Council or the European Parliament. It remains to be seen whether "the role of the Parliament in the appointment of the President of the ECB (109a) and the periodic reports and examinations (109b) actually prove to be acceptable mechanisms of control and accountability." Whether the balance of the system as a whole functions satisfactorily "can only be tested when the first major price shocks rock the system."[17]

Economic discipline, in the form of strict convergence criteria and avoidance of excessive budget deficits, was a second cardinal principle for the Federal Republic during the EMU negotiations. Otherwise known as an "economist" approach, as opposed to the "institutional" or "monetarist" approach espoused by the French, the Germans believe that EMU will come about only when a significant degree of economic convergence is achieved among EC member states. Both of these issues figured prominently in the debate about the timing of the progression to EMU. Once again, Germany was in the forefront of the negotiation. Three issues were at stake: "the timing and duration of Stage II, the conditionality that should be attached to the entry into force of Stage III, and the political and economic implications of a 'two-speed' EMU."[18]

On the timing and duration of Stage II, the German position supported 1 January 1994 as the starting date. On the duration of Stage II, the German Finance Ministry was against setting a specific timetable since it is not a priori possible to foresee when the convergence criteria will be met. As a corollary, the Federal Republic maintained that the creation of the ECB should be postponed until the beginning of Stage III for two reasons. First, it was necessary to avoid establishing a Central Bank prior to achieving significant economic convergence among the Twelve. Second, in order to encourage public trust in the ECB, it was best not to introduce the institution too early. The Central Bank would thus establish a good reputation from the start as a body capable of assuming substantial functions in the final phase.[19]

At the informal meeting of economics and finance ministers at Apeldoorn on 21–22 September 1991, agreement was reached on the fact that the EMU Treaty should be signed by all twelve EC member states. A consensus also emerged on the conditions of entry into Stage III of EMU.[20]

The decision taken on Stage III entry confirmed that three years after the start of second stage, the Council of Economics and Finance Ministers (ECOFIN), based on a report of the Commission and the European Monetary Institute (the forerunner of the ECB during Stage II), will evaluate the progress in fulfillment of the convergence criteria. The Council will then determine if passage to Stage III is possible and which member states are eligible. The European Council, taking note of the evaluation of the ECOFIN Council, will then make the final decision on the start of Stage III. For those member states not fulfilling the convergence criteria at the outset, temporary derogations will be possible until they can join EMU at a later date.

At Maastricht, Stage III entry was made automatic so as to emphasize the irreversibility of the EMU process. Britain was given an opting-out clause from the outset with the possibility to join EMU at a later date. According to the Maastricht Treaty, by 31 December 1996 the European Council will decide by qualified majority whether a majority of states fulfill the criteria for entry into Stage III. If this is the case, the European Council determines the date to begin the final phase. If, by the end of 1997, no date has been fixed, then Stage III will begin automatically on 1 January 1999 (Article 109j). Germany had urged that the Council decision to enter the final stage be taken unanimously. The fact that the decision will be taken by qualified majority vote, and that entry into the third stage is automatic, are examples of compromises made in order to achieve a final accord. Such willingness to compromise would be even more difficult during the negotiations on political union.

German Diplomacy and Negotiations on Political Union

In contrast to bargaining on EMU over precise and technical issues, the political union agenda was broad and messy. In order to facilitate analysis, the aims of German diplomacy in four essential areas are considered.[21] First, German goals on the extension of Community competences, including institutional questions, European citizenship and the subsidiarity principle, are assessed. Second, German diplomacy regarding the Common Foreign and Security Policy (CFSP) dossier, one of the most difficult despite the key role played by the Franco-German couple, is examined. Third, Germany's goals vis-à-vis the provisions in Home and Justice Affairs, the so-called third pillar of the Maastricht Treaty, are evaluated in light of domestic problems such as asylum. Finally, the German position on treaty structure, the relationship between the competences belonging to the European Community, or first pillar, and those belonging to the second, or CFSP, and third pillars, is explained. The German viewpoint on an area of contention that emerged in the conference on political union, namely, economic and social cohesion, is also outlined.

From the outset of the IGC, the Federal Republic attached primary importance to institutional questions. The German delegation submitted important contributions on codecision for the European Parliament with the Council of Ministers in approving EC legislation. Germany, in coalition with Italy and Belgium, wanted to go the furthest on this dossier in exchange for agreement on EMU. The notion of European citizenship, introduced by Spain, was advanced by Kohl and Mitterrand in the Franco-German letter of 13 December 1990. This underlined German concern for "A People's Europe" introduced previously in the Adonnino Report. The subsidiarity principle was one of the most important for the Federal Republic due to its federal government structure and the states' threat to veto any treaty that did not enshrine this principle in its test. Finally, while Germany advocated the extension of Community competences on dossiers such as environment and social policy, it had greater reserves in matters of state competence, i.e., education and culture as well as in areas where too much centralism in Brussels was feared, such as trans-European networks and industry.

Germany, together with France, played a crucial role in the negotiations to advance the Common Foreign and Security Policy dossier. In their letter to the Italian presidency, dated 13 December 1990, Kohl and Mitterrand foresaw an enhanced role for the Western European Union (WEU), by establishing organizational links between the WEU and the future European Union. Following the French lead, Germany supported a more prominent role for the European Council as the extra-Community institution that would give the highest political definition to the Union and implement the CFSP. This upset the Dutch presidency, in particular, which was sensitive to any shifts in the institutional balance in the Community.[22] Furthermore, it indicated the delicate compromise that Germany had to find between two competing concepts of democratic legitimacy: that of France, in which the executive can state "la démocratie c'est moi"; and its own system, in which parliamentary democracy can bring down chancellors. The former position explains French support for the European Council.[23] The latter phenomenon explains why Germany also championed Parliament's cause.

The discussions on the gradual inclusion of defense matters in the Union continued to be the subject of heated debate throughout the political union negotiations. As a reaction to an Anglo-Italian test on a CFSP, presented on 11 October 1991, Kohl and Mitterrand issued the last of three Franco-German letters in which they tried to give further impetus to the discussions. The political leaders submitted a proposal translating their earlier ideas into concrete draft treaty articles on CFSP.[24] Reference was made to strengthening the Franco-German brigade, which could serve as the first step toward a European army. Chancellor Kohl was also aware, however, of the impact of such a step on relations within the Atlantic alliance. In the area of CFSP, the Franco-German proposals were to a large extent inserted into the Maastricht Treaty. The role of WEU, as "an integral part of the development of the Union" is strengthened while a clear reference is also made to NATO (North Atlantic Treaty Organization). Only the trials of experience, like the situation in the former Yugoslavia, will reveal how workable these arrangements are *in der Praxis*.

On the dossier of Home and Justice Affairs, the Federal Republic was in the forefront of negotiations. At the domestic level, Chancellor Kohl's initiative in this area was decisive. In contrast to the CFSP, Home and Justice Affairs highlighted the urgency of matters of internal security to Germany, in particular, and the European Community in general. There are several reasons for German concern regarding this dossier. First, the asylum problem in Germany was a particular case among member states due to the liberality of Article 16 BL prior to its revision on 26 May 1993. Therefore, Germany placed much emphasis on the formulation of a European asylum policy in the Council of Ministers. Second, as internal barriers within the EU fall with the completion of the single market, increased cooperation in the fight against international drug trafficking and terrorism becomes a necessity. Therefore, Germany also saw the need to create a European police agency, EUROPOL, to counter criminality across borders. In a memorandum to the Luxembourg presidency in June 1991, the German delegation proposed that these ideas be incorporated into the *acquis communautaire*, or European Community competences. This proposal met with resistance from at least four member states—namely, the United Kingdom, Denmark, Ireland, and Portugal—throughout the negotiations. At Maastricht, a compromise was found in the form of a *passerelle*, Article K9, by which, over time, parts or the entirety of the third pillar could be transferred to the *acquis communautaire*.

The inability of some member states to agree on the inclusion of the Home and Justice Affairs or CFSP dossiers into the sphere of Community competences led to a debate on the treaty structure. The debate came to a climax on 30 September 1991 when the General Affairs Council (or foreign ministers of the EC Member States) voted against the draft treaty on European Union presented by the Dutch Presidency. In the Dutch draft treaty, both the CFSP and Home and Justice Affairs areas were to be subsumed under the European Community and, therefore, subject to its supranational decision-making procedures. Germany was in favor of the Dutch draft treaty, which in many respects recalled ideas suggested in the Genscher-Colombo plan. However, in the face of firm opposition from at least four member states, the United Kingdom, France, Denmark, and Portugal, the Federal Republic agreed to maintain the pillar structure eventually agreed on at Maastricht. In the treaty structure, the European Community, or first pillar, exists alongside the second (CFSP) and third (Home and Justice Affairs) pillars. The European Union, established by the Maastricht Treaty, is thus comprised of three pillars plus common and general provisions.

During the course of negotiations on political union, Spain, supported by Ireland, Portugal, and Greece, championed the cause of the poorer member states. Economic and social cohesion, emphasized alongside the completion of the single market and economic and monetary union in Article 130a of the Single European Act, became an integral part of the IGC. The Federal Republic's position was that this dossier was better left until after the Maastricht negotiations. It would thus be included in the debate about future financing for the Community, otherwise known as the Delors II Package. This position was shared by England and France as net contributors to the Community budget. However, it was totally unsatisfactory for the Spanish prime minister, Felipe Gonzalez. Chancellor Kohl was instrumental in facilitating a compromise on this dossier. In November 1991 Ruud Lubbers, as spokesman for the presidency, assisted by the Council Secretariat, visited Chancellor Kohl in Bonn. There the origins of a compromise were outlined that would take Spanish interests into account. The results obtained at Maastricht on this dossier owe a great deal to Kohl's political artistry and personal commitment to European integration.

During the IGC on political union, the dossiers on the negotiating table were numerous enough to detract from the balance of the negotiation. Balance is necessary to keep a limited number of goals firmly in mind and to hold a negotiating line in order to achieve specific diplomatic objectives.[25] Moreover, negotiations on political union were not as well prepared as those on EMU. Diplomatic success is often the result of careful attention to prior preparation and requires a substantial amount of time for dossiers to mature. The IGC on political union, which France and Germany called for because of the speed of change on the Continent, was prepared in haste. Valuable time during the actual conference was lost on an exchange of ideas normally conducted in a prenegotiation phase.

The Ratification Process in the Federal Republic

On 13 December 1991, in a speech before the Bundestag on the results obtained at the Maastricht European Council, Chancellor Kohl underlined the irreversibility of the path to European Union.[26] Although subject to stark criticism owing to the lack of progress on political union, especially from the opposition party, the Social Democrats, the Chancellor maintained that the EMU Treaty was strongly influenced by Germany in all essential respects. Three themes dominated the ratification debate in the Federal Republic. First, was the intense public fear of the loss of the Deutsche Mark in exchange for "Esperanto-Geld." Second, the states called for a constitutional amendment that would allow them to participate in negotiations at the Union level within their exclusive sphere of competence—i.e., education, culture, and health. A firm definition of subsidiarity, stated in the text of the Maastricht Treaty, was necessary for the states. In this way, the division of labor between the EC and national levels would be taken into account. Finally, all political parties in Germany disparaged the EC's inability to eradicate the "democratic deficit" in the Union, in part because it increased the powers of the Parliament.

The Treaty on European Union would be ratified in two bills. The first was the bill on the ratification of the treaty proper, creating the necessary conditions for the treaty to come into force. Here the Foreign Ministry was *federführend* (in overall charge of the ratification process). The Treaty on European Union contains provisions that, to be applicable at the national level, required a change in the Basic Law. Thus, the government tabled a second, parallel bill modifying the constitution. The Ministry of the Interior was responsible during the process for the modification of two articles of the Basic Law and to introduce a new "Europe" article. The articles modified were Article 28 BL, pertaining to the right of nationals of other member states to stand and vote in German local as well as European elections, and Article 88 BL, dealing with the transference of competences to the European Central Bank.

The Danish rejection of the Treaty on European Union by a narrow margin of forty thousand votes on 2 June 1992, coupled with increasing public skepticism on EMU within a country reeling from the costs of unification, led Chancellor Kohl to take the offensive to defend the results obtained at Maastricht. The Chancellor warned against a spreading "virus of nationalism" in the Federal Republic. It was clear, however, that insufficient knowledge about the treaty led the public to fear Maastricht as an attempt to keep Germany down. Responding to a critique of Maastricht by sixty economics professors, Jürgen Möllemann, then minister for economic affairs, expressed his unequivocal support for EMU.[27] Möllemann criticized, however, the weak compromises on the completion of political union and the provisions on industrial policy, which strike Germans as *dirgisme* by fostering greater interventionism from Brussels.

Meanwhile, the Constitutional Committee, consisting of members of the Bundestag and Bundesrat, which was established to prepare German constitutional reform, approved amendments on 26 June. In order to take states' concerns into account, a compromise was achieved. Under the new Article 23 BL, the basic principles of the federal constitution have to be preserved when transferring German sovereign rights to the EU. Both the Bundestag and the Bundesrat have to give their consent (two-thirds' majority) if a transfer of sovereign rights has an impact on the constitution. Thus, the government has to obtain the approval of the Bundesrat in areas where the states have exclusive competence. This is of particular importance for the new states, where difficult economic and social conditions hamper support for European integration. Essentially a distinction is made here between Union affairs, in which the states have a right to speak if their areas of national competence are involved (23 BL), and classical intergovernmental cooperation in which only the federal government may transfer sovereign powers to international institutions for reasons of collective security (24 BL). In the federal-state debate over treaty ratification, the threat of a veto revealed an element of poker. The states tried to obtain as much as possible in exchange for consenting to union.

The debate in the Bundestag focused on the lack of sufficient progress on political union as promised by Chancellor Kohl during the IGCs. The president of the SPD, Björn Engholm, did not consider the lack of sufficient powers for the European Parliament and the need to specify a role for the regions of Europe to be a "German problem" but rather a "democratic problem." Other themes prominent in the debate included criticism of the intergovernmental nature of both the CFSP and the provisions on Home and Justice Affairs. In the latter sphere, the debate in the Bundestag emphasized a more restrictive European asylum policy than the one presently allowed in the Federal Republic under Article 16 BL.

Moreover, some parliamentarians across the political spectrum called for a national referendum on the Maastricht Treaty, stating that European union would work only when legitimized by the people. The counterargument was that Article 20 BL did not provide for a referendum in the Federal Republic. The need for greater transparency in decision making was underlined, as was the need to inform citizens about the Union. In the fall, rather late in the game, the federal government started a DM 20 million public information campaign. The federal government also assured the Bundestag, and particularly the SPD opposition, of its right to vote on the passage to the third stage of EMU.[28]

Due to the limited number of constitutional amendments required to ratify Maastricht, the Federal Republic stuck to its agreed ratification timetable. The first reading in the Bundesrat took place on 25 September, followed by a first reading in the Bundestag on 8 October. After three weeks of debate in committees came a second and third reading in the Bundestag on 6 November, followed by a second and third reading in the Bundesrat on 27 November. The ratification process in the Bundestag and Bundesrat concluded with the approval of the Bundestag on 2 December and that of the Bundesrat on 18 December.

Changes in Domestic Structure

The politicoinstitutional consequences of the Maastricht ratification in Germany include the establishment of an EU committee in the Bundestag, according to Article 45 BL. In the future, the Committee for European Union will examine all European directives while obliging the federal government to take parliamentary views into account in the course of negotiations in Brussels. Thus, the Bundesrat and the Bundestag will exercise influence on European legislation in addition to that already obtained by the European Parliament.[29] This is a significant development in the direction of greater democratic legitimacy for the Union in the Federal Republic. The establishment of a European division in the Foreign Ministry, as well as a division for international and EC monetary issues in the Finance Ministry, is significant for EU policy coordination at the domestic level. These changes certainly do not lend credence to the idea of creating a European ministry in Bonn. Instead, as State Minister for European Affairs Seiler-Albring explains, the interaction of the European divisions at the Economics, Finance and Foreign Ministries will shape EU policy-making in the Federal Republic.[30]

Conclusions

The European policy of the Federal Republic of Germany in the 1990s will focus on both widening and deepening the European Union. The expansion issue, while given little attention during the negotiations throughout 1991, has gained momentum with the completion of negotiations on the admission of Austria, Sweden, Norway and Finland into the Union.[31] The impact of recent changes in the European Monetary System and prospective enlargements on the realization of the EMU timetable is difficult to predict. It is certain that the evolution of the domestic economic situation in the new states will also influence the speed of transition to EMU. During the second half of 1994, the German presidency of the European Union will work toward maintaining the integration dynamic in preparation for another intergovernmental conference on political union in 1996. The goals of German diplomacy at the second IGC will focus on further defining the CFSP, strengthening the EU's institutional structure (by expanding the use of qualified majority voting in the Council and augmenting the powers of Parliament) and strengthening European cooperation in judicial matters. The establishment of EUROPOL in the Hague was a concrete step toward institutionalizing "third pillar" issues.[32] The notion of *Parallelität*, namely that substantial progress must be made on Political Union in order to achieve EMU, will remain a key element of German European policy. In sum, Germany will continue to champion a federal union that is open to competition on world markets and conscious of its democratic responsibility to the citizens of Europe.

Notes

1. "German Court Rejects Appeal to Halt European Union Pact," *New York Times*, 13 October 1993, A8. Throughout this chapter the term "European Community" is applied when referring to dates prior to 1 November 1993, and "European Union" is applied when referring to the time period after 1 November 1993.

2. Reinhard Stuth, "Germany's New Role in a Changing Europe," *Aussenpolitik* 43 (1/92): 22.

3. Jürgen Kühn, "EG und Drittlandsbeziehungen aus der Sicht der Bundesrepublik Deutschland," in *EG und Drittstaatsbeziehungen nach 1992*, ed. Meinhard Hilf und Christian Tomuschat (Baden-Baden: Nomos Verlag Gesellschaft, 1991), 17–30.

4. Gerhard Rambow, "L'exécution des directives de la Communauté économique européenne en République fédérale d'Allemagne," *Cahiers de Droit Européen* 4 (1970): 379.

5. One example is the influence of EC legislation on French law. Interview, Council of State, 10 March 1992.

6. François Duchene, "Jean Monnet's Methods," in *Jean Monnet: The Path to European Unity*, ed. Douglas Brinkley and Clifford Hackett (New York: St. Martin's, 1991), 203.

7. "Rede des Bundesministers des Auswärtigen, Dr. Klaus Kinkel, bei der 2./3. Lesung des Vertrages über die Europäische Union und der damit verbundenen Gesetzentwürfe im Deutschen Bundestag am 02. Dezember 1992" (Nr. 1192/92), 11.

8. Irmgard Adam-Schwaetzer, "The German Role in the European Community—Basic Interests and Present Policies," in *The Federal Republic of Germany and the European Community*, ed. Wolfgang Wessels and Elfriede Regelsberger (Bonn: Europa Union Verlag, 1988), 14–17.

9. French Permanent Representation to the European Communities, interview with the author, 25 November 1992.

10. Ross Tieman, "Bundesbank Will Still Rule in Paris, However France Votes," *Times*, (London), 23 February 1993, 11.

11. Europe. Document 1658. Conclusions of the European Council of 27–28 October 1990.

12. Peter Ludlow, "Europe's Institutions: Europe's Politics," in *The Shape of the New Europe*, ed. Gregory F. Treverton (New York: Council on Foreign Relations Press, 1992), 69.

13. Wolfgang Neumann, *Auf dem Weg zu einer Europäischen Wirtschaftsund Währungsunion* (Stuttgart: Deutscher Sparkassenverlag GmbH, 1991), 148–162.

14. Andre Szasz, "The Politics of a European Currency," in *The European Community at the Crossroads*, ed. Alfred Pijpers (Dordrecht: Martinus Nijhoff) 149–160.

15. German Finance Ministry, interview with the author, 26 April 1993.

16. Szasz, "Politics of a European Currency," 151.

17. Andrew Britton and David Mayes, *Achieving Monetary Union in Europe*, (London: SGE, 1992), 31–32.

18. Ludlow, "Europe's Institution," 70–71.

19. German Finance Ministry, interview with the author, 26 April 1993.

20. *Agence Europe*, 23–24 September 1991, 9.

21. Philippe de Schoutheete de Tervarent, "L'apres Maastricht," *Journée d'Études*, 21 February 1992 (Brussels: Institute d'Etudes Européennes, 1992), 17–18.

22. Dutch Permanent Representation to the European Communities, interview with the author, 23 November 1992.

23. John Pinder, "Vital Tasks for the Dutch Presidency," in *The European Community at the Crossroads*, ed. Alfred Pijpers, 26–27.

24. Christa van Wijnbergen, "Germany and European Political Union," in *The Intergovernmental Conference on Political Union*, ed. Finn Laursen and Sophie Vanhoonacker (Maastricht: EIPA, 1992), 54–58.

25. French Foreign Ministry, interview with the author, 8 March 1993.

26. "Regierungserklärung von Bundeskanzler Dr. Helmut Kohl vor dem Deutschen Bundestag in Bonn am 13. Dezember 1991 zu den Ergebnissen des Europäischen Rates in Maastricht," (Nr. 485/91), 1.

27. Jürgen W. Möllemann, "Von Maastricht zum vereinten Europa," *Frankfurter Allgemeine Zeitung*, 15 July 1992, 7.

28. Kinkel, 5.

29. European Union Committee-Bundestag, interview with the author, 29 April 1993.

30. German Foreign Ministry, interview with the author, 16 April 1993.

31. "Europe Opens Way to 3 New Members," *New York Times*, 2 March 1994, A11.

32. "New European Police to Fight Regional Crime," *New York Times*, 17 February 1994, A11.

5

Standort Deutschland: Can a Changing Germany Compete in the Changing World Market?

Michael Zumwinkle

In 1989, when the Wall fell, the Federal Republic of Germany (FRG) had prospered under a decade of economic growth marked by low inflation, strong expansion of employment, and positive trade balances. The German economy had gained respect and admiration around the world, with the label "made in Germany" symbolizing quality and reliability. German machine tools, chemicals, household appliances, and automobiles were highly regarded for their dependability, as were German workers for their efficiency and competence. Germany boasted a developed infrastructure, an effective and efficient distribution system, and a technologically advanced and innovative economy.

Renowned as an export nation, Germany had alternated for a number of years with the United States as the world's export leader. By the end of the 1980s more than 30 percent of Germany's gross domestic product (GDP) depended on exports, mostly within the European Community (now formally known as the European Union). Germany's reputation as a strong export nation was enhanced by its competitiveness across a wide range of goods.

Now, five years later, many economists believe that the German economy faces its greatest hurdle in the postwar period. Following a postunification boom in 1990–1991, economic growth has faltered. The German economy contracted by nearly 2 percent in 1993 and is projected to grow at only .5 percent in 1994. Companies such as Bosch, Volkswagen, BASF, Siemens, BMW, and Stihl have increasingly invested abroad—

71

locating factories and production facilities in foreign countries instead of
at home. The reason: Germany has become too expensive.

In the 1970s, investment in Germany by foreigners exceeded that of
German investment abroad; during the 1980s the situation reversed itself.
According to statistics from the German Economics Ministry, foreign
companies invested some DM 34 billion in Germany between 1981 and
1990. In comparison, German investment in foreign countries totaled
almost DM 150 billion during the same period. By 1990, German companies invested ten times as much in foreign countries as foreigners did in
Germany.

Although a large share of this foreign investment can be traced to
securing markets, providing services to customers, and preparing for the
EU's integrated market, companies have also invested outside of
Germany to take advantage of more flexible employees, less bureaucracy,
lower employment costs, and lower taxes.[1] Recent reports by the Japanese
External Trade Organization (JETRO) and the American Chamber of
Commerce in Germany echo similar findings. Chancellor Helmut Kohl
has recognized this problem and made it a goal to increase foreign investment in Germany, especially in eastern Germany.

Public awareness of Germany's competitiveness and its problems as a
manufacturing center has been raised with renewed insistence by business leaders, who fear the country's competitive advantages have deteri-
orated. Many believe Germany will need to undergo significant
restructuring in order to improve its economic performance. Others argue
that the debate has more to do with the unexpected economic surge from
reunification and subsequent slowdown than with a deterioration of Germany's economic base. The question remains open: Has Germany lost its
appeal as an investment and production location in the changing political
and economic realities of the 1990s?

The so-called *Standort* discussion—the debate about attractiveness of
economic location and international competitiveness—emerges when
either economic goals are not attained or imbalances within an economic
development program occur or threaten to occur. *Standort* quality is
determined by a complex interaction of quantitative factors (employment
costs, work hours, productivity, taxes, and interest rates) and qualitative
factors (education, mobility of workers, social insurance system, political
stability, infrastructure, and monetary stability). The overall effect and
influence of these factors vary from industry to industry.[2] While some
factors of production may be natural or inherited, others must be culti-
vated and developed. The creation of international free trade zones and
the globalization of international firms have placed additional pressures
on governments to create competitive business climates. Governments

worldwide are interested in promoting their countries for business investment and production. The world economy is now dominated by investment capital and worker mobility. This permits production lines to be shifted quickly from place to place. The result is an intense competition for international investment and business activity. A wide range of policies and measures are available to governments to promote growth: currency devaluation, deregulation, privatization, relaxation of standards, tax reform, regional development, and expansion of government funding of research projects. With open borders, enterprises react very quickly to differences in *Standort* conditions.

The quality of a *Standort* is influenced not only by internal factors but also by changing *Standort* factors in other countries. Thus, an improvement in the investment conditions of another country without a subsequent change in Germany implies a net deterioration of Germany as a business location. Although Germany possesses many *Standort* advantages, its competitors have recently proved to be attractive production and investment alternatives.

The German government wants to increase its attractiveness as a *Standort* for growth and investment, especially in the eastern states. If developments there are to succeed, *Standort* conditions need to be improved throughout the country. Until now, the advantages of *Standort* Germany were enough to compensate for its weaknesses. Many German manufacturers compete to a large extent on quality and product differentiation rather than on price. But are consumers still willing to pay high prices for German products when comparable goods can be purchased from lower-cost producers? If not, the consequences could be loss of market share, reduced investment, uncertain job creation, and a need to restructure.

The *Standort* discussion in Germany first surfaced at the end of the 1970s with the oil crisis, the devaluation of the Deutsche Mark, and a global recession. As the 1980s ushered in a new export orientation and a stronger dollar (rising DM 1.72 in 1980 to DM 3.5 in 1985) the German economic position improved and the *Standort* debate subsided. The debate flared once again in 1987, as the dollar lost value and the German economy's growth rate slowed. By the close of the 1980s, Germany once again entered a phase of export growth, fueled in large part by purchases of German capital equipment, as the Continent prepared for EC 1992, lessening concern about Germany's economic competitiveness.

The recent economic recession in Germany has exposed a number of weaknesses and structural deficiencies in the German economy, and Germans have once more begun to question the country's economic competitiveness, continued high levels of subsidization, and social demands of an aging population. Following the initial euphoria over reunification and the first wave of eastern demand for consumer goods, the task of rebuilding the East's economy became almost overwhelming. Economic growth and development in eastern Germany have not met expectations, wages have risen faster than productivity, unemployment measures have been largely ineffective, and the government has been forced to borrow large sums of money to offset financial transfers to eastern Germany.

In 1991 the German government transferred some DM 170 billion to the five new *Länder*, DM 30 billion of which was raised by taxes in the East. Transfer payments to the East in 1992 have been estimated at DM 180 billion—more than 6 percent of Germany's GNP. This is roughly 25 percent of all public spending. Most of these transfers will be used to cover pensions, health care, and welfare.[3]

Although the Bundesregierung has sought to control expenditure growth at all levels of government, including the social security system, public sector expenditures are predicted to grow 4–5 percent in 1994. According to the Institut für Wirtschaft in Kiel, public debt in Germany is approximately DM 1.4 trillion, roughly 46 percent of GDP. If unification costs continue at current rates, public debt could escalate to DM 1.8 trillion or 51 percent of gross national product (GNP) by 1995. This is well below the average debt to GNP ratio of other industrial economies, but still an unwelcome development for a country that prides itself on fiscal responsibility.[4]

The prospect of further European integration has also intensified longstanding concern over the country's efficiency and competitiveness. With open national borders for people, goods, services, and capital, production and investment options will greatly expand. Many Germans have begun to question whether the many benefits and advantages they had won through hard work and efficiency might be lost because other Europeans are ready to accept lower standards of living.[5] Price competition from Eastern Europe has increased pressure on several industrial sectors. Subsidized less than its eastern rivals, the German steel industry, for example, is struggling to match East European steel prices.

The German economy is also stressed by demands for economic assistance from the former Soviet republics. For political and economic reasons (partly as a payoff for early Soviet troop withdrawals and to stem the tide of economic migrants from the east), Germany has expanded its aid to economically unstable East European nations. Soviet and East European debt has been accumulating for years, by some measures totaling $130 billion in 1990. Repayment is likely to be both in kind and slow in coming. In addition, neighboring East European nations now offer an enticingly inexpensive, well-trained workers, luring German companies to invest just across the border. The likely inclusion of these countries in the European Union serves only to heighten their attractiveness as low-cost investment sites.

Finally, to add to the list of woes, Japanese businesses are intensifying their sales efforts in Europe in an effort to diversify away from their heavy reliance on the U.S. market. Japanese producers have made impressive inroads into traditionally strong German markets such as consumer electronics, automobiles, and machine tools. As a consequence, many German industrialists consider Japan to be their primary economic rival. Japan's lead in computer and microelectronic technology gives them advantages in markets where Germans need to compete. The above factors and influences are forcing Germany to look inward. How will it maintain its industrial base in the face of rapidly changing economic and political realities?

Germany's attractiveness as an industrial site varies from industry to industry. The most successful sectors feature traditional German strengths: a well-trained, skilled workforce; a developed infrastructure; a large, dynamic market; a central European location; and a belief in working hard and producing quality products. Other industries that are energy-intensive, require more flexible cost structures, and/or utilize less-skilled workers have tended to relocate production facilities outside Germany.

Although the quality of Germany as an investment and production location is industry specific, recent surveys by the American Chamber of Commerce and the Institut der Deutschen Wirtschaft, among othters, reveal several common themes that are of concern to foreign firms doing business in Germany. Among the most frequently cited weaknesses of *Standort* Deutschland are high employment costs, worker flexibility, a heavy tax burden, environmental costs, energy costs, administrative delays, and bureaucracy. The next section will examine these factors and *Standort* determinants vis-à-vis Germany's primary economic competitors.

Employment Costs

Since 1989 West Germany has had the world's highest industrial employment costs per hour. In 1991, employment costs were DM 40.48 per hour, almost 43 percent higher than the OECD average. Between 1987 and 1991, employment costs rose 23.9 percent in Germany, compared with 18 percent in Japan and 4.1 percent in the U.S.[6]

The primary reason for the rapid escalation in employment costs is the incidental employment costs. When comparing just hourly wages,

Germany has a competitive position vis-à-vis other developed countries: DM 21.73 per hour. But the incidental costs of employing a German worker (social insurance, sick pay, paid vacations, bonuses, and other related employee benefits) make the overall costs skyrocket. Incidental costs now account for 86.3 percent of workers' direct pay in Germany, or 46.3 percent of workers' overall salary.[7] This situation is not likely to improve quickly, as social insurance premiums and payments for health insurance (*Sozial Versicherungsbeiträge und Entgeltfortzahlung im Krankheitfall*) continue to climb. In 1991 the average contribution to social insurance rose to 36.7 percent, a new high.[8]

Traditionally, Germany has been able to offset its high labor costs through high productivity, a German *Standort* advantage. But German labor costs have recently outstripped worker productivity. According to recent statistics from the European Union and the Institut der Deutschen Wirtschaft, Germany now trails Belgium and the Netherlands in worker productivity. Italy is not far behind. The employment costs of all three of these countries are roughly 20 percent less than Germany's —DM 8 to 9 per hour.[9]

Perhaps a more revealing statistic is the unit wage cost—the relationship between employment costs and productivity. By this measure, western Germany is the most expensive *Standort* for labor-intensive production. The unit wage costs in Germany are some 20 to 25 percent higher than those of its main competitors in Japan, France, the United States, and the United Kingdom.[10] Japan has improved its productivity since 1987 by 9.1 percent over Germany (3.7 percent through cost savings and 5.4 percent through productivity increases). The United States has improved its position by 11.2 percent for the same period of time, largely through exchange rate differences.[11] The United States Bureau of Statistics reveals that since 1982, the unit labor costs for Germany have risen 17 percent when calculated in Deutsche Marks, the largest increase in the world. German industry has so far been able to live with higher costs by producing goods of exceptional quality, diversifying, concentrating on market share in specialized products, relying on specialized production processes, and devoting research and development to selected fields.[12] With global competition increasing, only some of these costs can be passed on to consumers. Companies in competitive markets that cannot transfer these costs will face decreased market share, reduced investment, unemployment, and layoffs.

The situation is even more critical in eastern Germany, where unit costs are some 60 percent higher than in the West, largely because salaries have risen faster than productivity. In regions, professions, and factories where there is a shortage of qualified workers, higher hourly wages are justified. Where the transformation process has not produced sufficient results, the additional unit costs are not economically warranted.[13]

The Workweek

The length of the traditional workweek is an important criterion for determining the competitive advantage of a company. Germans work 37.6 hours per week—one of the shortest workweeks in the world. Only Norwegian and Danish workers enjoy shorter workweeks. To make matters worse, Germany is expecting further reductions in workweeks in several sectors of the economy. The IG Chemie Union has already secured a 37.5 hour workweek for its members, and the IG Metall has succeeded in lowering the workweek to 36 hours. In 1995 IG Metall members will have another hour shaved off the workweek: a four-day workweek is not far off.

The situation is even clearer when one considers personal vacation, holidays, and sick leave. German workers enjoy an additional forty-two days of vacation and national holidays—the highest in the world. Japanese and the Americans have on average twenty-five and twenty-three days respectively. Hubert Staerker, head of Zeuna Staerker, a maker of auto-exhaust systems, argues: "Each holiday costs German industry an average of 5.5 billion marks."[14] There has been some discussion of eliminating two federal holidays, but so far no action has been taken. If Germany were to restrict the number of vacation days, as some of its competitors do, it could add up to 7 percent its GDP.[15]

While German workers are working fewer hours per week, their allotment of sick days has increased. Germans now claim on average 148 hours of sick leave per year, giving Germany the shortest annual effective work time. Hence, on average, for each employee, a German company must pay for two and one-half months of worker absence.

Working lives are also abbreviated by extended university years and early retirement. A typical graduate in Germany starts his or her first job at age twenty-nine and retires at sixty-two. German Chancellor Kohl has recognized this problem and proposed shortening primary and secondary schooling to twelve years from thirteen.

The number of machine hours is also a matter of concern for potential investors and entrepreneurs. The difference between Germany and the European leaders, Belgium and the UK, is roughly 40 percent. More astonishing is that the number of machine hours exceeds work hours by only 41 percent.[16] The average number of machine hours in Germany is fifty-three, this is thirteen hours less than the European Union's average. German firms such as BMW have recognized the problem and have attempted to compromise with workers. According to *Der Spiegel*, BMW is prepared to offer its employees four-day workweeks in exchange for more flexibility on weekends and longer work days during the week to maximize machine hours. This would, of course, permit BMW to produce on Saturdays.[17]

Recent public opinion polls indicate that many Germans recognize that their wage levels, short workweeks, and leave benefits cannot be maintained. This same realism has created more conciliatory negotiations between unions and management. German labor has shown unprecedented flexibility in its most recent negotiations in order to help employers survive in the face of intensified global competition. Unions have, in fact, made a number of concessions in pay and working hours in the auto and chemical industries.

Taxation

Before a German, or for that matter, a foreign firm decides where to invest, a number of factors, including taxation, are considered. One reason that foreign investment in Germany has remained relatively low can be traced to high levels of taxation. In terms of tax structure, rates, and the variety of taxes levied on corporations, Germany has one of the highest tax burdens in the world. Taxes and social charges in Germany are estimated at 43.7 percent of GDP, and are the highest among industrial countries except for France. In Japan and the United States the comparable figure is around 30 percent. Statistics like this have important psychological aspects for potential investors, especially with the increased internationalization of corporate decision making and free movement of capital and personnel.[18]

Recognizing this problem, German lawmakers passed the Business Location Improvement Act (*Standorsicherungsgesetz*) on 2 July 1993. This law is intended to improve Germany's economic competitiveness by lowering marginal tax rates, building on the three-tier tax reform from 1986 to 1990 and the first stage of the Tax Amendment Law of 1992. It brings corporate and income tax rates down toward the lower international level. Elements of the package include the following provisions: (1) the 50 percent tax rate on retained corporate earnings was reduced to 45 percent; (2) the 36 percent rate on taxable income of resident companies, to the extent distributed to shareholders, was reduced to 30 percent; and (3) the 46 percent rate on taxable income of nonresident companies, irrespective of whether it is distributed or not, was reduced to 42 percent.

For the first time in postwar history, corporate and income tax rates will clearly be below 50 percent.[19] While this is a step in the right direction, tax reduction policies in other countries have, nevertheless, resulted in the continued disadvantage of German tax rates. Corporate tax rates are still much lower in the United States (34 percent), Japan (37.5 percent), and France (33 percent), irrespective of tax assessment bases.[20]

The German federal government will continue to push for further reductions of nonearnings-related taxes (trade capital and operational wealth tax), that inhibit operational efficiency. The German government will seek further reductions in earnings tax rates while widening the assessment base at the same time. Further harmonization of indirect taxation and interest rates within the European Union has also been identified as a priority. The tax reform also envisages the elimination of local business tax by 1996. Local governments will instead be compensated with funds from the income tax or value-added tax revenues.

While many applaud the reduction of marginal tax rates, the Association of Chemical Industries (VCI) cautions that restrictions on taxable deductions will negatively affect capital-intensive industries. Initial indications reveal that the law could lead to an additional DM 300 million per year in corporate taxes for chemical manufacturers. Industries that deduct a high percentage of their taxes, such as the machine tool industry, will also be hurt by the package. The German Chamber of Commerce and Industry and the German Federation of Industry criticize the tax reform as well, arguing that needed investment capital will be taken from firms. The Deutsche Institut für Wirtschaftsforschung has also raised questions about the ability of tax rate reduction and the restrictions on tax write-offs to increase investment and create jobs.

Research and Technology

Research and development (R&D) are critically important and are often the engine for economic growth and development. Improvements in technology lead to improved efficiency, better quality, and often higher prices. Only through continued innovation, improvement, and product development is company expansion possible. Although Germany is considered to be very competitive in several high-tech fields, the five major economic institutes have criticized industry for not moving quickly or assertively into *spitzentechnologie* (the most advanced technologies, such as microelectronics or microtechnology) as firms in the United States, Japan, and other Asian countries have done. Many fear that Germany's reluctance to develop and apply these technologies could give competing nations and firms advantages in attracting investment and technical talent.[21]

The fields in which Germany is considered to be very competitive include machine tools, automobiles, optics, electronics, and chemicals. In 1990 the chemical industry invested DM 11.3 billion in R&D—approxi-

mately 25 percent of overall industrial research. Of this amount, 98 percent was funded by private resources.[22]

Germany is second only to Japan in patent registrations in research-intensive products. A German patent office study revealed, however, that by 1989 Germany was trailing in three out of four major domestic patent areas, compared with the United States and Japan.[23] These numbers, however, can be misleading. Companies often protect a new development or invention by filing tens and hundreds of single patents to prevent others from slightly modifying a product and producing it. The customs of international patent registration vary widely from country to country. Furthermore, the number of patent registrations do not address the quality of innovations.

R&D is risky. Opportunity costs are high and the key to product success often hinges on the speed with which it is implemented. The time needed to develop new products is often more critical in determining the loss or win potential than the investment itself. For example, the time needed at BASF to develop and market a new product is ten years, at an average cost of DM 120 million. Thus, shortening the development time for new products, especially in the innovative field of chemicals, has become a priority for managers at BASF.[24]

Government policies play a significant role in the success or failure of many research products. German companies complain loudly about how long it takes the government to approve pilot projects; it sometimes takes up to two years, an average of thirteen to eighteen months longer than in most other European countries. Once approval is granted, companies are allowed to devote two to three years on a project—not nearly enough for many technologically advanced procedures. Similarly, the approval process for many production facilities is said to take too long.[25]

Government intervention and its detrimental influence on innovation is evident, for example, in gene technology. Gene technology is considered a key future technology with medical, agricultural, and environmental applications. Jürgen Strube, chairman of the board of BASF, noted during an April 1992 speech that Germany has only 3 gene technology-related products; Denmark has three production locations; Japan has some 130; and the United States many more. One of the main impediments in this field is said to be the German government's extended approval process. BASF recently waited twenty-seven months to receive authorization to produce a pharmaceutical product. Companies in the United States typically need three to six months for similar authorization. Strube concludes that with examples like this, it is easy to see why Eli Lilly selected Alsace and not Germany as the location for its new gene technology plant. In fact, during the past few years no foreign firms have invested in gene technology research in Germany. Even BASF has selected Boston, Massachusetts, as the site for its new research center for biological and gene-related research. The reason for this *Standort* decision was to avoid restrictive environmental and procedural requirements in Germany.[26]

Environment

Environmental protection laws are highly developed in Germany; many companies consider their costs to be excessive. Although there are severe environmental problems in the eastern part of Germany, the western part is considered one of the cleanest industrial locations in the world. When environmental costs are measured as a percentage of a nation's GNP, only the Austrians devote more resources to environmental protection than the Germans. According to the Institut der Deutschen Wirtschaft, 1.74 percent of Germany's GNP from 1991 can be attributed to environmental expenditures, compared with 1.94 percent in Austria. Countries such as the United States and Japan lag considerably behind, with environmental expenditures at 1.36 percent and 1.02 percent of their respective GDPs. It should also be noted that from 1986 to 1991, environmental expenditures in Germany increased 14 percent while the United States experienced a 7 percent decline and the Japanese a reduction of 24 percent.[27]

The chemical industry is severely affected by Germany's stringent environmental laws. Statistics collected by the Verband der Chemischen Industrie reveal that during the period 1986–1990, the percentage of investment in environmental protection was approximately 13.4 percent of overall investment in the chemical field. This amounts to roughly 2.74 percent of total sales in the chemical industry for the same period of time. Jürgen Strube recently noted in a speech that in 1991 alone, BASF AG spent approximately DM 1.1 billion on environmental protection, an amount that roughly reflects the total tax liability for the BASF Group in the same year. Strube expects additional laws and regulation aimed at restricting environmental pollution to create additional investment needs for BASF of some DM 700 million in Ludwigshafen alone. This entails additional costs of DM 400 million per year for BASF.[28]

BASF is proud of its accomplishments in reducing emissions. BASF air emissions have been cut by 75 percent since 1970, while production has simultaneously increased 80 percent. Organic wastes deposited in the Rhine have decreased by 90 percent since 1974, the year BASF installed its sewage treatment plant. The Rhine is now considered one of the cleanest of the ten major rivers feeding into the North Sea; it is in fact cleaner than many of its tributaries. In spite of the progress, new environmental requirements and new definitions require ever-greater compliance costs.[29]

Wolfgang Jentzsch, deputy chairman of the board at BASF, notes that since the *Bundesemissionsschutzgesetzes* (German emission protection law) was enacted in 1974, it has been changed fifteen times; also, a number of administrative regulations and decrees which have further specified and amended the law. In comparison, the changes in the Clean Air Act signed by President George Bush in November 1990 marked the first change to this law in thirteen years.[30] The additional time, planning, measures, and costs incurred by German firms detract from its efforts to compete against its rivals in the United States or elsewhere.

Energy

Germany is an energy-poor land and consequently needs to import most of its energy needs, as do most other industrial countries. Germany imports 97 percent of its oil needs. As in many other countries, the energy sector in Germany is heavily influenced by government regulation. Stringent environmental regulations, higher than average security precautions, and a heavy reliance on coal as a source of electrical power have led to more expensive energy prices in Germany. In 1990 the industrial electric price was 14.42 pfennigs per kilowatt hour, 23.6 percent above the average electric price in other countries of the Organization of Economic Cooperation and Development (OECD), up from 14 percent in 1980. When one considers that the annual electrical demand in West German industry is around 200 billion kw-hours—about 60 percent of total industrial energy needs—a *Standort* disadvantage of some DM 5.5 billion results.[31] Germany's electric costs are 47.2 percent higher than the United States.

Germany's expensive electric costs have political reasons. Most of Germany's electricity comes from brown coal, one of Germany's few natural resources. France, a country with relatively modest electric costs, derives most of its electricity from nuclear sources. The nuclear reactors that Germany does have operate under strict security standards, thus making electricity from this source more expensive relative to other Western countries.

Reduced energy costs are not expected for Germany. The cost of establishing an efficient energy production capacity in the eastern part of Germany has been estimated at DM 100 billion. The German government has also taken a leading role in reducing CO_2 emissions. The government's goal is to reduce emissions by 25 to 30 percent by 2005. This will add extra costs to an already expensive system. The majority of other Western countries, in contrast, will strive to meet EU requirements for stabilizing CO_2 emissions at 1990 levels until the year 2000. This may mean that German electrical prices may continue to climb even more vis-à-vis other European countries.[32]

Many companies support the EU Commission's proposal for more competition in the energy markets. The primary issue at stake is the availability of gas and electricity from other EU countries. The result would be the subsequent elimination of monopolistic pricing from regional energy producers, thus resulting in lower costs for consumers. Larger, more integrated markets are generally less susceptible to disturbances and offer a higher degree of security.

Can Germany Compete?

What are the implications of the challenges outlined above, and how might the government respond? In many ways, the German economy was confronted with similar economic problems at the beginning of the 1980s. At that time 900,000 individuals were unemployed. By 1983 the number had climbed to 2.3 million and deficit spending was threatening to slip out of control. The newly elected Kohl administration responded with painful measures: it defered social security increases, restricted wage and salary increases for civil servants, and restricted welfare and other programs. The corporate tax burden was reduced to help overcome a sluggish economy along with deregulation. The result was a period of stable growth. Germany's GNP achieved a 28.5 percent real growth between 1982 and 1991 and 3 million jobs were created. Perhaps this experience contains lessons for the 1990s.

Chancellor Kohl has vowed to make *Standort* issues a major theme in the 1994 election campaign. An economic recession, increasing unem ployment, and social tensions, particularly regarding foreigners, are issues of paramount importance. Public opinion polls and recent elections in Germany have shown a growing dissatisfaction with the established parties. Given this background, and considering that the measures proposed to improve German competitiveness will be quite painful to major social groups, the prospect for their short-term implementation is slight.

Germany's industrial and economic policies in the 1990s must promote economic growth and job creation—East and West. To accomplish this, the ruling Christian Democratic Union/Christian Social Union/Free Democratic Party coalition presented a thirty point growth and employment action program on 18 January 1994. The program draws heavily on the September 1993 government report on German competitiveness. It contains no additional spending measures, but rather emphasizes the need for supply-side financial and economic policies. The program's proposals seek to reduce tax burdens and reduce public sector spending. The proposals concentrate on new business promotion, privatization, deregulation, and wage moderation. Support for the action plan has been mixed. Not surprisingly, the program to stimulate economic growth and employment was welcomed by all industry associations, although it was seen as ambitious. In contrast, labor union leaders argue that the plan would not improve Germany's attractiveness as a business location, but would rather prolong the recession.

Government and industry have made a number of recommendations to assist the unified German economy to meet the challenges of the 1990s and beyond; some of them are listed below.

Redefine success—To be successful in developing eastern Germany, it is important to be realistic about the time it will take. If growth rates in the west continue somewhere between 2 and 3 percent per annum for the next ten years, the East will need a yearly rate of 15 percent to equalize living standards.[33] More work needs to be done to develop the infrastructure, resolve ownership claims, and settle environmental liabilities in eastern Germany to promote investment. German taxpayers need to be informed about the real cost and duration of rebuilding the East.

Set priorities—Transfers to the East should be directed more to investment needs and not consumption. Concentrate investment efforts in areas that need it. Strategic sectors should be identified and supported.

Increase employment—Germany needs to create 5 million jobs. This problem is especially serious in the five new *Bundesländer*, particularly among women. One problem hindering job creation in the new *Bundesländer* is the planned equalization of wages with western salaries. One fifth of eastern German workers are on contracts that call for equal wages with their counterparts in the West by 1994.[34] The net effect will be layoffs and further job uncertainty. In order to secure jobs, increases in wages need to reflect gains in productivity. One way to accomplish this is to promote regional, sectoral, and occupational differentiation in wages. In those areas or professions where shortages of qualified workers exist, increases in wages should be offered to attract people to fill these deficiencies. Where this is not the case, increases in wages should reflect productivity gains. Wage agreements should include revision clauses that allow wage increases to reflect political and economic conditions. There needs to be more flexibility with work hours and machine time, including weekends and holidays. This implies cooperation from Germany's powerful unions.

Decrease deficit spending—The tempo of deficit spending needs to be slowed. The high degree of state indebtedness burdens capital markets and hinders private investment. To accomplish this task, the government needs to curtail expenditures and limit subsidies. Consequences of continued government spending are inflation, high interest rates, and slow growth. The creation of new subsidies in the East need to be restricted—once they are in place, it is very difficult to do away with them.

Lower taxes—As previously illustrated, Germany is a heavily taxed country. Germany needs to lower its marginal tax rates and overall tax burden to an internationally comparable level in order to attract direct investment. This will alleviate pressure of the tax-price/wage-price spiral.

Deregulate—One way to invigorate and promote entrepreneurship is to deregulate. This will help create healthy competition and generally result in lower costs for related industries.

Privatize—Measures should be taken to privatize uncompetitive state monopolies. The Bundesbahn, Lufthansa, and Telekom are ideal candidates. Individual states and communities should also be able to avail themselves of these opportunities—privatization opportunities for harbors, airports, energy facilities, autobahns, and other modes of transportation should be examined. Legal questions concerning property rights and privatization in eastern Germany need to be cleared up to encourage future investment.

Simplify the planning and approval process—Bureaucratic barriers and excessive delays need to be reduced. The process needs to be simplified and accelerated in both western and eastern Germany.

Avoid unilateral environmental measures—Germany can and should maintain a leading position in environmental protection, but not unilaterally. Germany should continue to work through multilateral bodies to ensure worldwide environmental protection measures. Unilateral measures will only produce additional costs for enterprises and consumers.

Encourage free trade—Every third job in Germany depends on exports. The successful completion of GATT could lead to a 20 percent increase in the world's output of goods and services in the next ten years. This would certainly create additional trade opportunities for an export nation like Germany. The German government should actively work toward the elimination of the remaining trade barriers within the EU. The German government needs to take a more proactive role in reducing subsidies and barriers to trade.

Modernize—Firms need to move early to take advantage of global advancements in technology. The reluctance to take risks and failure to think long term have prevented many sectors in Germany from advancing into several high technology areas.

Increase R&D on new technologies—German firms are considered to be great improvers of existing technologies, but have experienced limited success in developing new ones. A higher rate of investment in new technological fields will lead to the creation of new industries and jobs. Large government-sponsored research and development projects with the support of multinational firms are unlikely to succeed. The best method of achieving success is by fostering competition among firms, in consultation with leading universities and research institutes.[35]

In conclusion, the reunification of Germany, the revitalization of Eastern Europe, and continued economic integration of the European Union offer challenges and opportunities for the German economy. Germany has many competitive advantages—a highly developed infrastructure, well-trained, qualified workers, political and economic stability, and a central position in the heart of Europe. Germany's future lies not in producing low-cost goods, but rather in creating new, sophisticated, and highly specialized products.

The recent *Standort* discussion in Germany has exposed several competitive disadvantages in the German economy—disadvantages that are mostly transitory and correctable. High wages, high taxes, and liberal vacations are a problem for Germany's competitiveness and an impediment to foreign investment. The solutions to these shortcomings are neither painless nor politically easy. They will require courage from all parties. The German trade unions will need to adopt conciliatory policies with employers. Politicians will need to create an environment conducive to international investment and production. German workers will need to show more flexibility and mobility. And businesses will need to be more aggressive in modernizing and advancing into new technologies.

Creating competitive advantages in sophisticated industries demands constant improvement and innovation. The fact that government, unions, and companies have undertaken a review of *Standort* Deutschland and have sought to find solutions to Germany's competitive weaknesses are grounds for optimism. The resiliency of the German economy should not be underestimated. As one Japanese businessman recently noted: "The German star may be flickering, but I don't see it waning."

Notes

1. Globus Kartendienst GmbH, 13 August 1990, as cited in "Information zur Wirtschafts- und Strukturpolitik," *Deutscher Gewerkschaftsbund Bundesvorstand,* No. 1, 5 February 1992, 5.

2. *Qualität des Wirtschaftsstandortes Deutschland und Ansatzpunkte zur Verbesserung,* Bundesministerium für Wirtschaft, 2. Auflage, no. 317, 1.

3. "There She Blows," *The Economist,* 23 May 1992, 5–6.

4. Ibid.

5. W. R. Smyser, *The Economy of United Germany: Colossus at the Crossroads,* (New York: St. Martin's Press, 1992), 220.

6. Institut der Deutschen Wirtschaft, *Industriestandort Deutschland—Ein Graphisches Portrait*, (Köln: Deutscher Instituts-Verlag 1992), 6.

7. Nomura Research Institute Deutschland, "Deutschland—Musterland der kurzen Arbeitszeiten—und seine künftige Wettbewerbsfähigkeit," September 1992, 17.

8. Rainer Gerding, "Wirtschaft Standort Deutschland," *Trend*, September 1992, 30.

9. Institut der Deutchen Wirtschaft *Industriestandort*, 7.

10. Ibid.

11. Rolf Kroker and Heinz Salowsky, "Indikator: Arbeitskosten, Productivität," *IW Trends*, Institut der Deutschen Wirtschaft, 2/1992, 27.

12. Nomura Research Institute.

13. "Strategie für den Standort Deutschland: Wirtschaftspolitik für die neunziger Jahre," Bundesministerium für Wirtschaft, N. 327, Bonn, 15 September 1992.

14. Daniel Benjamin, "Losing Its Edge: Germany Is Troubled by How Little Work Its Workers Are Doing," *The Wall Street Journal*, European Edition, 7 May 1993.

15. Institut der Deutschen Wirtschaft, *Industriestandort*, 10.

16. Ibid., 14.

17. "Der Exodus hat begonnen," *Der Spiegel*, No. 4, 1992, 94.

18. Winfried Fuest and Rolf Kroker, "Indikator: Unternehmensteuer," *IW Trends*, Institut der Deutschen Wirtschaft, No. 2, 1992, 35.

19. "Report by the Federal Government on Securing Germany's Economic Future," Federal Ministry of Economics, Bonn, 2 September 1993, 34–35.

20. Ibid., 34.

21. Smyser, *Economy of United Germany*, 107.

22. Jürgen Strube, "Das Innovationsklima in Deutschland—Sind wir für den internationalen Wettbewerb gerüstet?," Vortrag am 1 April 1992, Landesvertretung Rheinland-Pfalz, Bonn.

23. Smyser, *Economy of United Germany*, 109.

24. Elmer Frommer, "An Welchen Standortkriterien orientiert die BASF ihre Investitionsentscheidungen?," *Standortkriterien bei Investitionsentscheidungen*, Vorträge des 3. BASF-Geschprächs zwischen Politik, Wissenschaft und Wirtschaft, Mannheim, 13–14 September, 1991, 38.

25. Jürgen Strube, "Rahmenbedingungen des Wirtschaftsstandorts Deutschland–aus der Sicht der Unternehmen," Vortrag am 14 Januar 1993 im Rahmen der "Bitburger Gespräche," 14.

26. Strube, "Rahmenbedingungen," 18.

27. Institut der Deutschen Wirtschaft, *Industriestandort*, 19.

28. Strube, "Rahmenbedingungen," 14.

29. Dr. Wolfgang Jentzsch, "Einführung," in *Standortkriterien bei Investitionsentscheidungen*, Vorträge des 3. BASF Gesprächs zwischen Politik, Wissenschaft und Wirtschaft, Mannheim, 13–14 September 1991, 13–14.

30. Jentzsch, "Einführung," 16.

31. Gerhard Voss, "Indikator: Energieversorgung," *IW Trends*, Institut der Deutschen Wirtschaft, (Köln: Deutscher Instituts Verlag, N. 2, 1992), 52–54.

32. Ibid.

33. "There She Blows," *The Economist*, 23 May 1992, 11.

34. Ibid., 6.

35. Michael Porter, *The Competitive Advantage of Nations*, (New York: Free Press, 1990), 716–719.

PART TWO

German Unification:
Social and Cultural Consequences

Introduction

Kathryn S. Mack

Today, fellow countrymen, we have founded our common state. What we make of unity in human terms will not be decided by any government treaty, constitution, or law. It depends on the attitude adopted by each one of us, on our own openness and our care for one another. It is the "plebiscite of each single day" (Renan) which will determine the character of our community.
— President Richard von Weizsäcker, Day of German Unity Speech,
3 October 1990

On 3 October 1994 Germany celebrated its fourth anniversary as a united country. The whirlwind of events that led to unification created, especially in eastern Germany, excitement, high expectations, and optimism about the future. During the last four years, however, these positive sentiments have diminished as both parts of the country have had to make sacrifices to rebuild the nation. The tasks were enormous. The eastern part of the country was incorporated into the West, requiring it to change completely its laws, its government, its economic orientation, its customs, and its way of thinking. The western part of the country financed these changes while undergoing major restructuring made necessary by a prolonged recession. The process of unification was far costlier than anyone imagined, both in economic and social terms.

Given the magnitude of dislocation, one might ask whether the process could have proceeded differently. A review of how the unification process began, however, demonstrates that the political revolution could not, and probably should not, have been controlled or slowed.

In early 1989 East German citizens began to flee to the West in increasingly large numbers. In May the Hungarian government began to dismantle fences along its border with Austria. On 10 September it announced that it would no longer enforce a 1969 agreement with the German Democratic Republic (GDR) whereby citizens without valid travel documents were deported to the GDR. By the end of September more than 55,000 East Germans had fled across the border. This massive flight was dubbed *Abstimmung mit den Füssen* (voting with one's feet).

Meanwhile, demonstrations were occurring in Leipzig, Dresden, East Berlin, and elsewhere across the GDR. Demonstrators demanded democratic reforms to address the political and social problems fueling the mass exodus. On 19 September, New Forum, an umbrella organization formed to coordinate the activities of informal political groups and to campaign openly for democratic reforms, applied for permission to establish local organizations throughout the GDR. The Interior Ministry refused the request.

In October the demonstrations continued unabated. Prodemocracy protesters in Leipzig chanted "We want new leaders" and "We are the people." Two days later Egon Krenz replaced Erich Honecker as the party's leader. On that same day, in a nationally televised address, Krenz stated: "The door is wide open for earnest political dialogue. ... It is clear that we have not realistically appraised the social developments in our country in recent months and have not drawn the right conclusions quickly enough."[1] Nonetheless, large demonstrations persisted; among the demands: dismantling the Berlin Wall and free elections.

On 9 November 1989 the Wall fell. The chants from demonstrators transformed from "We are the people" to "We are one people." The exodus continued: 157,813 in November; 54,000 in December; 73,729 in January 1990; 63,893 in February.[2] In view of these numbers, free elections in the GDR were moved up from May to March 1990. In the elections, the mainstream West German democratic parties won a clear mandate.

What had begun in the East as a spontaneous, grass-roots movement rapidly changed into a West German effort to reconstruct the GDR's economy, its cultural institutions, and its political, educational, and legal systems. The process involved the transfer of West German money, institutions, professionals, financing and know-how to the East. The transition was fast and East Germans had very little control over the process.[3]

This section of the book attempts to convey the enormity of the social and cultural challenges facing Germany in this transition. Many Germans from the new eastern states are struggling to keep their jobs and a sense of security. The real rate of unemployment in the East is about 40 percent if early retirements, government make-work projects, and worker retraining programs are taken into account. The strong "cradle-to-grave" social net that the East German government provided, including the guarantee of a job, is gone. Homelessness, drug addiction, and unemployment are increasing; mounting evidence of inequality creates tension between men and women, employed and unemployed, and haves and have nots. Feelings of frustration, fear, inferiority, inequality, and anxiety prevail. Not anticipating the harshness of the transition to capitalism or how long the process of social equalization with West

Germany would take, many easterners feel that they have been unfairly treated in the unification process. Exploiting these feelings, the former Communists, known now as the Democratic Socialists (PDS), are emerging as a political force in eastern Germany.

Politicians from the new eastern states talk of *Lastenausgleich* (equalization of burdens) and about *Überwindung der Teilung durch Teilen* (overcoming division through sharing). These concepts are not well received in the western German states, where citizens feel they have shared enough. The Bonn government annually transfers well over $61 billion to the eastern part of the country. To help finance these huge expenditures, the government has announced plans to cut unemployment and welfare payments, the first reductions of social benefits in West Germany since World War II. Compounding the strain of unification are serious structural problems that hinder Germany's international competitiveness, create frictions between labor and management, and threaten many of the benefits West Germans have come to enjoy, including the longest vacations, the shortest work weeks, and the earliest retirement age in the industrialized world. The frustration of westerners who feel they are being asked to sacrifice too much is captured by the popular T-shirts reading "I want my wall back."

Chapter 6 attempts to convey the depths of the Germans' frustration and pain by comparing the situation in Germany after the fall of the Berlin Wall to that facing the United States at the end of the Civil War, when a nation divided was reunited across a deep emotional divide. In both the American South and the German East a complete Reconstruction or *Rekonstruktion* had to take place.

The former East Germans are also in the process of reflecting on their past in the GDR and coming to terms with the inhuman face of that state and the crimes it committed. On 2 January 1992, pursuant to a new law, the Stasi archives, widely known as the "Horror Files," were opened. The Stasi kept files on six million of the GDR's eighteen million citizens, and people are now free to review their own file. Shockingly, most of the information for these files did not come from professional spies but from part-time informers, private citizens who provided information to the political police on their friends and colleagues. Chapter 7 explores various reasons why many East Germans collaborated in the state's efforts to control them.

What must remain clear, however, is that it was the East German government that failed, that was corrupt, that exploited its citizens; most of the East German people were neither cowards nor collaborators, but rather were victims. They were people trying to survive under a government installed by the former Soviet Union that permitted only the most limited political expression and employed the Stasi to ensure conformity. The state indoctrinated and coerced them, using fear and blackmail to ensure obedience to the regime. Even now, when attempting to determine who the collaborators were, the lines between resistance, self-protection, and guilt are blurred.

As East and West integrate, both sides must attempt to reaffirm and continue the positive aspects of life in the former GDR. The joke in the eastern states these days is that the only thing remaining from the former GDR is the green traffic arrow allowing a right turn on red. Although this is how it might feel to those experiencing the social and economic upheaval of the past few years, other aspects of life in the former GDR have continued and have grown stronger, particularly in the area of culture. The strong tradition of opera, music, and theater in eastern Germany remains. In addition, youth groups and other grass-roots cultural initiatives have not only continued, but, given their new-found freedom, have multiplied. Chapter 8 presents a snapshot of the issues challenging the cultural organizations in Leipzig in 1993. Although it depicts the difficult financial struggle many of these organizations are facing, the majority, from opera houses to jazz clubs, are overcoming the obstacles and learning how to operate under new economic conditions.

Other positive aspects of life in the former GDR have suffered more in the transition. One is the role of women in society. The percentage of women working in so-called male professions was far higher in the East than in the West. In the GDR it was expected that women should receive the same training and have the same career aspirations as men. Indeed, while women comprised only 38 percent of the work force in West Germany, they accounted for 52 percent of the East German work force. The East German state provided generous maternity benefits and child care. Now, as eastern Germany undergoes major restructuring, women are the first to lose their jobs and it is harder for them to be reemployed. Day-care centers are no longer as affordable. Furthermore, East German women, who for the past twenty years had access to state-funded abortion, are now subject to a 1993 Constitutional Court ruling that holds that abortions are unconstitutional (because they violate a constitutional provision requiring the state to protect human life). The court went on to say that women who undergo abortions in the first three months of pregnancy would not be prosecuted, but it imposed various restrictions on obtaining an abortion and banned state funding for the procedure. As a result of the numerous changes women are facing, birth and marriage rates in the five eastern German states are plummeting.

Chapter 9 discusses the various factors that account for the rise of rightist violence among youth in Germany. Minister of Saxony Kurt Biedenkopf emphasizes in his address (later in this book) that each obstacle eastern Germany faces in some way also represents a possible future opportunity. This maxim might be difficult to apply with respect to right- ist violence directed at foreigners and others considered to be outsiders. Yet this violence can be seen as a clear warning to Germany of the need to remain alert against prejudice and hate and to deal directly and openly with issues of immigration, integration, and minorities. The gov- ernment must take the lead in building mutual understanding between different ethnic groups rather than depending, as it has in the past, on the unhelpful and inaccurate position that "the Federal Republic is not a country of immigration." The political parties, election campaigns, and media must all adopt a responsible attitude and stop employing scare tactics to exploit the issue.

As Germany moves slowly forward, bowed under its heavy burdens, it is important not to forget the power of the autumn of 1989. The use of force was imminent and yet the East German people did not back down. Chanting "We are the people," they brought down the government and obtained their freedom. It is this power to achieve political change that gives hope for the future, despite the growing *Politikverdrossenheit*, or political disgruntlement. Step by step economic and social advances are being made, and step by step the fading dreams from 1989 will become a reality.

Historically, in their political thought, however, Germans have longed for harmony and perfection. Democracy, in contrast, requires tension and lively conflicts; it requires individual initiative rather than conformity. In a 1991 speech President Richard von Wiezsäcker emphasized the impor- tant role of the individual in a democracy by quoting Heinrich Heine's famous line, "Germany means each one of us."[4] Thus it is by continuing to address and debate openly and honestly as a society the problems and tensions they are facing that the Germans will meet the challenges unifi- cation poses.

Notes

1. *Facts on File*, 20 Oct. 1989, 786.
2. Stephan Eisel, "The Politics of a United Germany," *Daedalus* 123 (1994): 152.
3. Jürgen Kocka, "Crisis of Unification: How Germany Changes," *Daedalus* 123 (1994): 176–177.
4. Speech by President Richard von Weizsäcker, 13 December 1991.

6

Passages: East-West by North-South

Thomas A. Hagemann

Ruined cities; beaten land. Destruction, chaos, scars of a nation torn apart, everywhere: dilapidated, outmoded machines; brick and stone ruins; occupying forces that will, someday, if all goes well, be gone. In the news are the faces of need, soon to be joined by those of frustration and resentment. To a stubborn-willed people, brought to terms with total, systemic failure, the present seems a threat and the future an uncertainty. The new loyalty demands that the past be declared a shame. Fundamental principles, those that had given life to this peculiar economy and this complex society, have been eviscerated, and, somehow, new principles must be erected, accepted, and sustained.

The Confederacy, After the Fall ...
Eastern Germany, After the Wall[1]

This is an essay about the experience of Reconstruction—or *Rekonstruktion*—a word that had taken on no particular meaning in Richmond 1865, or Berlin 1990. Then, a struggle's end and a reunion's beginning were preeminent. But the state of affairs was diametrically opposed in these two lands. Unlike the U.S. South, eastern Germany chose to *join* a union and stood perched on a breathlessly high tidal wave of optimism—one formed with the cathartic opening of the Berlin Wall in November 1989, one which not one year later had swollen into the decision for and the fact of one Germany. Prosperity and an era of good feeling, the imagined cash crops of capitalism and democracy, were surely just around the corner.

Times change; reality intervenes. If the fanciful words of 1990 were, "I never dreamed I'd see this in my lifetime," the sobered voice of 1992 was, "I never thought it would be this painful." Sadly, after the Wall, the emotions of eastern Germany have moved much closer to the Confederacy's sense of loss. In both lands, Reconstruction was—and is—a painful passage.

Past Tense: The Passage of Time

"Every wall falls sometime."[2]

Imagine that the Civil War had lasted not four but six years and that, at war's end, seemingly every inch of the South had been overrun, burned, and destroyed. When peace finally came, the Union decided— perhaps in light of the economic nothingness that remained—to let the Confederacy have its way. With no reunion, the South was left to its own empty devices to reconstruct itself. Imagine then that a ruthless group of foreign investors had somehow taken control of the South and that a bitter enmity had developed between that controlling group and the North—an enmity so bitter that, in 1883, they built a cordoning wall around their investment from Virginia all the way to Texas. This wall stood, walling in and walling out, until 1911. And, behind this wall, the investors bled the South—its land, its people, its spirit.

In the next year, however, events suddenly, unexpectedly, careened in another direction. The wall came down, the investors obtained the best close-out price they could, and in a decisive flashpoint, the North and South were reunited. Yet what was left to reunite? On the eve of the Age of Wilson, who remembered the Age of Lincoln? Johnny Reb, a young man in the Wilderness campaign, was then in his late sixties. Time had marched on.

In 1865, the North was substantially similar to the North of 1861 from which the Confederacy had tried to secede. Within the North itself, absent internal revolution or external takeover, four years was simply too short a period of time for the land to undergo fundamental change. If grudgingly, Johnny Reb returned to a union and a system that he surely knew. In eastern Germany, by contrast, only those fifty or older can recall the unity that was—when the industry was in the East, not the West; when Germany was thoroughly centralized in Berlin, not decentralized through federalism; when, of course, the Third Reich was the tie that bound.

The specter of the Third Reich spread its deadly, twelve-year shadow in every direction; unlike the one-sided wreckage of 1865, both sides of the soon-to-be "German Question" lay in shambles in 1945. Both sides had to be reconstructed. By force, by choice, and by necessity West Germany did not remain in a state of suspended animation, waiting for reunion with its former sidekick. New forces of occupation, alliances, and enemies; a new constitution and federal framework; new economic wonders; new political problems; hundreds of new McDonald's—these were signposts along the way to the fact of modern West Germany, a country remade in the image of a materialistic, enterprising, westernized, parliamentary democracy.

For eastern Germans, the passage of time alone has created formidable barriers to reentry that American southerners never knew. For many, any word with "re-" before it is a misnomer. Having never experienced unity, they have not reunited; having never left, they have not returned. Even the older generations have been away a long time, so that even the identical home would feel strange. But, lastly, after so much time, "home" cannot be what it used to be. The doors are new and the furniture has been rearranged. The house is framed by golden arches.

Past Imperfect: The Passage of Identity

"Bearing the responsibility to point the way for the entire
German nation toward a future of peace and socialism…
The people of the German Democratic Republic…"[3]

Time did not pass idly by in the east after 1945. Time brought those "foreign investors." Time witnessed a wall. But what came first in time was a nightmare.

The South, too, had its nightmares. But the South faced its worst nightmare at the endpoint of disunion, while eastern Germany confronted the worst at the beginning. In other words, although conditions were unpalatable, in some aspects miserable, for this land in 1990, they seem almost serene when compared to May 1945. In German history, that is *Stunde Null*, zero hour; nothing for food or warmth; nothing for shelter save ruins. This nothingness at origin leads logically to one easily overlooked consequence: the history of the German Democratic Republic (GDR)[4] is one of huge *progress*. Given its mangled economy, environment, and governance, that notion may sound a bit far-fetched today. Yet, as the GDR began its own march to self-destruction, bombs and buildings, at least, had stopped falling. Buildings began to be built, people to be fed. This undeniable fact of progress would form an oft-repeated, socializing cornerstone of the curious structure that took shape over the next forty-five years in the GDR.

In year one, however, there was no GDR and no West Germany. After total war and total surrender, the whole of Germany was divided into two parts, for all practical purposes: the Russian and the Western sectors. For the next four years, although the two entities were forming from the rubble of the thousand-year Reich, Germany itself did not exist. In national limbo, a war-torn people had to begin to define itself in a vacuum. From the first days of peace, the questions "Who are we?" and "Who will we be?" were also pieces of the puzzle of survival.

And then the puzzle split in half. With the founding of the two Germanies in May and October of 1949, there began a forty-year period in which the citizens of the GDR would have four different ways—all partially correct, none completely accurate—to define themselves as Germans: We are the true Germany. We are part of what will again someday be Germany. We hope to be part someday of what is now Germany. We are a new nation of German descent. For forty years, however, it was still another definition that would make the biggest impression upon the East German identity: We are a socialist state and part of the Soviet constellation.

Elemental facts of life flowed from this definition and worked their effects on nearly every citizen of the GDR. One of these, affecting all Germans, was the fact of crisis. The peak crises of the cold war are all too well-known, but these were only heightened reflections of a daily fact of life in Germany from 1949 until well into the 1980s. That is, if the cold war reverted to war unmodified, then Germany would be the central battlefield from the outset. As a nation parceled, as the line for international tug-of-war, Germany lived for decades on the cutting edge of destruction. The armored divisions massed on either side of the border were daily confirmation of that edge.

A second impact of socialist adherence was the rise and fall of the GDR. While there was never an "economic miracle" to rival West Germany's, it remains clear that times were not uniformly bad in the GDR. In general, the country's economic well-being and political morale seems to have followed a parabolic curve, reaching its peak somewhere in the late 1960s and early 1970s. As the 1960s unfolded, signs of that peak could be found both inside and outside the GDR. After some nearly catastrophic economic and worker crises in the 1950s, the GDR's industry—allowed at least to whisper the word "profit"—proved itself the most productive of the Eastern Bloc countries. While parity with West Germany was never within sight, gaps of disparity were at least temporarily closed. (For example, if 84 percent of West Germans owned a refrigerator in 1969, so did 50 percent of East Germans—as compared to a mere 6 percent in 1960.) At the same time, the international community recognized the separate existence of the GDR, with gradual diplomatic recognition and with immediate recognition of profound athletic achievement in Mexico City in 1968, when the GDR sent its first team to the Olympics.

The size of a peak is both absolute and relative. In West Germany, what had been an unending chain of success throughout the 1950s began to display a few weak links. In 1966, a budget crisis; in 1973, the oil crisis. Across the political landscape stormed the student movement, the Baader-Meinhof gang, and, most significantly, Vietnam, which shifted the moral balance between Russia and America and stiffened the resolve of the former's allies. By 1969, to East (and many West) Germans, the socialists' two favorite words—"militaristic" and "imperialistic"—seemed fitting enough to describe a Kafkaesque "Amerika."

The seeming accuracy of that description was exacerbated in the GDR by a third fact of its life: propaganda. By that, I refer not only to the banal speeches of politicians, but also to the writings of academicians and the press. The Marxist-Leninist spin was put on a staggering array of publications, speeches, and information—namely, anything that remotely touched the proper, dialectical development of the GDR. With dialectics construed rather broadly, that could range from a basic travel guide describing how the GDR was "saved" by Russia in 1945 to a history textbook declaring "Victory over the Monster" in 1980—the monster, of course, being America.

Propaganda, however, is not necessarily false; its truth value depends on the underlying gap between rhetoric and reality. That gap became a chasm in the late 1970s as the fall of the GDR began. To fasten upon a precise turning date would be pointless, but it is more than a coincidence that, in 1971, Erich Honecker replaced Walter Ulbricht as the GDR's leader. Ulbricht's partly successful effort to turn the GDR into a model for socialist countries, a model that mixed in the spice of capitalism, had been ultimately taken for presumptuous by the Kremlin, and so it fell to Honecker to remodel his country after the Soviet Union's fashion—thoroughly centralized, rigidly socialized, and dogmatically acculturated: the seeds of economic and popular failure. That is not to say that Ulbricht's policies were destined to succeed, merely that Honecker's were destined to fail. As incentive faded, as West Germany again surged, vivid signs of the fall came to dominate the last two decades—decaying buildings; contaminated waste sites; collapsing infrastructure. When Honecker proclaimed in October 1989 that the GDR had developed an economy of modern structure and huge capacity, "propaganda" had been stretched too far. That, quite simply, was a lie, the proof of which was everywhere to be seen.

Yet rarely to be heard, thanks to a fourth fact of life in the GDR. As with Nazi Germany, the hallmark of this distorted state was not government propaganda; it was the unwillingness to tolerate dissent from the opposition. Emanating first from Stalin's own paranoia, the stench of repression gradually seeped through every seam in the GDR structure, with most of the sewage generated by the state security police, or "Stasi."

In the annals of government security, history may well judge the Stasi the most frighteningly inefficient yet efficiently frightening organization for its ludicrously unfocused overinclusiveness in the quest for useful information. The Stasi tried to know *everything*. Open every letter; turn everyone into an informant; make everything an undercover location. (There were almost 600 in Leipzig alone.) The title of a permanent exhibit in Leipzig captures the terrible irony: "Power and Banality." The latter, because who really needed to investigate a fourteen-year-old boy's essay on why the Trabant was not a very good car? And yet the former, because the Stasi did not simply gather information. It used it to barter away people's private lives; to turn the GDR into a land of docile, would-be paranoiacs. "Would-be," only because Big Brother was usually watching. Listening. Or trying to.

All, however, was not propaganda and repression, for one must recognize a fifth strain of the socialist identity. That is the power of an idea. In a time when capitalism looks like a landslide winner, it is tempting to view socialism as nothing more than another loser, gone the way of monarchy into the ideological graveyard. That would be to underestimate the force of this principle: from each, as able; to each, as needed. The sensitivity for underdogs, the notion of sharing with and caring for each other—no matter how utopian—has always given pure socialism a certain conceptual advantage over the harsh market realities of pure capitalism. People know they are property-acquiring animals but strive, to varying degrees, to be property-sharing Samaritans, and, since its theoretical inception, socialism has always seemed to lay strong claim to the future. To the time, someday, when we will all be *better* people.

Ideology alone can affect a person's identity; the results of its praxis the more so. And, while socialism in the GDR failed to keep its promises in myriad ways, everyone had a job, no one was homeless, and crime, unnourished by unemployment and homelessness, was an exception in daily life. Such a society is, to say the least, not the worst imaginable, and it would not be surprising to find that a society long without these problems, experiencing them *en masse* for the first time, might soon find itself looking for the baby thrown out with the bathwater, remembering a rosy past and the pristine beauty of an idea.

An outsider can scarcely presume to say what forty years of socialism meant to the sixteen million citizens of the GDR. Nor, from what I have seen, can any insider. Taking socialism as a faith, there are still true believers, atheists, agnostics, and every perspective in between in eastern Germany. Taking socialism as a parent, which may be the closest analogy, it was a stringent, cruel, nosy, but not uncaring parent—constantly changing and never simply a ubiquitous, Stalinesque monolith. The socialist state remains an experience subject to radically different interpretations in this land because it was the experience by, through, for, or against which individuals defined themselves.

By 1989, from the multiple complex of identities a number of characteristics had taken deep root in the GDR. First, over the years, the sense of physical and emotional edge—honed by the two superpowers, not the two Germanies—forced the two Germanies into pawn-like helplessness in the presence, so to speak, of kings. This was especially true in the GDR, where the red king was always much closer and more visible at critical times. Global helplessness was mirrored and magnified by helplessness in miniature; as the forces of repression took their toll, many resigned themselves to a passive public voice. Similarly, leadership, initiative, and drive were rarely welcomed—too "disturbing"—and so these once distinctly Prussian characteristics atrophied from disuse.

Second was a consistent tendency among East Germans to measure themselves against their former countrymen, the West Germans. Over the GDR's history, the grass was almost always greener there than to the east. The barometer of progress and decline was on the western front.

No matter the scale, no matter the reading, however, a sense of pride and achievement survived the seasons of the GDR. Part of that pride stemmed from the basic fact of progress; their world was better than it had been in 1945. In part, pride stemmed from certain self-sufficient economic successes over forty years. The socialist economy fed itself from the massive *Kombinat* farms, clothed itself through its textile industries, kept itself warm largely with lignite strip-mining. The educational system was good and the culture, when it avoided the dialectic, was spectacular. There were things to be proud of: individual achievements, communal efforts, the abstraction of an idea.

At journey's end, however, there was one decaying, invidious thing that almost no one was proud of: the GDR. A former citizen of the GDR may speak warmly of his apartment, her family, an orchestra, chemical company, hometown—even of "the way we did things"—but not of the state itself. That state wiretapped his phone. That state enforced its will on the voices of dissent for too long. That state promised her the future only to deliver relics of the past. As a nation, there was nothing left of the GDR by the late 1980s in which to take pride, and, thus, a sixth political identity had risen to highest prominence, an identity that was in fact no identity at all: I do not think in terms of "we." I do not have or envision a political existence.

Not knowing whom to trust, afraid to display what one truly felt, people turned inward. They cherished a private, and learned to cultivate a public, persona—the one authentic, the other functional. Everyone knew that, too; the dichotomy of self, of truth and appearance, was hardly a secret. Thus, public interaction rested, at some level, on something that did not really exist. Politics had become the supreme fiction. And the GDR—having become nothing more than a bundle of unreal public interactions held together only by coercive forces—had ceased to exist for its people long before the borders opened and the Wall came down.

During this long passage, whatever happened to the Confederacy? That is the point: the Southern experience never approached the complexities described here. The background of the South's disjointed experiment is one of gradual evolution and, finally, the story of a region carving its direction for itself—a region urging the theory of states' rights and the practice of slavery, fighting to preserve that identity in secession. As with the passage of time, the passage of identity took a far greater toll on the GDR, leaving an identity so meaningless by the end that its people would choose that their nation should commit suicide.

Past Perfect: The Passage of the Festival
"Wir sind das Volk."[5]

It did not look like suicide at first; it looked like rebirth. In October 1989, after Hungary had opened its border with Austria, as East Germans began to stream in that direction and the demonstrations began, the word was "freedom." The thrill of a word. "Now or never — democracy." The joy of a festival. Freedom from repression, freedom from a decaying system, freedom to change the GDR—these were the initial hopes behind the slogan of 1989: *"Wir sind das Volk."* "We are the People"—straight out of America 1776, or France 1789—and revolution, not reunion, was in the air.

This revolution succeeded and failed on the same day: 9 October 1989. Two days before, on 7 October, Honecker and the GDR had celebrated the nation's fortieth birthday in Berlin. Part of the unintended festivities included demonstrations, which were quashed quickly and brutally by the Stasi and police. Now, on 9 October in Leipzig, as part of the Monday demonstrations begun a few weeks earlier, seventy thousand people poured into the streets. The festival had grown in size and seriousness. At the same time, government forces waited for but one word: "Shoot." It was time to put an end to this festive nonsense; Honecker's signed orders simply needed to be passed on to the troops.

At the last minute, however, six men—three from the ruling party, three from the street party—turned the night away from confrontation to dialogue. The people stayed in the streets. No one was killed. After that, in one city after another, the demonstrations kept coming. Growing. Nine days later, Honecker was gone.

The revolutionary success of that evening is plain; its failure lay somewhat hidden behind all the fanfare. It rested in the identities of the three revolutionary representatives: Masur, the director of the Leipzig orchestra; Lutz-Lange, a cabaret player; and Zimmermann, a theologian. Three men whose professions remain unchanged to this day; three heroes from different walks of life who filled a vacuum for a day. As 9 October showed, and as future events would confirm, the main reason why there would be no revolution in the GDR as there had once been in America or France was that there were no revolutionaries to direct it. There was a massive citizens' movement—which ended up moving nowhere. A "revolutionary" agenda would soon be drafted—but not by anyone from the GDR. Having never been allowed to, no one in this country knew how to lead a body politic—save those who had done so by force and would soon not be allowed to lead. There was no Jefferson, Washington, or Paine; nor was there a Mirabeau, Lafayette, or Danton. There was only Helmut Kohl, who was no revolutionary.

Past Undone: The Passage of the Sword

"Wir sind ein Volk."[6]

On 28 November 1989 Chancellor Kohl announced his "Ten-point Plan" to the West German Bundestag. Its ultimate goal: reunion of the two Germanies. A torch had been passed. The revolution was dead. Change directed from within would be effectively supplanted by change orchestrated from without. Slowly at first, but picking up speed as events outpaced them, the East Germans gave up—or lost—control of their destiny. As in April 1865, when Lee handed over his sword to Grant at Appomattox, so in May 1990 the GDR and West Germany signed the contract that would regulate their monetary, economic, and social union. While the actions seem radically different, they were in fact two variations on the same theme: surrender. The difference is that Lee knew it at the time.

Premonitions

"I have confidence in confidence alone."[7]

One thing the South always had going for it was pride. Southerners believed in their peculiar cause and fought fiercely on the battlefields in desperate demonstration of that pride. In the process, they erected many legends, none more mythical than Robert E. Lee. From the moment he stood by Virginia in secession, Lee was the epitome of Southern pride: a man of tradition, bravery; a man of unfailing courtesy; a man who carried his nation through four years of war and into reunion with head held high. Through forty years, the GDR had not one Lee, but from the glory of 1989, its people had created the myth of themselves as self-willed, peacefully conquering revolutionaries. Before anyone realized the festival was over and the sword had been passed. Before anyone knew that a few months could not possibly erase forty years, *they* had taken to the streets. *They* had overcome. *They* had brought the free vote to the GDR. They were "The People" and their heads, too, were held high in the delirious spring of 1990.

Now they were going to get rich.

Unlike the South in 1865, expectations in the GDR were raised even higher than heads. After all, they had not lost a war; they were the victorious champions of freedom. Now it was time to reap from the land of plenty. The passage of the GDR was over; it was time to come home. In this heady atmosphere, no one dreamed that reunion might cause or expose more problems than it seemed capable of solving. And, surely, no one would have believed that the specters of the past, far from buried, were just preparing to emerge from their graves.

Present Tense: The Passage of Ghosts

"What the people here have swallowed is unbelievable.
In Stuttgart, civil war would have broken out long ago."[8]

From a distance, it is rather simple to describe eastern Germany today. A society, its machines and its infrastructure worn down and misdirected by forty years of repressive socialism, must suddenly operate at the accelerated speeds of forty years of democratic capitalism in West Germany. Fast train, slow track, and the resultant frictions can be felt at every turn in this society. That they are operating under these conditions at all is, at present, almost completely due to massive infusions of capital from western Germany into various eastern German sectors. Yet, more closely viewed, it is easiest to see the problems in this one-time country if one follows the passing traces of old ghosts.

The Ghost of the Sword

There is a different word used by the disaffected of eastern Germany today to describe the events of 1990: *Anschluss*. It dispenses altogether with the semantic difficulties of "union" versus "reunion" and makes brutal reference to another form of accession, another time: the *Anschluss* of 1938, when Hitler's Germany peacefully yet inexorably swallowed Austria whole. Although there are indeed parallels between these events, most broadly encompassed perhaps by the totality of change required in 1938 Austria and 1990 eastern Germany, as opposed to the total lack of change in 1938 Germany and 1990 western Germany, the word choice is rather more a reflection of frustration, a realization of just how much control was given up in the early phases of reunification.

The ghost of the sword of sovereignty appeared first in eastern Germany on 1 July 1990. Although the sword had long been passed to West Germany, the effects of its loss were first felt within days of the currency union. At that time, one West German mark was worth about four or five GDR marks. The exchange rate, however, as established by the 18 May 1990 contract, was (with unimportant exceptions) one for one: thus, an East German employee making 10,000 GDR marks per year on 30 June 1990 was making 10,000 West German marks on July 1. Salaries inflated 400 to 500 percent overnight, and only massive transfer payments from the West prevented total chaos. Overnight, the GDR became not a welfare state but a state on welfare.

In the late 1860s, the economy of the U.S. South was also in a state of collapse, and all control had been ceded, at least on paper, to the North. Yet the collapse may have been less painful psychologically because of the South's diminished expectations in surrender. Only the strangest of thinkers in the 1800s expected the state to take care of its downtrodden; certainly the South had no such expectations.

One of those strange thinkers was Karl Marx. History may well judge Marx's greatest contribution to be his inspiration of the movements that led in part to the kinder, gentler social welfare states of the late twentieth century, but it is a great irony that the states that held most closely to Marx's economic tenets—the Soviet Union and, more or less forcibly, the states of the Warsaw Pact—would become the developed states most in need of a helping hand in the 1990s. Governments today face people who need *and expect* help—a problem compounded in Germany by the eastern Germans' bargain precisely to that effect: help, in exchange for sovereignty.

Those with hands outstretched are scarcely in a position to dictate the course of human events, however, and the loss of economic control in eastern Germany has been followed swiftly by substantial losses of political, administrative, and, for lack of a better word, self-actualizing control. The carpetbaggers have taken over: savvy, western politicians; clever, western bureaucrats; and facile, western businessmen and economists, screaming eastern Germany's needs in shrill, western tones: "Management ability! Know-how! Technical infrastructure!"

In the East, with synergistic effects upon the loss of control, nearly all former politicians in leadership positions are, unsurprisingly, gone.

Teachers who taught the wrong subjects are out. All things political, legal, administrative, and macroeconomic now work, from the eastern-er's perspective, in frustratingly mysterious ways.

The head-spinning sense of unfamiliarity, of important events occur-ring outside and beyond a person's control, which would be felt by members of any society undergoing such fundamental changes, have been multiplied by vestiges of the GDR's years. The sword in the people's hands during late 1989 and early 1990 was, after all, only a brief anomaly. The helplessness which existed before that for forty-five years has translated itself quite naturally into submissiveness, as one "Big Brother" has followed another. Forty years of an ideology which prom-ised to take care of its people has fostered a people with no small need to be taken care of. The planned economy and society, as well as the repres-sive hand that steered the distortions of the ideology, have left a large number of people in eastern Germany with little will, small desire, and limited ideas of how to participate effectively in an unplanned, process-oriented, less "helpful" society.

All of this aggravation is compounded by the new "Big Brother." In one of the great sibling rivalries in history, the GDR and West Germany competed on every front for forty years. In the end, all the medals that seemed to matter hung on the western brother. In the end, the GDR, like the South, lost. Now it is that western brother who is establishing the rules of the new game—a game he knows far better than his eastern brother yet which the eastern brother is forced to play. The sibling meta-phors could be extended for some time, but the heart of the matter is this: it is one thing to take orders from a stranger and quite another to take orders from a brother. While it was grating and regrettable to lose control to the Russians, it is insufferable for the East Germans to have lost control to the West Germans—their enemy, their brethren, their benefac-tor.

The Ghost of the Festival

As fond longing for the sword has left many East Germans frustrated, the bygone festival has left many others, especially the young, curiously disappointed. Democracy turned out to be an empty vessel, a salesman without the merchandise. Where once people took to the streets and gov-ernments toppled, now the German leviathan known as "Bureaucracy" has inserted itself between the people and their causes to ensure the properly lethargic, procedural reign of law and order. The freedom equated with democracy in the fall of 1989 was uplifting, energizing, lib-erating—*fun*. Where have the daily expressions of freedom gone—the demonstrations, placards, and speeches? What happened to the revolu-tion?

In part, nostalgia is playing its standard tricks on memory. As with the dream of the deliriously courteous, chivalrous, and serene antebellum South that developed after the Civil War, the vision of a "third way" continues to hold sway in the hearts of many eastern Germans long after its demise: an intermediate primrose lane combining the best of socialism and capitalism. There is something terribly understandable in that wishful thinking, coming from people who for so many years could scarcely dream of having their cake and eating it, too, but it has set up roadblocks in the path of unifying forces. To be sure, the Southern romance with antebellum times was also somewhat divisive, but it was rocking-chair nostalgia, not nostalgia for another upheaval. In eastern Germany, however, there is something more at work, a sense that, somehow, the causes of 1989 were not properly settled by the results of 1990. The trouble in eastern Germany—as the force of entropy roams at will in the former Soviet Union and Yugoslavia—is that the third way, a movement born of revolt, remains an unexercised option. As disappointment with this brand of West German—based democracy grows, that option seems to leave open a second chance for the freedom of the festival.

The promises of that festival were so rich, and the promises that turned the people from their own party toward a reunion now seem so empty. The core promise, because the bargain was money for sovereignty, was about the wages of time: How long will it take before we East Germans are as wealthy as you West Germans? In 1990 it was three to five years; by 1991, a few years. Now, estimates range from ten to twenty years, conceivably more. Leaving aside why the original projections were so wrong, the problem with the slippery promises of time is that everyone from the GDR has heard it before. The echoes of the voice from the past: "It's just a matter of time. ... Our time is coming. ... Wait." That is what Erich Honecker said at every party rally for almost twenty years, and no one in eastern Germany wants to hear from Honecker—or anyone who sounds like him—ever again. They want payoffs and festivals in conjunction with a very short but very important word—"now." They have waited on time long enough.

The Ghosts of Time and Identity

Erich Mielke was tried in Berlin for murder. Allegedly, he and an accomplice shot two policemen, a heinous crime for the Stasi's former head. Except that the shots were fired in the dying days of Weimar, in 1931, when right-wing Nazis and left-wing Communists, including Mielke, roamed the streets as vigilantes in uniform. The police came down hard on the leftist demonstrators roaming the streets and looked the other way as the right marched. The prosecutor's office said the left was obviously looking for a fight. Swastikas are the graffiti of choice.

Except it is no longer 1931, or 1939, but yesterday, today. ... Young men in the East German army followed orders in 1989. Their orders were to shoot, and they did, and other young men died in the death zone. Those young soldiers now answer to charges of murder, but under whose law can they be judged? They will be judged under the laws of humanity, and the ghost of Nürnberg has reappeared in Germany once more. ... Karl Marx Stadt is Chemnitz once more. The countless statues of Lenin have, by and large, been torn down. Streets with overtones of the socialist past have been given their old names, but Karl Liebknecht Strasse in Leipzig is still Karl Liebknecht Strasse. It has to be; its old name was Adolph Hitler Strasse. There were 16 million citizens in the GDR. Some estimates say that five hundred thousand were Stasi informants; some say 1 million. There are literally miles of Stasi informant files in Berlin and elsewhere. A bishop announces that he had contacts with the Stasi to help members of his church; some days later, his imbalanced daughter commits suicide, leaving a note ascribing her death to the horror of her father's revelations. ... *Aufarbeitung* has returned to Germany, working out the past. What did you do in the cold war, daddy? I didn't know. We didn't know that. How could we have known that? ... All property confiscated by the GDR after 1949 is to be returned to its rightful owners. Property taken between 1945 and 1949 remains where it is. Property taken by the Reich between 1933 and 1945 will be returned to those who can show they were persecuted. ...

Sixty years of history are, at once, banished and summoned, past and present.

Front-page items from an east German newspaper, looking East, then West: In Dresden/Bitterfeld, twenty-five thousand parcels of land in eastern Germany have been environmentally poisoned. The cleanup costs are incalculable. In Hamburg, ten men and women decided it is time to act and have formed the Union against Baldness. For 60 marks a year, one can join the union and learn about natural hair growth.

Priorities differ. Prices differ. Can the price of reunion be paid? The chancellor, who is bald, says, "I am optimistic." The ghosts say, "*Anschluss*," and refuse to go away.

It takes years to lose and years to find an identity, and that is the hardest search behind closed doors in eastern Germany right now. Some are looking West for their lost selves. Some are looking at 1989, wondering where they went wrong. Some are trying to take a new look at the GDR years. Some are staring at old files. Others read Marx. Others shave their heads. Others are painting swastikas on city walls. What did the GDR mean? What was my role? To whom can I talk about it openly? How could we let that go on for forty years?

Yet there is no time to figure it out, no time for identity crises; time has other priorities. New jobs must be created. Businesses must be made competitive; productivity must be enhanced. Streets must be widened and improved, old buildings torn down or renovated, new buildings erected. The cities need more apartments, telephone lines, railway lines, freeway connections; small towns need development centers, parks, more roads; the environment needs massive, unprofitable attention everywhere. The people do not need an identity; they need management ability! Know-how! Infrastructure! So it goes. Under such real, economic pressures, there is simply no time left for unreal therapies and so eastern Germany today has begun to take on the appearance of its nearest capitalist forefather, West Germany, a land filled with people too busy to look back, too aggrandizing to be reflective.

That is one way to deal with an identity crisis: to look the other way. Another way, in a country given to extremes, is the opposite extreme: to become obsessed with the question of identity. Nothing illustrates this obsession and its difficulties more than the saga of the "Tribunal." The Tribunal was composed of a number of important East Germans and was envisioned as a public forum for the telling of the GDR's history; a chance for East Germans to come together, to speak openly, and to judge the meaning of past events for themselves. Then people began to get nervous about where things might lead. Might the Tribunal conflict with the orderly processes of law? What would the Tribunal's judgment, if any, mean? Did not the word "Tribunal" smack of the tribunals that reigned during the Terror in 1792 France? (Yes, the resurrection of such revolutionary fervor was part of the point.) Propriety reigned, and the emotionally charged Tribunal changed its name to the politically palatable "Forum for Enlightenment and Renewal," which eventually waned into insignificance, leaving the vast majority of East Germans alone to discover the truth for themselves.

To be left "alone to discover the truth for themselves" would be innocuous if applied to Californians finding themselves at Big Sur. But the plain fact is that the truths that need to be discovered in eastern Germany are fundamental, communal truths—a shared understanding about this community, "these truths we hold self-evident"—and these are not truths so easily found in the privacy of one's home. They require, by definition, public agreement. They require a communal search based on open trust and essential confidence in each other, and these resources are in scarce supply in eastern Germany today.

There are two McGuffins in this psychic drama. One is the Stasi, which has been dead for a few years but whose ghost refuses to leave the stage, taking on shifting roles as lead villain, mysterious stranger, and scapegoat. It was long understood in the GDR that its government and media could not be trusted; however, revelations about the pervasiveness and insidiousness of the Stasi and its "unofficial co-workers" have completed the picture: the nation's citizens could not be trusted. For many, the conclusion is clear: trust no one. With that, the internal wall between private persona and public facade erected in the GDR years has, to a large extent, remained standing, ensuring that widespread, engaged, cooperative public activism at a time when and where it is most needed—activism in search of a consensus about each other's past and present—does not and cannot exist.

As the exaggerated specter of the Stasi has attacked whatever remnants of trust remained among the GDR's citizens, the image of the carpetbaggers in charge—the *besser Wessies*—has shaken whatever confidence resided in themselves. As eastern Germans are gnawed with insecurity, the West Germans come armed with the new, working, victorious system; they are proselytes brimming with the pride of success, with confidence and The Answer. "What economic concerns? Just stick with (our) capitalism." "What search for truths? You have the (West) German Constitution." "What national identity crisis? (West) Germany is your country." Truth imposed on them by another is the last thing that most eastern Germans want, however. They have seen that movie.

In short, reunion—far from healing old injuries and covering ugly scars—has poured salt on the wounds of the past, exposed them, and, in effect, said, "Look, see how bad it was." One does not know the distortions of propaganda or the full measure of repression until the truth comes out. One does not know how retrograde an economy was until the statistics are assimilated and the comparisons (endlessly) trumpeted. One does not know what could have been in eastern Germany until one sees what is in western Germany. Reunion has brought freedom, which has brought information, which has brought pain, which has bred distrust and uncertainty. Frustrated at their lack of control, disappointed with the fruits of democracy, distrustful and uncertain of their own worth and identity, more than two years after the blessed reunion but still trying desperately to shake off the ghosts of forty years, eastern Germans face the future reunited yet, in so many ways, terribly alone.

•

Two years after reunion was about the point at which Reconstruction began to founder in the South. Without forty years of separation to overcome, with no festivals celebrated while apart, with few Stasi-like traitors in its midst (united as the Confederacy was in its mass treason), Reconstruction foundered upon what was once called "an American dilemma." It foundered upon something which, while merely a problematic footnote in eastern Germany at present (what with all the other ghosts floating around), promises to become a "German dilemma" in the Germany of the future: East and West.

Future Tense: The Passage of Das Volk

"Wir sind das Volk—aber wer sind wir?"[9]

Shakespeare wrote that what is past is but prologue, which is undoubtedly true as a logical proposition but only half true insofar as this essay is concerned. Some pasts are largely written out of the play. In that vein, although it will always be worth an essay or two, I suspect that eastern Germany's forty years in the wilderness will soon be, to put it redundantly, a thing of the past. This past, the GDR's past, is not the stuff of prologue for the German future. For the past twenty years, few in the GDR really thought it would be; the prologue was too lackluster. Barring total crisis—a depression, a war—when any number of ghosts can be summoned up with alarming speed, when prologues can be rewritten overnight, the GDR's past seems destined to become a curio of German history; an anomalous, short-lived bundle of complexity that never really amounted to much insofar as the history of the German people is concerned. It was not really a German choice to begin with.

The identity crises of the excitable, transitional present will be buried, forgotten, or resolved. As we have seen, identities in the GDR were not very strong to begin with, and there is not enough consensus about what a national identity was to fuel a crisis for very long. There is not an "East German way" in the manner of a southern way. Similarly, the issue of control will probably be recognized for what it is—a red herring. For example, when a general strike in 1992 threatened to overwhelm western Germany, eastern Germans were already beginning to see that they have every bit as much—or as little—control of events as the "Wessies" in a parliamentary democracy. And past festivals will most readily be forgotten in a flurry of new cars, Oktoberfests, and vacations. It was a short festival to begin with.

The Bard, however, was never wrong, and what is past is prologue. It is just that we have to define our terms.

One part of this definition is simply the standard truism about the European sense of history. "The past" does not mean to Germans what it does to Americans. Americans tend to hold on to the past about as long as people's lives; that is, as long as there are people around who still remember World War II, the Depression, World War I, or Teddy Roosevelt, that past lives on. Once those generations die, the past dies with them, relegated to the history and civics textbooks and the occasional reminder that the long-distant events of the past still have meaning. To Germans—and to many Europeans—however, all that is past, all that is known about the past, remains somewhat alive in the present. To be sure, 1945, 1933, and 1914 live vividly in German hearts and minds, but so do 1871, 1848, 1793, 1648, Goethe, Luther, and the barbarians who fought off the Romans in the ninth century.

From that meaning of the past, from the length of the prologue, there is a second meaning that emerges: the meaning of the *Volk*—a partly historical, partly visionary amalgamation of people, nation, and culture that conjures up a millennial German heritage. It is a word wrapped around a feeling that takes Germans—eastern and western—back a long, long time.

Between 1863 and 1870, from the Emancipation Proclamation through the passage of the fifteenth Amendment, the United States undertook one of the most ambitious projects in the history of nations to redefine the notion of *Volk*: the inclusion and equality before the law of not simply a mixture of white nationalities, but a mixture of races, white and black, as Americans. If the goal of the Civil War had been merely reunion, it succeeded; if the goal of Reconstruction had been to ensure federal supremacy over the states, it succeeded; if another goal was the economic restoration of the South, it too succeeded, albeit less completely; but the utter failure of Reconstruction lay in the implementation of the new definition. The American *Volk* might be a mixture, but it was a white, not a colored, one and no one could tell many white Americans differently—North or South—until … 1941? 1954? 1964? 1992? Someday.

This entire line of thinking, however, is largely foreign to Germans. The vast majority of Germans have never sought and are not seeking a new definition of the *Volk*; the "melting pot" is not a goal. *Ausländer* are welcome, sometimes, as workers, but not as citizens. To this day, though there has been some tinkering at the margins of the definition, Germans are those born German—of German heritage, not those born in Germany; to this day, the dream of the ancient *Volk* lives on.

That self-perpetuating dream and its long view of the past lead to two predictions about eastern Germany and the German reunion. The first is that the identity crisis of the eastern Germans will be replaced by a stabler vision of a much greater, much older identity shared by eastern and western Germans; that is, the long view of the past will itself resolve the East Germans' search for identity and their presently felt sense of alienation from the West Germans. They may have missed forty years together, but what are four decades among a millennial *Volk*? Never mind that Germany actually united in 1871; the centuries in common will erase the decades apart.

The second surmise is that the German reunion and Reconstruction will go far more smoothly than the American example and will, one day, be viewed as far more complete than the American reunion. It will do so, first, because it has to. Unlike the South, which had spent itself in war and which could be left relatively untended because its borders—being water—were secure, neither the potential of civil unrest in eastern Germany nor of disturbance on the all-too-near eastern front can be discounted by the German government. Second and more fundamentally, however, leaving aside the "what ifs" of chaos, it will do so because it has brought together folk from a single race, east and west, who continue to share the same dream of *Volk*, and, as importantly, because this reunion has embraced no attempt to reshape that German dream.

In the long run, that may be the critical difference between the American and the German reunions. The American reunion was a reunion based—in part intentionally, in part fortuitously—upon new principles, looking forward to a future that would reshape the entire land; whereas the German reunion, to date, is one without new principles in which the West is still playing a pat hand and the East is to play West, and one whose internal dynamic of a shared past may well find Germany, instead of looking forward, looking back to the future.

That difference has its costs and its benefits. The Emancipation Proclamation, the Gettysburg Address, the thirteenth, fourteenth, and fifteenth Amendments, the early days of Reconstruction (when, for example, blacks were elected to national offices), and the fact that all these things took place within a seven-year span are a constant reminder to Americans of their failures. Almost 130 years after the Emancipation Proclamation, a suburban Los Angeles jury with no blacks on it acquitted four police officers who beat a black man nearly to death. The blacks in that city rioted, and the main conclusion was, "It had to happen sooner or later." No one knows how to stop "it" from happening again. Too many blacks live in ghettos; too many live on welfare, too many die young. Yet those seven years are also a reminder to Americans of their dreams: of equal justice and opportunity, of different cultures growing together as an American culture, of the energy produced by new ideas. Those seven years set the terms of America's most difficult experiment, and it is testimony to the greatness of the principles that 130 years of problems have not, as of this writing, triumphed over 130 years of dreams.

The German reunion, on the other hand, has a wholly different orientation: the financial equalization, not the reevaluation, certainly not any redefinition, of the *Volk*. On the eastern front, much seems new today, but it is in fact old western hat. Erich Maria Remarque wrote it: *,im Westen nichts Neues* (In the West, there's nothing new). What is new for all of Germany is only what is old: Germany lies, once more, at the center of Europe. The *Volk* are together again.

Yet they are together at a time when, ironically enough, the issues raised in the aftermath of the American reunion are among the most pressing in Europe; a time when new principles apparently cannot be avoided. How do you define a people? How do you treat those, can and will you integrate those, of different race, creed, or color? The European Union is seeking to redefine the European sense of *Volk* in supranational, economically bound terms.[10] Other European nations, at the same time, are splitting up along intranational, ethnic lines. In Austria, France, and Italy, powerful political forces are trying to prevent the ethnic lines from even entering the picture.

The forces of synergy, entropy, and inertia are colliding in Europe and in Germany, where a new problem of identity is building; not the problems of the East German past, but the dilemma of the German future. Neo-Nazi skinheads are not the problem. Nor is the political far right. Nor is the present treatment of asylum seekers, the law as it stands on citizenship, or the general, exaggerated hysteria about being deluged by foreigners. These are all symptoms, but the problem is the underlying disease: racism—or, as applied to Germany, "Volkism." If not in, then out. It is a problem Germany knows too well; it was a problem the world ignored when the *Volk* were last together, with terrible consequences for all.

Far be it from an American to cast stones, for the "American dilemma" of racism still rages and precludes any form of sanctimony. Still, there is general if imperfect agreement in the United States as to the goal: a society of many races, creeds, and colors, with liberty and justice for all. The German dilemma of Volkism is different, however, because the goal itself remains in question. On the one hand, Germans want to be a *Volk*—one color, one culture; a people who cherish their common past. On the other hand, Germans cherish the idea of progress and want an open culture. Reunion did nothing to ease this tension; if anything, the very fact of reunion, of the *Volk* defining themselves as they once did, has given a certain thrust to Volkism. Although unresolved in reunion, the debate over Volkism cannot be put off forever. With the lifting of the border restrictions by the European Union, with the Iron Curtain torn down, with the far right gaining significant, unmistakable support in several states, and with the number of *Ausländer* in Germany growing, Germany must decide, sooner or later, for what it stands. If not "melting pot," then what? If *Volk*—German or European—then how? *If "Ausländer Raus!,"* then why?

•

And so, a circle of sorts completes itself. At the end of its passages, eastern Germany faces the same questions that a reunited America faced over a hundred years ago; at the beginning of new passages, the same questions with which its own passages began: Who are we? Who will we be? And, this time, a third question: who do we *want* to be? No, they are not asking the questions alone. But yes, they can help to choose the answers.

Notes

1. The idea behind this essay came from a conversation with the only freely elected mayor of East Berlin, who served from May until October 1990. He suggested that perhaps one way to appreciate what is happening in Germany today is to reflect on the aftermath of the Civil War; that is, to consider themes and strains of our own effort to reunite two pieces of one (or two) land(s), in order to understand Germany's current complex of problems. In all that follows, my focus is on eastern Germany, not the U.S. South, but in the comparative terms of this essay, I want to derail any notion that whereas the American reunion was complicated—emerging, as it did, from the ashes of war and slavery—the German reunion was simple—blossoming, as it were, in the gardens of peace and freedom. To be sure, the American version was complicated; however, just as surely, nothing in Germany is ever simple.

There were four vital sources for this essay. Three of them were books: *Nach Vier Jahrzehnten: Ein Rückblick auf die deutsche Teilung* (Wiesbaden Universum Verlagsanstalt, 1990), which provided essential details about the history of the GDR from 1945 through 1989; *Jetzt oder nie—Demokratie!* (Forum Verlag Leipzig, 1989), which gave me some personal insight into the fall of 1989; and *Der Gefühlsstau* (Argon, 1990), by Hans-Joachim Maaz, which draws a psychological portrait of the GDR's citizens after forty years of repression.

The fourth source was the Robert Bosch Foundation in Stuttgart, Germany, which gave me the opportunity to spend a year in Germany. Under their auspices, I lived in Köln, Bonn, and Leipzig, traveled throughout Germany, and had the opportunity to meet countless people, ranging from Chancellor Kohl to Roland Wötzel—one of the party representatives involved in the confrontation in Leipzig on 9 October 1989—to an old comrade standing on a hill in Frankfurt an der Oder who simply said, "Capitalism kills one's humanity." If I have hit upon any truths in this essay about Germany, it is due solely to the Robert Bosch Foundation, which gave me the opportunity to find them in Germany.

2. Berlin Wall graffiti.

3. Preamble to the GDR's 1968 constitution (author's translation).

4. In this essay I have tried to use two phrases primarily to describe the area of Germany which, before 3 October 1990 was socialist Germany: "eastern Germany," when referring to that area at present, and "the GDR" (*German Democratic Republic*), when describing the entity before 3 October 1990. The point is only worth noting because Germany itself is, to some degree, still searching for the best way to describe this once and future part of its body. Choices, each with varying connotative weight, range to and from "the one-time GDR," "the ex-

GDR," "East Germany," "the eastern part," "East," "the five new states," "the new federal states," and "over there."

5. "We are the people," 1989 GDR slogan.

6. "We are one people," 1990 German slogan.

7. A line from the song "I Have Confidence" (Rodgers and Hammerstein, *The Sound of Music*).

8. "Der Osten Hängt am Tropf," *Stern*, 18 February 1992. The quote is from Rolf Bartke, manager of the Ludwigsfelder Mercedes branch (author's translation).

9. "We are the people—but who are we?" *Jetzt oder nie—Demokratie!* (Leipzig: Forum Verlag, 1989), 26.

10. The European Union's efforts to redefine the Europeans' sense of a people are beyond the scope of this essay. These efforts have their own parallels to the United States' efforts to bind a new nation after 1865; they, too, involve one of the most ambitious projects in the history of nations to redefine a people—with an equal, if not greater, number of attendant difficulties.

7

A Quiet Land: Reflections on Dictatorship in East Germany

Angela Kurtz Mendelson

When the East German state burst its concrete and barbed-wire seams in 1989 it unleashed a tide of protest that led virtually overnight to its collapse. The scenes of jubilant East Germans squeezing themselves through holes in the Berlin Wall confronted Americans with images with which they believed they could sympathize: a subject people running from persecution, seeking freedom. What many failed to realize, however, was that they were superimposing their own interpretation on events. East Germans were not fleeing political oppression but economic hardship. Their *primary* goal was not freedom; it was a good job and the concomitant material rewards long enjoyed by their West German counterparts.

These rather prosaic motives for an otherwise spectacular revolution may startle American sensibilities for they reflect an alien system of values. East Germans cherished diligence, order, and respect for authority more than freedom, liberty, and justice. The Weimar Republic (1919–1933), Germany's first experiment in democracy, collapsed too soon for the German people to develop any deep-seated attachment to democratic values. While the Allied powers effectively counteracted and reversed the legacy of autocracy in the West, the Soviet Union and its Communist surrogates reinforced it in the East. Perpetuation of an underdeveloped code of ethics—coupled with the psychologically debilitating effects of dictatorship itself (first National Socialist, then Communist)—destroyed all potential for widespread rebellion in East Germany.

In conversations with eastern Germans over a period of six months in 1992, I explored some of the reasons for the lack of significant resistance to the East German regime. To be fair, it is important to point out that the

119

German Democratic Republic (GDR) was a Soviet satellite state wholly dependent on the military might of the Soviet Union for its existence. It collapsed in 1989 when that might was withdrawn by Soviet leader Mikhail Gorbachev. What I hoped to better understand by interviewing eastern Germans, therefore, was not their legitimate fear of Soviet tanks but rather the reasons for their willingness to adopt as their own—*and perpetuate*—many of the state policies that served to enslave them.

Communist ideology as practiced by the Soviet Union idolized the working class, glorified diligence, and preached obedience to a higher authority, namely the ruling party. It thus catered to old-school German values and served as an extension of the authoritarian political culture to which Germans had long become accustomed. The result was a largely compliant, antirevolutionary citizenry. As psychoanalyst Erich Fromm observed: "The influence of any doctrine or idea depends on the extent to which it appeals to [the] psychic needs ... of those to whom it is addressed."[1]

East Germans never had the opportunity to evolve psychologically, to progress from an authoritarian to a democratically oriented mentality. Eberhard Brecht, an eastern German physicist and Social Democratic Party (SPD) member of the Bundestag, suggested in a 1991 speech that time had stood still for the East Germans. The West Germans by contrast were propelled into the future, forced by their western allies to adopt a genuinely democratic form of government and, most important, given the *time* to assimilate the values for which it stood. As Brecht asserted: "The transfer of the unchallenged secondary virtues and mentalities of one dictatorship to yet another is the reason why the habits of the East Germans and their political culture remind one so uncomfortably of the West Germans of the 1950s."[2]

East Germany never experienced a "Prague spring" or a Polish Solidarity movement. It was a quiet land founded on a subliminal social contract: The East German state would provide jobs and otherwise uphold the hallowed German virtues of diligence, love of order, faith in authority, and loyalty to convention. The East Germans in turn would contribute their labor and conform to—even reinforce—the dictates of the state. The first and essentially only uprising against the East German regime took place in June 1953 as a result of worker frustration over increased production norms and depressed living conditions, *not* over a lack of political freedoms. Although Soviet tanks crushed the rebellion and resolved the problem in the short-term, increases in the standard of living—that is to say, fulfillment of the social contract—lulled the population into submission over the long-term.

This sleep of submission was not to last, however. In the minds of its citizens, the East German Communist leadership committed the ultimate crime in the 1980s when it sent the economy into a nosedive. Years of living on credit, economic mismanagement, and skyrocketing energy prices overwhelmed state economic planners. Production slowed; basic consumer goods became scarce; more and more jobs became jobs in name only (the Communist version of unemployment). Diligence went unrewarded. This disastrous economic situation made a mockery of the German work ethic and poisoned the political climate, gradually creating the unrest that would precipitate the collapse of the state. As Peter Bender, western German journalist and long-time GDR observer, noted: "What wore the people down were less the blows of fate than the petty problems of daily life. That is why in all probability it was the failure of the economy rather than the many evil acts of state which ruined the internal stability of the GDR."[3]

Bärbel Plumbaum (age thirty-six), former secretary with the National People's Army, confirmed Bender's observations when she remarked:

> It became very difficult economically in the 1980s. People often left work two or three times during the day in order to see if they could find something to buy. How we survived as long as we did, I have no idea. People did not work full days anymore. Time was wasted in the endless search for basic necessities, and production came to a virtual halt for days on end. That was actually the worst about it. Everyone worked. Husband and wife both worked, and *still* there was no progress! In fact, things only got worse.[4]

In a discussion in his office in Potsdam in the spring of 1992, Brandenburg premier Manfred Stolpe (age fifty-seven) expressed his dismay at the exaggerated status given work and diligence in East German society. He emphasized that it was one reason why his constituents were so demoralized by the high unemployment in the new eastern German states. Stolpe explained that the regime's glorification of work had robbed the people of a balanced system of values, making them incapable of appreciating other peoples' need for greater freedom.

> For those people who lose their job, life loses its meaning. The deification of work ... that is, I think, a German characteristic. ... [W]hen the Poles began to strike in 1980, the average man in the street, the workers here, actually said, "The Poles are just too lazy to work!" That is so typically German![5]

This point having been made, values—lofty or pedestrian—would not have played such a large role in shaping East German behavior had it not been for the insidious psychological effects of dictatorship itself. The East German state was stabilized through the relentless and arbitrary use of terror and intimidation, particularly from 1949 to 1971, under Communist Party leader Walter Ulbricht. Although the system did mellow after the ouster of Ulbricht by Erich Honecker in 1971, harsh police tactics and other means of instilling fear continued to be used against those who threatened the system. At times, merely attracting attention could be seen as posing a threat. Rainer Speer (age thirty-three), former cabinetmaker-turned-political-campaign-manager, was accused of such a "crime" when he engaged in some harmless antics at a state youth festival. As he explained:

> In 1979 I attended a big, Free German Youth festival in Berlin. I was dressed somewhat "differently," jeans, parka, etc., and had run into some people at Alexanderplatz. We were joking around. I was pretending to play bass on a long shoelace. It turned out to be the *ultimate insult*, to behave like that at an organized youth festival. In any event, I attracted attention, was immediately arrested, and put into a police wagon. Across from me sat a man whom they had dragged in and were interrogating about the reason for his presence in Berlin. He explained that he had come to visit his sister who was working at one of the stands at the festival. He didn't let them intimidate him; his answers were nonchalant. So, they started beating him. I wanted to intervene to stop it. They told me that if I didn't stay out of it, they would beat me too, and harder. This experience … this feeling of utter impotence … was unbearable.
>
> The police wagon stood along a wide street called August Bebel Street that ran past Alexanderplatz. Outside, parades were marching by with people shouting in unison "G – D – R, our Fatherland!" and similar things. Thousands passed shouting this shit … it was a turning point for me, to be in a police wagon watching a man being beaten, black guard dog at my feet, sitting from morning until evening without being spoken to by anyone, without being told what would happen to me, while outside they shouted patriotic slogans.[6]

I heard many such stories from eastern German acquaintances, stories of extreme punishments meted out for modest displays of rebellion. Barbara Schumann (age fifty-two), Slavic affairs expert in the Office of the Brandenburg Premier, described witnessing the arrest of a seventeen-year-old boy at a Free German Youth Conference in 1956. Bored by the long speeches, the teenager drew across a picture of Lenin. For this act of "defacement" he was incarcerated for two years at the infamous prison complex in the city of Bautzen near Dresden to which political prisoners were sent.[7] (In 1989, discovery of the remains of more than seventeen thousand political prisoners from the Soviet occupation era confirmed Bautzen as the site of the largest mass grave of post–World War II Germany.) In his groundbreaking work, *The Captive Mind*, Polish-born writer Czeslaw Milosz graphically illustrated how the intimidation tactics used in Communist countries affected individual behavior:

> Before it leaves the lips, every word must be evaluated as to its conse-
> quences. A smile that appears at the wrong moment, a glance that is not all
> it should be, can occasion dangerous suspicions and accusations. Even
> one's gestures, tone of voice, or preference for certain kinds of neckties are
> interpreted as signs of one's political tendencies.[8]

The atmosphere of fear which the use of force created exerted an increasingly perverse influence on personal conduct. Individuals developed a mode of behavior which, they hoped, minimized their chances of being punished. In so doing, they conformed and even abetted. They also developed *psychologically palatable rationales* for their behavior, such as fulfillment of duty, obedience to authority, and professional advancement, which had nothing to do with the original motive (avoiding punishment). Particularly disturbing is that many East Germans actually came to believe these artificial rationales, which not only conformed well with long-held values, but also provided a way of escaping the guilt and shame East Germans felt for having "succumbed" to the dictates of an abusive system.

Erich Fromm noted in 1941 that people living under abusive regimes tended to develop lofty, self-convincing rationales for dubious behavior, behavior which—having been coerced—elicited painful feelings of humiliation and resentment. Fromm explained that:

> [the hatred an individual feels towards his oppressor] would only lead to
> conflicts which would subject [him] to suffering without a chance of
> winning. Therefore, the tendency will usually be to repress the feeling of
> hatred and sometimes even to replace it by a feeling of blind admiration.
> This has two functions: (1) to remove the painful and dangerous feeling of
> hatred, and (2) to soften the feeling of humiliation. If the person who rules
> over me is so wonderful or perfect, then I should not be ashamed of
> obeying him.[9]

Once convinced of the desirability of their own conformism, the newly converted in turn condemned those who did not conform. The mere existence of these "resisters" posed a threat to the new converts' painstakingly salvaged self-esteem. As the eastern German psychologist Hans-Joachim Maaz observed:

> Nonconformism was seen as a threat to the system, unnerving and fright-
> ening the average citizen, [because] alienated people can usually only feel
> truly comfortable in alienated relationships. Better, freer, and more natural

conditions would inevitably force them to confront their own alienation, inhibitions, and internal conflicts—something which is intimidating and unnerving, something thus to be avoided.[10]

Maaz echoed Fromm when he observed that it was easier for East Germans to treat the abnormal as normal—indeed to perpetuate the abnormality, however oppressive—than it was to confront feelings of shame and inadequacy. Many victims of East German dictatorial rule thus developed mind-sets that turned them to greater or lesser degrees into victimizers; greater, if they worked directly for the Ministry for State Security, or "Stasi"; lesser, if they simply blinded themselves to the regime's human rights abuses. Journalist Peter Bender referred to this phenomenon as the "internalization of the dictatorship."

Herr X (age forty-five) was one example of an otherwise decent man inured to abuse and suffering. He was a hardworking, soft-spoken state government official whom I came to know over a period of several months during my apprenticeship in the Brandenburg government. When I first met Herr X, he expressed a great deal of skepticism about the "new" society rising up around him. He criticized the West's obsession with money and material acquisition, the petty power games of party politics, the sensationalism of Western tabloids, and the general apathy of most people to the condition of their environment. As an example of the latter, he described to me his recent attempt to motivate his neighbors to clean up and repair their apartment complex only to have his mailbox vandalized by one of the residents.

Herr X graciously granted me a more "official" interview one bone-chilling March afternoon. He asked not to be taped or identified, and I have thus withheld his name to protect his privacy. Herr X explained that he came from a simple background. Both parents had worked on a farm cooperative and had been members of the Socialist Unity Party, or SED (the East German Communist Party), which he also joined. The party enabled him to study, something for which he would always be grateful, he emphasized, because it gave him opportunities he otherwise would not have had. Herr X explained that he eventually worked his way up to a position in the Infrastructure and Administrative Liaison Office of the "Ministerrat," the highest executive arm of the GDR government, and served there as a trouble-shooter responsible for the smooth functioning of state enterprises in fifteen separate districts.

He described the site visits he made to investigate problems and complained bitterly that his reports were always sanitized by headquarters. Problems he identified were thus ignored and went unaddressed. When I asked Herr X why he thought the system ultimately collapsed, he answered:

It failed because the leadership refused to acknowledge and confront problems, deeply mistrusted the people and their genuine desire for reform, was megalomaniacal, spending vast and precious sums of money on massive state events, and was obsessed with security, thereby diverting crucial resources to the military and Ministry for State Security.[11]

Herr X's critical tone suddenly changed, however, when I asked him about the more oppressive aspects of the system. He rigidly defended the building of the Wall and the shooting of would-be escapees, dryly observing: "After all, one wasn't really sure if these weren't just *criminals* trying to escape prosecution." Moreover, the people who tried to flee "knew the risks they were taking." Herr X showed no remorse, no appreciation of the injustice of this deadly use of force. He justified the Wall as necessary "to protect the GDR from negative, foreign influences during the cold war" and to prevent a brain drain. He added pointedly that people had received a subsidized education and professional training and could not just be allowed to *desert*. (Offering individuals the opportunity to pay the money back, however, had evidently never been considered by the party whose views Herr X had so unquestioningly adopted.)

Later, when I asked Herr X about the Polish Solidarity movement, he described it as having been driven by "foreign influences" designed solely to incite the Poles "to undermine the socialist system." He added that his view of Solidarity had evidently been proven correct "for what has changed in Poland [now that the socialist system has collapsed]? What did Solidarity in the end accomplish?"

Herr X refused to use his healthy skepticism fully to illuminate his own past. He could easily criticize the current system and society, as he had played no role in creating them; they remained something foreign and apart. He could also provide, to his credit, a rather sober assessment of some of the more salient shortcomings of the East German state system. He nevertheless felt compelled to defend the murder of individuals whose "crime" had been a desire for freedom and to denigrate, even in retrospect, Poland's Solidarity movement. The hostility that Herr X harbored toward such earlier acts of rebellion highlighted the extent to which he still clung to the narrow values and party-sanctioned worldview that had made resistance in the GDR so unthinkable.

Even more disconcerting than the seemingly thoughtful individuals who could breezily justify state crimes were the many who actively helped to commit them. The Ministry for State Security managed to recruit hundreds of thousands of secret, or "unofficial," informants. Some 86,000 to 100,000 people worked for the Stasi directly, and various estimates put the number of people who worked for them unofficially at a mind-boggling 1 million. Many East Germans told me that people used to say to one another that the Stasi were everywhere, yet no one imagined them to be as pervasive as the Stasi's own files now reveal. The pernicious spread of the Stasi can be considered the most tragic characteristic of the former GDR.

Der Schwarze Kasten (The Black Box), a documentary on the life and work of a Stasi official that premiered at the 1992 Berlin film festival, illustrates the extent to which ostensibly well-intentioned, "average" people can commit crimes by developing sanitized rationales for their actions and divorcing themselves from the consequences. The film probes the life of Dr. Jochen Girke, former lieutenant colonel and psychologist in the Ministry for State Security responsible for the psychological training of Stasi agents. Girke explains in the film how he instructed agents in the art of psychological manipulation to teach them to recruit, intimidate, and extract information. As he observed: "In order to break open the black box inside a man and illuminate it, you had to employ clean, scientific methods."

Girke himself was psychologically manipulated and abused as a child—particularly by his father, whose mistrust appeared to have been boundless. He recalls that his father once instructed his school teachers to observe his every move and to record their observations in a journal that he himself had to present to them after class each day. Girke later recounts that he always wanted to become a cameraman, no doubt having been influenced by his grandmother, who worked as a movie theater usher. (This comment provoked considerable audience laughter.) He was advised, however, to go into the army first for three years.

Once in the army, Girke remarks, he was recruited to work for the Stasi. The Stasi took him to a room where they showed him a file they kept on him. It not only revealed that he had written a letter to the Vatican many years earlier as a child, expressing pride and excitement that he had managed to tune into Vatican radio, but also that he had recently had a fight with his brother. Girke stated that he was shocked at how much the Stasi knew about him. This shock then turned into respect and admiration at the Stasi's efficiency and seeming omniscience. Girke stated that he thought to himself at the time: "Such an organization would be an honor to work for!" (More guffaws from the audience.) Girke's remark bears a chilling resemblance to an observation made by Adolph Eichmann at the time of his trial in Jerusalem: Hitler's "success alone proved to me that I should subordinate myself to this man."[12]

The film later depicts Girke teaching a class. The camera slowly pans an empty room as Girke explains the psychology of peer pressure and group dynamics, how the weaknesses of certain individuals can be exploited to compel compliance. He subsequently describes his own espionage activities and admits to a certain degree of pride about his success. Girke whitewashes his activities by maintaining that he tended to write more flattering reports about his subjects than did the other two or three Stasi agents usually assigned to the same case. He disassociates himself from the destructive consequences of his actions by restricting his attention and sense of responsibility to his own "area of jurisdiction." He taught. He spied. He administered, nothing more. When asked by the film's director, Tamara Trampe, if he had ever visited a prison, he answers that visiting prisons did not fall within "his range of duties."

The documentary illustrates the extent to which an individual can delude himself into thinking that he is behaving morally (that the means are normal) because he views his larger goals (or ends) to be moral. Girke believed he was helping to secure his state against subversion from within. The fact that people may have lost their lives or been maimed or imprisoned as a result he viewed as an unfortunate necessity that in no way detracted from the worthiness of the work itself. Hannah Arendt noted that Eichmann "claimed more than once that his organizational gifts ... had in fact helped his victims; it had made their fate easier. If the thing [extermination] had to be done at all, he argued, it was better that it be done in good order."[13] In other words, the individual thinks in categories. Within his own category, he is safe, honest, pure.

In a postscript to her coverage of the Eichmann trial, Arendt came to the startling conclusion that Eichmann had "merely ... never realized what he was doing." She observed that he was far removed from reality, that he suffered from a complete lack of imagination (and thus empathy). "He was not stupid. It was sheer thoughtlessness—something by no means identical to stupidity—that predisposed him to become one of the greatest criminals of that period."[14] Although Jochen Girke was not responsible for the death of tens of thousands of people, as was Eichmann, he too had managed to develop a mind-set inured to the imperatives of conscience.

Maaz attributes the fact that so many people in the GDR worked for the Stasi and saw nothing wrong with it as a symptom of psychological abuse suffered in childhood and perpetuated by the schools, the party, and the security services. The abuse created an emotional vacuum. Maaz emphasizes that "every form of oppression, injustice, force, betrayal, and denunciation is only possible through the cutting off of emotions. ... This is one of the reasons why we played along with, or at least tolerated, the tragedy in our country."[15]

While writing this chapter, I took a break to attend May Day celebrations in Potsdam. The festival was sponsored by the Party for Democratic Socialism (PDS), the successor to the former Communist Party of the GDR. My husband and I decided to attend out of curiosity and historical interest, as few expected the PDS to garner the 5 percent of the vote they would need in the next election to retain seats in the federal parliament. Among ice cream stands, balloons, and pony rides, a crowd had gathered and was listening to speeches by PDS Brandenburg parliamentary leader Lothar Bisky and others. Acting as moderator at Herr Bisky's side—to our amazement—stood none other than Jochen Girke. Bisky was at the time chairman of an investigative committee of the Brandenburg parliament looking into allegations that Brandenburg premier Manfred Stolpe had had contacts with, and might have worked for, the Stasi during his tenure as president of the Consistory of the East German Protestant church, charges that Stolpe has denied and that remain unproven.

The speeches came to an end. The crowd began to leave. Girke stood alone, gathering up the sound equipment. With more than a little trepidation, I approached to ask him some questions. Relaxed and friendly, Girke seemed eager to explain why he had agreed to make *The Black Box*. He stressed that he had done it in the hope that it would contribute to a greater understanding of the Stasi and thereby of the GDR overall. He admitted he also hoped that with understanding would come some degree of acceptance. When I asked whether he had also felt compelled to do the film out of a feeling of guilt or remorse, Girke evaded the question, repeating that he hoped to make a contribution to the public debate.

Girke explained that a probing analysis of German history had not taken place after World War II. Germans had suppressed it all, claiming that they had to devote all their time and resources to rebuilding the country. Girke emphasized the danger that this mistake would be repeated with respect to the GDR. Wanting to encourage debate, he was trying to coax other Stasi officials to go public as well. Only through honest dialogue between victims and perpetrators, he remarked, could one approach the truth and initiate a healing process. He made no mention of justice or compensation for the victims.

In post–World War II Germany, the need for democratic political institutions and civil education was perhaps greater than in any other western or central European country. It was a need which, in East Germany, went unrequited. There, a national character structure perilously susceptible to authoritarianism was prevented from developing into a psychologically secure, independent-minded, and freedom-loving one. The old ways of thinking were indeed encouraged by the new masters; progressive impulses among the populace were quickly crushed. The debilitating effects of authoritarian rule—from which no Eastern European country was immune—were consequently magnified in East Germany. A *widespread* resistance movement never had a chance in such arid soil; it never had a chance due to the heavy legacy of German history, the psychologically injurious nature of dictatorship, and the iron hold of the Soviet Union, which viewed the GDR as the final bulwark against invasion from the west.

Do the lessons that the history of East Germany teaches us offer clues to the future of a united Germany? Can the West German democratic experience be seen as a model for the larger state? The brief history of the Federal Republic appears to indicate that people can learn from history if encouraged, guided, and *given the time* to do so. Premier Stolpe at one point insisted that political maturation was an evolving process. Genuine democratic values, as Weimar proved by its demise, take time to root. This rooting process, Stolpe asserted, was as yet far from complete even in West Germany. As one example, he cited the western Germans' as yet superficial coming to terms with the crimes of the Nazis:

> When I experience how discussions go with representatives of Poland or with representatives of the German Jewish or American Jewish communities ... I still sense an enormous gulf, because the Germans have a certain arrogance towards others. They say, "Yes, it was very bad. We're sorry. It is now settled ... over ... the end. And besides, we have paid a lot and are still paying. What more do you want? And then this nonsense with the Holocaust Museum! What do you think you are doing with that Holocaust Museum?" Yes, they are very annoyed about it, the Germans ... the West Germans. The ones in the East haven't really caught on yet. But with our discussion partners the issue of the Holocaust is still very much alive. It is not "the past" for them.[16]

In their expressions of shock and disgust at the Stasi and their co-conspirators, Stolpe implied, the West Germans were failing to recognize that the seeds of this most recent tragedy lay in their own past as well. He suggested that one possibly positive outcome of the current Stasi debate was the new light it promised to shed on the German people's common Nazi past. After all, Stolpe observed, the Stasi had collected many files from the Nazi era.

In the process of analyzing the legacy of the East German state, the West Germans might do well to remember that their own democracy is the hard-won product of long years of civil education *initially imposed from without*. They cannot entirely disassociate themselves, as many do now, from the fate that befell the East Germans. Confronted by civil unrest and growing right-wing violence, German leaders would be wise to shed their complacency about the stability of the Federal Republic and to recognize that democracy, even West German democracy, is an ongoing process that is not—and may never be—entirely complete.

Notes

1. Erich Fromm, *Escape from Freedom* (New York: Holt, Rinehart & Winston, 1969), 83.

2. *"Zur politischen Kultur im vereinten Deutschland,"* speech by federal parliamentarian Eberhard Brecht before the Friedrich Ebert Foundation, Bonn, 24 September 1991.

3. Peter Bender, *Unsere Erbschaft: Was war die DDR—was bleibt von ihr?* (Hamburg: Luchterhand Literaturverlag, 1992), 33.

4. Interview with Bärbel Plumbaum, administrative assistant in the Brandenburg premier's office (Staatskanzlei des Landes Brandenburg), 25 February 1992. Ages are provided to place individuals in history. The GDR lasted a mere forty years. Older eastern Germans had experiences with National Socialism and the early years of reconstruction in East Germany not shared by the younger generation.

5. Interview with Manfred Stolpe, premier of Brandenburg, 9 April 1992.

6. Interview with Rainer Speer, director of the Economic Development and Internal Affairs Department of the Brandenburg Premier's Office, 3 March 1992.

7. Interview with Barbara Schumann, Polish and Slavic affairs analyst in the Economic Development and Internal Affairs Department of the Brandenburg Premier's Office, 26 February 1992.

8. Czeslaw Milosz, *The Captive Mind* (New York: Vintage, 1990), 54.

9. Fromm, *Escape from Freedom*, 188.

10. Hans-Joachim Maaz, *Der Gefühlstau, Ein Psychodramm der DDR* (Berlin: Argon Verlag, 1990), 54.

11. Interview with Herr X, state government employee, 2 March 1992. Identity withheld at interviewee's request.

12 Hannah Arendt, *Eichmann in Jerusalem: A Report on the Banality of Evil* (New York: Viking Penguin, Inc., 1963), 126.

13. *Ibid.*, 190.

14. *Ibid.*, 287–288.

15. Maaz, *Der Gefühlstau*, 20.

16. Interview, Manfred Stolpe, 9 April 1992.

8

Slouching Toward Capitalism: Cultural Transformation in Leipzig 1993

Lauren Stone

The Berlin Wall was breached more than three years ago, and the two Germanies have now been unified for more than two years. The city of Leipzig, birthplace of the revolution of 1989, is suffering the growing pains of a society and an economy in transition. The city has undergone a dramatic face-lift. Drab and crumbling buildings have received new coats of paint. Scaffolding and cranes foreshadow economic development and a bright future for the city known throughout the centuries for its culture and its trade fairs. Bach, Mendelssohn-Bartholdy, Goethe, Schiller, and many other well-known artists, composers, and writers lived and worked in Leipzig. The city has always placed a high value on maintaining its cultural tradition.

After managing to flourish through forty years of communism, the cultural scene in Leipzig is now struggling to meet the challenges of a new economic reality. Although many in the city, including the new mayor from the West,[1] recognize the ties between culture, city image, and economic development, budget cuts threaten lasting harm to Leipzig's cultural fabric. As one of many cities undergoing the transformation from communism to capitalism, Leipzig's experience is relevant for many other communities in eastern Germany and elsewhere in Eastern Europe.

The Meaning of Culture

Culture means different things to different people. The German word *Kultur* has a broader meaning than its English cognate. It includes everything from museums and galleries to youth clubs and rock concert and performance venues. In Leipzig much emphasis is placed on local "community culture" (*Stadtteilkultur*), culture that develops at the grass-roots level. This broad definition of culture has great political, economic, and sociological resonance. Although some in the West have asserted that culture is a luxury that eastern Germans can ill afford in these hard times, cultural infrastructure has played and continues to play a very important role in both the psyche and the development of eastern Germany. Indeed, many have argued that the closing of youth centers in the East has contributed to the rise of right-wing violence among youth. Thus, the question of the future of culture in Leipzig is one of extreme importance.

Leipzig's Cultural Landscape

Several important anniversaries in 1993 drew attention to the important role culture played in Leipzig's past. The Opera is celebrating its three-hundredth birthday; the Gewandhaus Orchestra, led by Kurt Masur, is 250 years old; and the College of Music is 150 years old.[2] The city's celebration of these events has been used as part of a marketing campaign intended to attract investors to Leipzig. Despite drastic budget cuts in the city's cultural budget since unification, these three institutions are still well-funded and remain financially stable.

In contrast, the rest of the cultural landscape, particularly community culture, has been badly shaken. These cultural institutions must now learn to support themselves without the substantial state subsidies that sustained them in the past. Few cultural institutions in the world can exist on box office revenues alone. Federal, state, and city subsidies, as well as grants from private organizations and foundations, are essential for their survival. Per capita municipal expenditures for culture in eastern Germany, however, are markedly lower than in western Germany. For example, in 1992, Frankfurt spent DM 734 per person on culture, Stuttgart spent DM 450, and Leipzig only DM 375.[3]

Thus in Leipzig, as elsewhere in the East, cultural institutions are reorganizing and cutting spending. They are seeking new audiences at a time when many citizens can barely cover the basic costs of living. They are defending their existence and proving that they were not tainted by the old regime. They are thinking about the bottom line—something that does not come easily to artists anywhere. They are competing for limited funds against myriad other needs and worthy causes in the East. They are being forced to stretch their budgets to make up for many years of financial neglect.

The problem of financing cultural institutions is made even more acute by the extraordinary number of contested property claims involving buildings that house cultural organizations. Resolving these claims will take many years and will involve expensive legal fees and potentially high restitution costs. In the meantime, the clouds over property titles will hinder the financing of artistic and cultural activities and the renovation of performance space. Perhaps only the Gewandhaus, the city's theater, and the Opera are entirely free of claims.

Despite these constraints, culture continues to flourish in Leipzig, testimony to the will and the spirit of its people. The cultural boom is based in part on the new spirit of democracy and freedom that followed the revolution of 1989. Much of the political will behind the revolution had its roots in the youth and arts scenes. Empowered by their successes on the political front, many citizens turned their energies to creating a new nongovernmental sector, providing needed cultural and social initiatives. These initiatives generally took the form of clubs (*Vereine*) or nonprofit organizations (*Freie Träger*)—giving the groups legitimacy and a measure of independence from the city and the state.

It is particularly ironic, however, that this burgeoning of the cultural scene is not something an economy in transition can easily support. Leipzig has made a valiant, if not always successful, effort to continue to support new cultural initiatives while encouraging cultural continuity.

Reform of the Cultural Council

There has always been a close relationship among federal, state, and city governments and cultural institutions in eastern and western Germany. Even today, private sources of funding, such as foundations, endowments, and businesses, are far more limited in both parts of Germany than in the United States. Thus, although the apparatus that supported culture in Leipzig has changed, it is natural that the cultural organizations and institutions continued to look to public entities for support.

The Cultural Council (*Kulturamt*) of Leipzig is the city's public arm for culture. In the German Democratic Republic (GDR), it was a very centralized, politicized bureau that determined which institutions received support and which did not. As the only source of funds for artists, museums, youth clubs, and other cultural organizations, the pre–1989 Cultural Council had tremendous control over culture in Leipzig.

After unification, the Cultural Council was depoliticized, streamlined, and debureaucratized. The city intentionally sought to reduce its power, hoping to make it more of an administrative support system and less of a direction-setter for culture. Gerald Biehl, appointed deputy director of the Council in 1991, spent several months establishing contacts with cultural councils in western Germany to examine other models and determine how best to restructure Leipzig's council. After a period of study, a new model for funding was devised: cultural organizations would no longer be supported institutionally. Instead they would receive funds for specific projects selected according to strict criteria. This approach was designed to provide more flexibility and transparency, as well as to encourage groups to seek other sources of funding. The Council convened impartial advisory commissions of local experts from each artistic medium and established funding criteria. This reduced the perception that certain organizations were "favorite sons" of the city.[4]

The new policies received a mixed reception. All cultural organizations were forced to find additional funding. Many groups were financially shaken and others distrusted both the reorganization process and its consequences. Whereas in other sectors western business people had come to the former GDR to help in the restructuring and privatization process, providing training and needed skills to the East Germans, this was only rarely the case in the cultural community. Most artists, gallery owners, directors, and other cultural figures in the East received little or no guidance in marketing, fundraising, and lobbying. As the euphoria of unification faded, a sobering economic reality set in, hitting the cultural scene particularly hard.

Nevertheless, a surprising amount of continuity in pre-unification cultural activity prevailed. Popular GDR clubs and venues, such as the *Moritzbastei* and the naTo Cultural Center, continued to run full cultural programs. The Leipzig Documentary Film Festival, a popular annual event before unification, continued uninterrupted and expanded its support base. Only two city-run cultural institutions closed: the Lenin Museum, which had a shaky historical connection to the city, and the Sports Museum, where the directors and staff chose to close down rather than reorganize.[5] In addition, from 1990 through 1993, many new groups were established, although some of these closed down almost as quickly as they were formed.

Cultural Restructuring and the ABM Program

The transition from a socialist command economy to a market economy was extremely difficult for many in the former GDR. A majority of eastern Germans lost their jobs, changed jobs, or were forced into early retirement. The federal government helped bridge the gap by establishing a federal program of work creation known as *Arbeitsbeschaffungsmassnahmen,* or ABM positions.[6] In 1992 and 1993, ABM positions were created at all levels of society in eastern Germany; the majority of the staff of many institutions were ABM workers. This was particularly true in Leipzig, which had one of the highest percentages of ABM jobs in all of Germany.

When the Federal Institute for Labor *(Bundesanstalt für Arbeit)* announced the ABM program in 1991, the promotional materials, in the liberating spirit of the times, promised:

> Where new ways are called for, the answer is ABM—something for everyone. ... Move forward with ABM! Develop new ideas! Develop more initiative![7]

The response in the cultural arena as well as other areas was overwhelming.

The ABM program provided a way for the fledgling nongovernmental sector to survive. Applicants from the cultural arena ranged from old GDR institutions that had found new life as clubs (such as historical societies), to organizations that had been developed through personal initiative during the period of change (such as Youth Media Center Leipzig, which is discussed later in this chapter), to new organizations that seemed to have been created solely to take advantage of ABM financing and were unlikely to survive on their own (such as the Tourism Sociology Club).

By early 1993, a broad spectrum of cultural institutions had become dependent on ABM positions. During a time of severe resource constraints, approximately 70 different groups in Leipzig used the ABM program to support at least 250 positions in the cultural community.[8] ABM, together with the Cultural Council's grant program, provided the most important source of financial support for these groups.

The Cultural Council also used the ABM program to broaden and expand its activities. Museum hours were extended, music lessons for nearly 150 students were provided, and cultural education and other activities for youth, seniors, and the handicapped were supported. At the outset, the ABM program seemed to be an effective way to ease the transition to a market economy.

The Demise of ABM: Consequences for Culture

Slowly, however, abuses involving ABM positions began to come to light. The abuse was not confined to the cultural community, and similar incidents were reported elsewhere in the economy. The local ABM offices gave positions to nearly all who applied, and the number of positions granted often did not match the actual needs of the organization. In some cases, a financially troubled organization would fire employees only to hire them back as ABM workers. Some ABM-funded employees did very little at work, and others would not even bother to go to work. A few organizations failed to produce anything to show for the ABM employees on their staff. The Federal Institute for Labor quickly recognized some of the problems and began to reassess the program. Regulations were tightened, and positions became harder to obtain. By early 1993, the ABM program and its future were a point of intense political controversy and a source of tension in the negotiations on the government's Solidarity Pact, a package of measures to address needs in the East. One week the ABM program would be slated for termination; the next only modest changes would be under consideration. The final result of the discussions was a scaled-back program in which very few ABM positions were to be renewed. For a renewal to be considered, the organization or firm had to guarantee a regular position at the end of the ABM financing.

The problem, however, was that the ABM program, intended only to provide jobs during a period of economic transition, had become the financial backbone of the entire nongovernmental sector in eastern Germany. Although it was clear that the program could not continue indefinitely, many organizations were slow to consider how their ventures could continue without the employment subsidy. By January 1993, realizing that the end of their personnel subsidies was near at hand, many groups began to take action.

Small groups of concerned individuals met to discuss tactical strategies. Group representatives believed that political pressure at the local and state levels to continue subsidies was their most effective tool and, in the spring of 1993, they organized demonstrations. Lobbying groups formed to pressure local and state government, but the groups were disorganized and unable to work effectively with one another. Rather than devising alternative funding models, the organizations called for the continuation of subsidies, which, given the budgetary cutbacks in the eastern cities, was unrealistic.

As the ABM dialogue continued, Leipzig's Cultural Council became increasingly concerned about the potential effect of the termination of ABM subsidies on the city's cultural landscape. The Council realized the need to make difficult choices about which organizations to fund and what types of projects to emphasize. Strategies for finding alternative sources of funding were refined and criteria established for allocating the limited funds still available. Emphasizing to the cultural community that the number of ABM positions would be dramatically reduced, the Cultural Council began to work with city and state authorities in an attempt to maintain some positions and to find new sources of funds.

The Debate Between High Culture and Community Culture

One of the more difficult issues that Leipzig faces is deciding how much to spend on "high culture" (the Opera, the Gewandhaus Orchestra, the city theater, and the large city museums) and how much on other cultural activities. The trade-off is clear: Many smaller institutions that reach out to a different, generally more local audience receive less because the internationally famous Opera and the Gewandhaus Orchestra, both showpieces of the former government, together consume 55 percent of the budget. Their high-profile directors (Udo Zimmerman and Kurt Masur) are strong lobbyists for their organizations.

By 1993, these premier cultural institutions had become both a boon and a burden for the city. Although they draw visitors to Leipzig and are, at least indirectly, critical to the economic development of the city, they also cost the city a substantial sum. Because they are municipal institutions, the state of Saxony does no more than match funds provided by the city. In contrast, the Dresden *Semperoper* receives all or most of its funding from the state.[9]

During a period in which culture is under threat and budgets are being cut, is it reasonable or fair to continue to fund high culture at the same high levels as in the past? Community culture, with an annual city budget of DM 50,000, accounts for a minuscule fraction of the culture budget.[10] This allocation has created no small amount of tension in the city. The budget clearly reveals the city government's priorities.

Studies in Cultural Transformation

The following case studies highlight the experiences of two cultural institutions and illustrate some of the problems and challenges facing such organizations during this transitional period. Both studies were prepared in the winter and spring of 1993.

Case Study 1: Leipzig Youth Media Center

The Leipzig Youth Media Center (*Jugendmedienzentrum*, or JMZ) was a child of the revolution. Five independent groups that shared a commitment to public education through the use of film, video, and broadcast media and a belief that the cultural needs of the community were not being met banded together to form a consortium in 1992. The groups covered their operating costs through a variety of means, relying heavily on the use of ABM positions.[11]

In 1992 the groups worked with more than 22,880 young people in the region. They began to pool their resources for joint projects to avoid redundancy. Apart from their regular offerings, they initiated special projects dealing with youth violence and foreigners. The individual and joint projects were tremendously successful, winning awards and grants and filling a cultural gap resulting from the closing of GDR youth clubs. They addressed current issues and provided important training for young people. Why then, was the JMZ in a state of crisis and uncertainty in 1993?

The answer is complex and cannot be attributed to a single reason. The greatest concern of the individual groups was the continued funding of personnel costs. Of nineteen JMZ staff slots, seventeen were ABM positions. Most were due to expire at the end of June 1993, and only one person had a guaranteed job through October 1993. The two non-ABM positions were funded by a private film distributor who until recently had provided housing for the JMZ and reaped positive publicity for his efforts. Most of the JMZ employees, who believed that their positions would be renewed or converted to permanent status with city funding, came to their jobs with a strong commitment to the project. Many had worked as volunteers while collecting unemployment benefits before the ABM positions were created. A common sentiment of the staff, one voiced at many other cultural institutions, was that once the ABM positions ended they would again volunteer at the JMZ while collecting unemployment benefits and searching for regular employment and for other sources of funding to keep JMZ—and their jobs—going. Although the staff's dedication to JMZ is admirable, volunteer staffing often leads to poor work performance, low morale, and half-hearted job searches. Such an outcome would be inconsistent with ABM's original purpose of placing and keeping people in the work force.

The JMZ's problem was also one of mind-set. Most of its employees shared the conviction that good projects would and should survive on their merits. They expected the state or the city to provide support because of the broad scope and importance of their projects, a viewpoint inherited from the GDR era when the state did support such projects, although always with firm ideological control. The members of the JMZ board also were disinclined to focus their efforts on marketing and lobbying.

Rather than pursuing a variety of solutions, the board insisted on a single approach to resolving JMZ's impending funding crisis. If the city could be persuaded to recognize the consortium as a nonprofit institution, the JMZ could seek state and federal funds. The board also tried to secure property to house the JMZ, but it expected the city to pay the bills. Alternative sources of funds were not sought, and compromise positions were not discussed.

In May 1993, the city's Youth Council, which together with the Cultural Council had been supportive of the JMZ, granted JMZ 50,000 DM for start-up funds and asked the board to consider sharing an already existing youth center with other groups. The proposal threw the board into a state of crisis. Board members began to fight among themselves, and some considered breaking up the consortium. Although pooling resources seemed an appropriate strategy on paper, the reality was somewhat more problematic. The JMZ had a difficult time planning for the future, even into 1994.

Case Study 2: naTo–A Cultural Success Story?

With its long history under the GDR the naTo Culture and Communication Center represents a cultural continuity in Leipzig that few institutions can claim. Founded in the 1950s as the National Front Pavilion by an alliance of all GDR parties and political organizations, its activities included organizing rehearsals and performances of local choirs, preparing special events for socialist holidays and festivals, hosting meetings of political parties and mass organizations, and even scheduling office hours for the local policeman. In the early 1980s the National Front Pavilion began to be known as a center for jazz events and independent art and culture. City officials tolerated the change because it created a manageable creative outlet in a somewhat controlled environment.[12]

A critical change for the organization came in 1987, when the GDR parliament passed a resolution to increase funding for youth activities, especially through the creation of more youth clubs. The National Front became the home of the local youth club, "On the Corner," and its activities and staff support grew. The club then closed for two years for repairs and reconstruction. When it reopened in early 1989, it quickly emerged as a center for jazz and art and was widely regarded as the center of the alternative scene.

When the Berlin Wall fell in late 1989, this particular youth club had five full-time positions, all financed by the city. By early 1990, even before unification was seriously discussed, the director of the club, Frank Fröhlich, adopted a far-sighted and pragmatic approach to funding. He was one of the first in Leipzig's cultural arena to look to the West for models of private financing.

In early 1990 the club was reorganized as "Club naTo e.V." Fröhlich, working closely with the city's Cultural Council, proposed a gradual privatization of the club. As unification drew closer, he realized that the cultural clubs like his were unlikely to be as well supported in a unified Germany. Negotiations with the city produced a contract for a five-year transition period in June 1991. The terms were extremely liberal and generous. naTo could work in its space rent free, receiving funding for two full-time staff members and 90 percent of its operating costs.

naTo was also a city leader in maintaining a quality program while securing its financial base. The club moved quickly to identify funding sources both within and outside of the government. Searching out old GDR assets that had transferred into public hands, such as funds from the now-defunct National Youth Club (FDJ), naTo was able to finance a complete renovation of the building in which it was housed.

In addition to its city-financed positions, naTo had three ABM positions in 1993. The entire staff participated in quarterly retreats to refine goals and ponder the economic future of the center. naTo also began to seek out partners to co-sponsor its activities by initiating contacts with private foundations.

Conclusion

The picture painted here of culture in Leipzig in 1993 is one of struggle and fear. A return visit to Leipzig early in 1994, however, reveals a remarkably resilient cultural sector. A mood of optimism prevails among cultural activists and employees of the Cultural Council. The city still boasts a very wide choice of events, venues, and activities. Most of those who were involved in the arts before the Revolution remain active and dedicated; others have found new activities or settled into long-term unemployment. When discussing the impact of the phase-out of the ABM program and the reduction of other government subsidies, people frequently repeat the following phrase: "The changes have separated the wheat from the chaff."

JMZ still exists in a somewhat scaled-down form. It maintains its profile in the communities it serves but has suffered financially and structurally by failing to cultivate a base of support at the city level or in the wider cultural community. It has secured one full-time position with financing from the city's Youth Council and has also received some operating funds from the state of Saxony. The work of the JMZ is now carried out by officially unemployed workers acting as volunteers.

naTo continues to run a full program and has achieved a certain level of financial security. It is a center for cutting-edge music, art, and culture and a very popular meeting place for a broad cross-section of the city. As the result of a restitution claim, however, naTo will have to move from its building in 1995. The current site was once a Jewish-owned apartment building that was expropriated by the Nazis. naTo has made the right moves at almost every step and its future prospects are good. Nonetheless, much depends on maintaining a good relationship with the city. A strong lobby for culture—which currently does not exist—would help to ensure support for the arts in the future. Furthermore, the elections scheduled for the fall of 1994 could also play a determining factor.

Much of Leipzig's success in continuing its cultural tradition can be attributed to the dogged persistence of its artists. The threat, however, is great. With its gradual phase-out, the ABM program that gave birth to so many democratic cultural initiatives will take many of those initiatives along with it. ABM was created to help ease the East's transition to a market economy, but the long-term consequences of ending the program were not considered.

Cultural transformation was indeed necessary after the revolution of 1989 and unification, and the cultural landscape today looks very different than it did only five years ago. Many of the bureaucratic structures supporting culture, particularly at the city level, are much more democratic than before. But the philosophical questions behind the process of transformation have never been addressed. In the GDR, members of the arts community—artists and administrators—enjoyed a high level of support provided they cooperated within the system. Ironically, unification has brought greater artistic freedom, but artists of all kinds face an uncertain future and likely unemployment.

Because the benefits provided to an unemployed worker are more costly than supporting a cultural position, the government should carefully assess the costs and risks of reducing support for the arts.[13] Culture touches everyone's life, and the costs of maintaining it at a certain level may be less than would first appear. Failure to support the arts in an adequate manner poses a threat not to the GDR inheritance but to the cultural fruit of the revolution, the fresh ideas born in a remarkable time.

Notes

1. Hinrich Lehmann-Grube, SPD, elected as mayor of Leipzig in 1990, came to the position from Hannover, where he had served as city manager. Widely admired, he is considered to be quite sensitive to the needs of the East and is expected to be reelected in 1994.

2. This event is being celebrated by the city under the motto "*Leipzig Lobt Kultur*" and has been officially integrated into the city's marketing campaign. The year-long program has received funds from the city and from private sources.

3. Figures for Frankfurt and Stuttgart come from the Leipzig Cultural Council's internal report "*Grosskonzeption für die Kulturentwicklung der Stadt Leipzig*," 2 February 1993. Figures for Leipzig's per capita expenditures come from financial reports prepared at the author's request, 16 April 1993.

4. Interview with Gerald Biehl, deputy director of the Cultural Council of the city of Leipzig, 9 February 1994.

5. Further inquiry in 1994 indicated that the Sports Museum had reopened with a new staff and a new format.

6. Paragraph 3, Article 249 of the Employment Promotion Act of 1992 establishes the right of the Federal Institute for Labor to fund environmental, social, and youth work that would not otherwise be carried out. These funds are provided in the form of employment for registered unemployed workers.

7. As quoted in "Zauberformel ABM," *Kreuzer–Die Leipziger Illustrierte*, January 1992, 15–17.

8. Internal report of the Cultural Council on the issue of ABM. Statistics on ABM workers in the cultural realm are surprisingly hard to come by; the Employment Office in Leipzig, which should have an overview of the situation, has no statistics. These numbers were compiled by the different departments of the Cultural Council in order to create an effective position paper for lobbying the City Council.

9. Figure is for fiscal year 1993, from a financial report prepared on 16 April 1993 by the Administrative Department of the Cultural Council at the author's request. In 1992, the combined financing of the Opera and the Orchestra took up 52 percent of the annual budget.

10. This amount does not take into consideration the potential funds that community cultural initiatives can receive from city grants. This amount is 2,202,500 DM for 1993.

11. The following case study is based on interviews with board members, work the author did with the group from January to March 1993, and materials produced by the JMZ. The five groups that make up the consortium are: *AG Kommunales Kino*, a group that screens and promotes noncommercial films for children, young people, and adults; *Multi-Medien-Werkstatt "Die Fabrik"* ("The Factory," a Multi-Media Workshop), which works with children and youth to produce television, video, and a school magazine; *Filmschule e.V.*, which uses children's films as a starting point for creative work and media training; *Radio Verein Leipzig*, a group that produces radio for and by children and young adults; and *Landesfilmdienst Sachsen* (Saxony State Film Service), which supports children's, youth, and young adult education through video and film production and distribution.

12. This case study is based on an interview with Frank Fröhlich, director of naTo from 1989 to 1991 and currently a city employee responsible for community culture in southern Leipzig. It is also based on several months of the author's personal experience with the club and discussions with naTo co-workers and other cultural figures in Leipzig from January to May 1993.

13. Thomas Flierl, "Kulturarbeit und Gesellschaftliche Modernisierung," *Kulturstrecke*, No. 9 (1993), 12–18.

9

Rightist Violence as a Youth Phenomenon in United Germany

Bradden Weaver

In September 1991, rightist radical youth and Nazi skinheads attacked the homes of asylum seekers in the East German town of Hoyerswerda, shouting "Germany for the Germans. Foreigners out." But Hoyerswerda was only the prelude. In the following months, the nightly attacks against asylum hostels escalated, culminating in the August 1992 Rostock riots. Three months later, in November, three Turkish women burned to death in a fire-bombing in the town of Mölln, and the following April another fire-bombing claimed five Turkish victims in Sollingen.

These events, graphic representations of thousands of others that have erupted since 1990, have forced Germans to acknowledge that they must deal not only with specters from the past but also with a new and unique form of youth violence. As in other Western countries, alienation, weakened social control, and visionless futures have driven young German men to acts of street savagery. But whereas elsewhere youth violence is anarchic and materialistic but decidedly non-ideological, Germany's present violence has a pronounced right-extremist bent. People of color and foreigners are not the only targets. Other imagined enemies exist: the handicapped, the homeless, gays, leftists, and others deemed "un-German." In a youth subculture once dominated by punkers and the left-extremist *Autonomen*, rightist youths are establishing a foothold with their own brand of brutality.[1]

This chapter explores the various factors that contribute to the rise of right-wing youth violence. First, the motivations and socioeconomic background as well as the personality traits and *Weltanschauung* of the youths involved are examined. Second, the economic and social turmoil caused by unification and by the great influx of refugees and asylum seekers to Germany are discussed. Third, the role of public discourse that portrays asylees and refugees as threats to German society is analyzed. Lastly, the renewed search in Germany for a national identity and the need of eastern Germans to come to terms with their past are considered.

Recognizing some of the causal factors behind the rightist violence is the first step in combatting the problem. At this point, the youths associated with the violence have not coalesced into a viable political force, nor has their violence become an effective political tool. But conceptualizing today's violence as acts of frustration and social protest by an underclass youth counterculture in no way lessens the danger that Germany now faces. Even the smallest societal fringe, once established and rooted, may cause considerable domestic disturbance and international embarrassment, exactly what Germany does not need as it faces a myriad of post-unification problems.

Youth Offenders: Motivations and Socioeconomic Backgrounds

Although they commit similar crimes against similar victims, violent rightist youths are more notable for their differing motivations and backgrounds than for their commonalities. They can be divided into four major groups:

- politically motivated youths with strong ties to or membership in a rightist extremist organization
- followers or "groupies" of the fascist political groups who search for acceptance from these groups but are not politically motivated
- non-ideological and apolitical youths assembled in loose rightist groups who consider themselves to be socially disadvantaged and use violence to gain attention
- youths from dysfunctional homes who learned violence as a means of communication[2]

Although the borders between these categories may be blurred, it is important to differentiate between violent youths who are rightist-oriented but have no political agenda and hardened rightist extremists who use violence to promote national socialism. A key factor common to all groups appears to be neglect and estrangement from family.

For all the media hype about "neo-Nazi" youth, the first category of hard-core political extremists is quite small, composing only 7 percent–15 percent of youth offenders.[3] Despite their small numbers, however, they are extremely dangerous and responsible for about 20 percent of rightist violence, including a majority of the most brutal acts.

These youth are fanatically committed to resurrecting national social-ism as a political and social order.[4] They belong to regimented groups such as "Nazi-Skins," "Party Skins," and "Faschos." Often they have multiple memberships in or strong affiliations with fascist organizations such as the Free Workers Party (FAP), the German Alternative (DA), the National Offensive (NO), and the National Front (NF).[5] Most of them lead a disciplined life focused on martial sports and street fighting, polit-ical agitation, and male camaraderie. True to the National Socialist ethos, they take pride in their proletarian roots, remain firmly integrated in the working class, and disdain the soft lifestyle of the bourgeoisie. Most have completed vocational school and are employed in the construction and electronics industries.[6]

The second category of youths differs from the first in that its members are not card-carrying, active members of a fascist organiza-tion. They are "part-time" fascists who often serve as security guards at political meetings.[7] Usually, they are poorly informed about the tenets of national socialism, and their commitment to fascism is wavering. Their motivation for associating with fascist groups stems more from personal and family problems than from a messianic vision of recreating the Third Reich.

Members of these first two categories do not fall into the typical underclass stereotype usually seen in the media. Although the majority come from poorer working class families or unemployed eastern German families, many also come from middle and upper-middle-class back-grounds, including professional, two-parent families from western Germany.

The last two categories are far larger and more fluid than the first two. It is difficult to determine either their exact number or their potential for violence. The youths in these categories tend to come from a lower socio economic milieu. Their parents are frequently struggling to make ends meet and to keep their jobs, creating an atmosphere of perpetual crisis.

These youths are also marked by their social and educational failure. Most dropped out of high school or vocational school without profes-sional certification and have difficulty finding steady work and housing. Their counterparts in eastern Germany are generally better integrated into the working class as unskilled tertiary labor.[8]

Despite their alarming rhetoric and slogans, youths in these last two categories cannot be called Nazis in any formal sense of the word. Despite their racist *Weltanschauung*, they reject Nazi tenets, including the concept of allegiance to a *Führer-based*, single-party dictatorship. They fall into one of the less hard-core groupings such as the eastern Oi-Skin Head faction or the Hooligans. Frequently they are called "baby skins" or "free time skins" because their "skin" activities are so wavering.[9]

Although extreme-right political groups have attempted to mobilize these youths, they have generally not been successful. Skin groups have no firm organizational structure and distrust political organizations that attempt to exert control and discipline over their lives. This results in a direct clash with the approach of rightist extremist parties that exist by order and party line.[10]

Personality Traits and *Weltanschauung*

Despite their differing backgrounds and motivations, the four categories of youth share common personality traits that vary in intensity. These commonalities bolster the youths' predisposition for racist and xenophobic violence.[11]

First and foremost, these youths are unrooted and disoriented, possessing little in life except their "Germaness." They are pessimistic about the future, have low self-esteem, and are extremely insecure about economic and social competition. Rightist scenes and cliques provide them with adventure, acceptance, direction, and security. Through special clothes, hairstyles, symbols, and slogans, these youths find empowerment in the group's identity.[12]

Xenophobic violence, usually accompanied by heavy drinking, provides excitement in an otherwise tedious daily life.[13] In the words of many youth offenders, they are *Geil auf Gewalt*, or "turned on by violence" and engage in such violence "just for the fun of it." On a deeper level, however, violence functions as the core rationale for these groups. Since most groups are not predicated on ideology or political programs, camaraderie in drunken violence against "the enemy" functions as a unifying sacramental act.[14] Foreigners and people considered "un-German," such as gays, Jews, and the homeless, provide clear and definite "enemies" against which the group can define itself.

Second, the world of these youths consists of clear hierarchies of winners and losers; conflict between the two is resolved through physical force. Most of these youths have learned this type of conflict resolution from their families. Furthermore, they are aware of their disempowered social status and feel threatened by forces beyond their control, such as unemployment, that could bring them further down the social ladder.

For such people, foreigners and "un-Germans" represent the next lower level in the social pecking order. Attacks on them serve as tests of strength through which these youths can experience feelings of supremacy and reinforce their threatened masculinity by winning clique respect.[15] The foreigner, however, serves not only as a whipping boy for displaced aggression, but also as a scapegoat. By launching attacks under the banner of "German virtues"—cleanliness, law and order, manliness, and morality—these youths attempt to portray foreigners as the cause of Germany's increasing social problems and thereby justify their violence against them.

Finally, these youths are unable to deal with the controversy, diversity, complexity, and ambiguity of today's multicultural society. Their black-and-white thinking is dominated by enemies, the evil oppressors of Germany, and the heroic but persecuted German *Volk*. This simplistic understanding of the world is based on racial and ethnic prejudices. It is also the outgrowth of poor education and, frequently, of limited intellectual capabilities and life experiences. For youth who need order and clarity, the closed *Weltanschauung* of rightist extremists is very attractive.

Unification and the Dimming Future

Particularly for the youth of eastern Germany, the economic and social disorientation caused by unification has been overwhelming. As the future and the hope of the socialist fatherland, they had an honored role in society in the German Democratic Republic (GDR).[16] State programs channeled them automatically into apprenticeships, technical training, and universities, after which assured work places awaited them. Youth organizations such as the Free German Youth and the Young Pioneers ordered every aspect of their lives, keeping them busy with political meetings and public service projects. Although much maligned today, these organizations served an important role, providing recreational activities and free vacations in the Eastern Bloc.

Today the youth infrastructure in eastern Germany is in shambles. Gyms, movie houses, and libraries, once funded and administered by the state, have been drastically reduced due to budget cuts. Youth discotheques, camping trips, free vacations, and athletic clubs have also been discontinued. The Free German Youth and Young Pioneers have been disbanded. At best, rooms at an underfunded "recreational center" may be kept open as a coffee house.[17]

As a result, eastern German youths must structure and take responsibility for their own lives. They must face their own failures in a free market society without the cradle-to-grave social net they had known. They must compete in an extremely tight labor market. Of the 9.8 million people employed in eastern Germany in 1989, the Deutsche Bank estimated in 1992 that only 5.4 million still had jobs in the East and that industrial output had slumped by 70 percent.[18] In the East in 1993, 1,117,000 people were searching for work without success, an unemployment rate of approximately 15 percent.[19] If people in temporary work programs are included, unemployment is more than 30 percent. (It is more than 45 percent if early retirees and those obliged to work in the West are counted.)

After years of Western television seduction, easterners had placed great hope in Chancellor Kohl's promise of a blooming landscape in which life would be better after unification. The realization that Western living conditions were at least a decade away brought with it great feelings of betrayal. With the old dictatorship gone, eastern German youths can now openly vent the fury they feel about the hopelessness of their lives.

Going Multicultural at the Worst of Times

The fall of communism left permeable borders across which people from Eastern Europe, Africa, and the Balkans came to Germany searching for security and a better life. The new arrivals compete for limited housing, jobs, and economic resources. They also shatter Germany's social and ethnic homogeneity at a tense moment in the country's history.

The Federal Republic of Germany (FRG) receives most of Europe's asylum seekers and refugees (about 79 percent of the European total). From 1988 to 1992 the number of asylum seekers arriving annually in Germany grew from 103,076 to nearly 450,000. In the first quarter of 1993, there were 118,064 asylum seekers, a 21 percent increase over the same period in 1992. Nearly all claim that they were politically persecuted in their country of origin. Only a small portion of such claims can be proven, however.[20] In addition, since 1988 about 520,000 refugees have come to Germany fleeing war and strife in their homelands. Most come from the former Yugoslavia and will not be repatriated until the civil war ends. The reunification treaty stipulated that 20 percent of all asylum seekers would be sent to eastern Germany, and asylees and refugees began to arrive there in the late autumn of 1990. From the beginning, however, it was clear that the eastern German states were not prepared to handle this new responsibility.

The problem was both logistical and psychological. Because the supply of housing was inadequate, towns had to sacrifice their hotels, rooms for rent, sports halls, and civic centers. Smaller communities were especially hard hit. Most of the asylum seekers come from vastly different cultures and have been unable or unwilling to fit in with German mores and lifestyle. For communities that had known few social problems, the arrival of thousands of asylum seekers unfortunately meant an increase in petty crime.[21]

Most eastern Germans had never really dealt with resident foreigners.

Although the GDR had imported foreign workers from other socialist countries, the numbers were extremely small. At the time of unification, there were only 191,000 such workers living in the GDR (60,000 from Vietnam, 14,000 from Mozambique, and 5,000 from Cuba), or about 1.2 percent of the population.[22] In addition, despite all the talk of socialist internationalism and the friendship of peoples, foreign workers were extremely isolated from the eastern German population, living in barracks and hostels on factory grounds.

In the words of Bernd Mesovi of the Workers Benevolent Society in Frankfurt:

> The distribution of refugees to the East went too fast. There was no thought, no overall concept, no organization. These refugees were viewed as solely a problem of order by the authorities. They were worried about protecting the German population from the foreigners. It was only later that they realized that it was the foreigners who needed protection. ... The speed with which reunification and these transfers occurred contributed to the violence. The population was unprepared for the refugees. They were too preoccupied with themselves. The problems were obvious.[23]

Political and Media Discourse on Asylees and Refugees

The German media and German politicians, particularly but not exclusively politicians from conservative parties, have reinforced antiforeign sentiment by painting negative images of asylees. The most ubiquitous image portrays them as ingrates, intruders, swindlers, and parasites. Tabloids such as *Bild Zeitung* regularly run inflammatory headlines. An article on 7 August 1991 is one of many that have portrayed asylees and refugees as ungrateful guests who take advantage of their hosts' gracious hospitality. In a "A Report on a German Problem," readers were asked to

> Imagine this situation: A man rings your doorbell and asks to come in. He says that he has powerful enemies who want to take his life. You give him shelter. But you quickly learn that the man wasn't persecuted at all; he only wanted to live in your house. What's more he behaves very badly. He hits your children, steals your money, and wipes his shoes on your curtains. You would like to get rid of him, but you can't. This is the reality of German asylum laws in 1991. The house is the city of Frankfurt, and the man is a Yugoslav who in the underworld is known simply as "Cento."[24]

Another image is the foreigner as a "natural disaster." Interior minister Seiters has repeatedly referred to the "continuing flood of economic refugees," while the Christian Social Union's Manfred Ritter compared refugees to "locusts who leave a desert in their wake." The "flood" endangers nothing less than European culture and the health of Germany cultural integrity. In the words of Stefan Reicher, Social Democratic Party state chairman in Brandenburg: "The great streams of refugees from the east could bring an end to European culture. They could be more dangerous for Europe than the Red Army in the time of the Cold War."[25]

Eckart Schiffer, chief advisor to Wolfgang Schäuble, Christian Democratic Union parlimentary leader, repeats this theme when he claims that the arrival of foreigners will lead to the "ghettoization" of Germany, which could bring Europe back to the Middle Ages. Even Helmut Schmidt has spoken of the country as being "overrun" and has warned that a country with Germany's lengthy history cannot be turned into a melting pot without societal "degeneration."[26]

So threatening was this "wave" to the integrity and security of the German state that in November 1992 Chancellor Kohl raised the possibility of invoking a "state of emergency." The state of emergency was not needed because of extremists such as the neo-Nazis but because of the "flood of refugees."

The strongest statements come from the Republikaner, a rightist political party. The Republikaner have moved beyond crude slogans of "Foreigners out!" They now speak in terms of "protecting cultural identity," "rejecting the multicultural society," and "protecting the purity of the German language." Party boss Franz Schönhuber, who declares he is proud to have been an SS member, has called for the protection of Germany's *Lebensraum* from foreign "infiltration."[27]

Yet another image used by conservative politicians has been that of Germany as a boat overloaded with passengers. Even the most unlikely sources now mirror this image. The 9 September 1991 edition of *Der Spiegel*, traditionally a magazine critical of the government, brought this image to life better than any Republikaner could have. Under the title, "The Onslaught of the Poor: Refugees and Asylum Seekers," the cover depicts a black, red, and gold boat in a sea of struggling humanity. The vessel is massively overcrowded, with people falling out and others fighting to clamber aboard. In the article, the poor of the world are portrayed as sitting on their suitcases with only one aim—to come to Germany and partake of its prosperity.

All of these images and the highly loaded words that accompany them—such as *Scheinasylant* (sham asylee)—have become part of daily discourse in Germany. They can be found on the front page of newspapers and on the evening news. They are heard in conversation in homes, schools, and government offices. In this atmosphere of national alarm, it is not surprising that youths have been incited to acts of violence.

Reawakening and Redefinition of National Identity

The cold war division of Germany into the FRG and the GDR meant the end of a pan-German national identity and consciousness. Given the radically different political and social orders, all discussion of what it meant to be German in the post-Nazi period was centered on what it meant to be a citizen of the FRG or the GDR. Germany's unification opened up the long-postponed debate on *die National Frage* (the national question). In the post-unification turmoil, once taboo questions are now open for soul-searching public discussion: What does it mean to be German? Dare Germans be openly proud of their nation, celebrating events in national history and "traditional" German values in the way the Americans or the French do? To what exent has the German national character evolved, and what are its constituent properties? Who is German, and who can become a German citizen? Why is it so difficult for Turks who have lived and worked in Germany for three decades to become German citizens, when Poles and Russians, whose forefathers immigrated from Germany two hundred years ago, have an automatic right to citizenship?

Some German youths, especially from the East, answer such questions by turning to an elitist and exclusionary national pride. It would be misleading, however, to view a resurgence of an elitist national identity as a simple product of unification. Public opinion data gathered on youth attitudes by GDR survey organizations in the summer of 1990 show that East German youth were particularly susceptible to exaggerated feelings of national identity months before unification and the first arrival of asylees in eastern Germany. In one survey, for example, 50 percent agreed in full or in part with the statement, "Germans possess good characteristics such as industriousness, perseverance, and loyalty that other peoples don't have." In another survey 20 to 28 percent of eastern German youths agreed that "the Germans have always been the greatest in history." A third showed that 11 percent agreed with the proposition, "We Germans are fundamentally more advanced than other peoples," while 30 percent agreed with slogans such as "Germany for the Germans."[28]

How could a country based on principles of "socialist internationalism" and the "friendship of peoples" produce young people who espouse nationalism, antisemitism, racism, and xenophobic violence?

The answer lies in part in the East German dictatorship's espousal of antifascism. The regime identified itself and its people as antifascist resistance fighters, but for the young people of the GDR, antifascism was not something freely chosen or internalized. It was an ordered doctrine forced upon them by state authorities. For youths unable to fit into the world of the GDR's "real existing socialism," the old, gray men of the politburo and the ubiquitous icons of Communist martyrs could never evoke anything but derision.[29] By attacking their society's "holy of holies," GDR youth could shock and provoke, avenging the frustration dealt them by their state leaders.

Unlike the FRG, which underwent an agonizing period of collective soul searching after World War II, the GDR never openly and honestly discussed and confronted its fascist past. The official state line was that the socialist people of the GDR had been "liberated" by the Soviet Red Army and were victors of the war against Hitler. Rather than admitting the complicity of its own people and the danger that fascist thought could be passed on to successive generations, the Socialist United Party (SED) proclaimed that Nazism had been "eradicated" within the borders of the workers' and farmers' state.[30] Hitler, said the party, was a child of capitalism; therefore, fascism was a problem for the imperialist-capitalist FRG and not for the GDR. Under socialism and the progressive leadership of the SED, so the propaganda went, only the "friendship of peoples" and socialist internationalism would flourish.[31]

The truth was otherwise. The ideological remnants of fascism still present in people's minds in the GDR were reinforced by the SED's brand of socialism. In an attempt to fortify the cultural identity of the GDR, the regime turned to promoting the country's Prussian heritage and values: hierarchical order, duty, discipline, hard work, and cleanliness. Socialism as practiced by the SED strove for social uniformity and homogeneity. The "conflict-free" society of which the GDR boasted came at a great price: East German society was one in which every expression of individualism, pluralism, and personal eccentricity was suppressed by social conformity. Foreigners, by virtue of their different skin colors, languages, and cultural traditions, disturbed the homogeneity and familiarity of the GDR's ordered society. If ever there was fertile ground for the resurgence of fascist thought, it was in the totalitarian society of the GDR.

Conclusion: The Appeal of Destruction

This chapter offers an interpretation of Germany's rightist violence as a phenomenon of marginalized, apolitical youths who know that Nazi symbols are effective in gaining society's attention. Painting a swastika on a school wall or raising a "Sieg Heil" salute brings the immediate attention of parents and teachers, the press, the government, and the world. Alienated young people have found a way to dominate the evening news with sensationalist coverage, invoke colloquies of academics and bureaucrats, convene cabinet meetings, and spark debates in parliament. The message behind their crude invocation of fascism is a bitter cry of frustration and anger against the emptiness they feel. It is an appeal for attention: "We have something to say. You cannot ignore us. You will take serious notice."[32]

The FRG faces a danger that merits the loudest of warning bells. The danger is not, as some journalists would have it, that Germany is reverting to the ideals of its Nazi past. The danger is that as long as the sources of youth frustration are ignored, the rightist violence will remain an enticing and viable form of youth protest. Rightist groups will continue to consolidate their hold on the youth subculture. Germany is facing nothing less than a struggle for the soul of its youth.

Notes

1. Heinrich Sippel, "Aktuelles Lagebild des Rechtsextremismus im vereinten Deutschland," in *Texte zur Inneren Sicherheit, Extremismus und Fremdenfeindlichkeit,* vol. I (Bonn: Der Bundesminister des Innern, 1992), 7, 9.

See also, Heinrich Sippel, "Rechtsextremismus im Vereinten Deutschland unter besonderer Berücksichtigung fremdenfeindlicher Gewalttaten," Lecture delivered at a seminar organized by the Federal Ministry of the Interior held at Bad Lasphe on 10 November 1992. (Bonn: Bundesverfassungsschutz, Der Bundesminister des Innern, 1992), 6, 9; and Bundesverfassungsschutz, *Verfassungsschutzbericht,* (Bonn: Der Bundesminister des Innern, 1991), 74–88.

The sharp upward spiral began with *der Wende.* In 1990 there were 1,578 non-violent, rightist-extremist offenses. These included threats of violence, distribution of illegal propaganda and agitation, and harassment and insults. There were 270 acts of violence: 2 deaths, 47 cases of arson, 102 bodily assaults, and 119 cases of vandalism. Of 1,848 rightist crimes, only 10 percent were violent.

In 1991 there were 2,401 nonviolent rightist crimes and 1,483 acts of violence. Among those were 3 deaths, 384 arson attacks (354 against foreigners), 449 bodily assaults (336 against foreigners), and 648 cases of vandalism (562 against foreigners). Of the 3,884 rightist crimes, 2,598, 66.8 percent, were xenophobic.

In 1992, there were 2,285 rightist crimes, a 54 percent increase over 1991. Of these, 1,760 were acts of violence: 11 deaths, 586 arson attacks (539 specifically against foreigners), 12 bombings, and 600 critically injured victims. Of these, 1,566 were xenophobic.

The first six months of 1993 saw 971 acts of rightist violence including 195 cases of arson, four bombings, 261 cases of bodily injury, and 364 acts of vandalism.

2. "Merkel Bericht," *General-Anzeiger,* 20 June 1993, 4.

3. Sippel, "Rechtsextremismus im Vereinten Deutschland," 11. Of the 1,088 known offenders arrested in 1991, 199 were on file with the Federal Constitution Protection Agency as members of rightist extremist organizations, as participants in events sponsored by these organizations, or as having been charged earlier with rightist extremist crimes and violence.

4. Amin Pfahl-Traughber, *Rechtsextremismus. Eine kritische Bestandsaufnahme nach der Wiedervereinigung* (Bonn: Bouvier Verlag, 1993), 18–21. Rightist extremism is based on five tenets. First, the democratic constitutional state is rejected. Adherents disdain the soft lifestyle of the bourgeoisie under liberal democracy. Second, authoritarianism and hierarchies of power are the main ordering principles for social and political life. Disciplined obedience to an omnipotent leader is the key value. Third, social pluralism is completely spurned. In the *Volksgemeinschaft*, individual and group interests are subordinated to the service of an ordered nation. Fourth, the *Volk*-based nation is valued above the rights of the individual. This glorification goes beyond national chauvinism. Because rightist extremists believe that their nation is the apotheosis of culture, other nations and cultures must be devalued. At worst, this nationalism justifies the conquest of other national groups. Fifth, rightist extremism is based on an ideology of natural inequality and is supported by reference to "natural hierarchies" and social Darwinism. Rightist extremists view Asian and African people as biologically inferior.

5. Bundesverfassungsschutz, *Verfassungsschutzbericht*, 72–74. The Federal Constitution Protection Agency estimates that there are 60,000 rightist radicals in such "patriotic" parties as the DVU and the Republikaner. Considerably more militant are forty thousand rightist extremists who belong to 76 additional organizations. About 6,000 of these are dyed-in-the-wool neo-Nazis, or Hitlerites, who belong to organizations such as Freie Arbeiter Partei (FAP), Deutsche Alternative (DA), and National Offensiv (NO). Of these, between 4,200 and 4,600 are the fanatical "hard core" responsible for almost all of the violence. About 4,200 are Nazi skinheads who belong to various rightist extremist parties and gangs. The remaining 400 are activists without affiliation.

6. Peter Koedderitzsch and Leo A. Mueller, *Rechtsextremismus in der DDR* (Göttingen: Lamuv Verlag, 1990), 13.

7. Thomas Assheuer and Hans Sarkowicz, *Rechtsradikale in Deutschland* (Munich: Beck'sche Reihe, 1992), 86.

8. Koedderitzsch and Mueller, *Rechtsextremismus in der DDR*, 19–20. One police report in a GDR district broke down the social status of its rightist extremist offenders as follows: high school students, 5 percent; apprentices, 24 percent; piece laborers, 3 percent; skilled laborers, 53 percent; vocational school students, 2 percent; jobless, 13 percent.

Employers of these workers were surveyed and 75 percent stated that the workers performed well at their job.

9. Peter Frisch, "Die Bekämpfung des Rechtsextremismus durch den Verfassungsschutz," *Texte zur Inneren Sicherheit, Extremismus und Fremdenfeindlichkeit*, band 2 (Bonn: Der Bundesminister des Innern 1992), 37. See also; Bundesverfassungsschutz *Verfassungsschutzbericht*, pp. 5–6, 91. Although most attention is given to the Nazi-Skins and Faschos, the skinhead movement is quite diverse. The movement started in England as a Pan-European countercultural group based on a stylized appearance, not fascist politics. The Oi-Skins, known for their drunken rioting at public sporting events, are similar to the Hooligans. Although they are nationalistic, they are nonfascist and apolitical. Presently the Oi-skins are most numerous in the West. The Red-Skins are antifascist and leftists, and the

Skinheads against Racial Prejudices categorically reject racial prejudice. Before unification only 10 percent of the skinheads were politicized. Now approximately 1,500 of the 3,500 skinheads belong to the neo-Nazi splinter group. *Volkszorn*, *Endsied*, and *Störkraft* are but a few of German skinhead bands. Great Britain's National Front movement has many. Skinhead magazines include publications such as *Heimatfront, Stahlfront, White Power*, and *Outsider*.

In contrast, East German skins, because they developed as a protest to the GDR communist apparatus, are much more politicized, and their ties to Nazi ideology are much stronger. Nonpolitical or leftist skins are the exception in East Germany. In the East there are about 3,000 neo-Nazi activists. Almost all of the actual and potential neo-Nazi violence in East Germany comes from skinheads.

10. Bundesverfassungsschutz, *Verfassungsschutzbericht*, 6–7.

11. Richard Stoess, *Die extreme Rechte in der Bundesrepublik* (Opladen: Westdeutsche Verlag, 1989), 230.

12. "Schläger, Kämpfer, Helden," *Der Spiegel*, 17/93, 91.

13. Baden-Württemberg Landesverfassungsschutz, *Landesverfassungsschutzbericht*, (Baden-Württemberg: Ministerium des Inneren, 1992), 5. Experts estimate that 90 percent of youth offenders have been drinking before their crimes.

14. *Der Spiegel*, 17/93, 91. See also, Bundesverfassungsschutz, *Verfassungsschutzbericht*, 10.

15. Frisch, 37.

16. The following words of Erich Honecker, delivered at the VIII party convention of the SED, typify the rhetorical place of youth in the canon of the GDR:

> The Party convention turns to the young generation of our Republic: You are the inheritors of the revolutionary German workers movement. Socialism alone gives your life sense and meaning. Be selfless, brave, true to ideals and totally devoted to your socialist fatherland, the German Democratic Republic. Strengthen and protect her, because it is about your future.

17. Köderitzsch and Muller, *Rechtsextermismus in der DDR*, 20.

18. Roger Cohen, "Deceived and Sold, East Germans Weigh Down Europe," *International Herald Tribune*, 9 March 1993, 1.

19. *Die Welt*, 7 May 1993, 13.

20. *PZ*, No. 69 (Bonn: Bundeszentral für politische Bildung, July 1992), 6. At the heart of the asylum problem has been Article 16 of the German Basic Law, which stated, "The politically persecuted shall enjoy the right of asylum." Until the article was amended on 1 July 1993, a potential asylum seeker had only to reach the German border and utter the word "asylum" to receive a hearing and protection while pleading his or her case. Although only 2–4 percent of applications are finally approved, asylum seekers come to Germany knowing the review procedure will be protracted. Only 20 percent of those claiming asylum arrive with personal documents, a tactic used to encumber the investigations of the German asylum bureaus.

21. "Das alles nervt total," *Der Spiegel*, 3 May 1993, 72. See also, "Streit um eine Unterkunft für Asylanten," *Frankfurter Allgemeine Zeitung*, 9 July 1992, 10.

22. Kurt Hirsch and Peter Heim, *Von Links nach Rechts: Rechtsradikale Aktivitäten in den neuen Bundesländer* (Munich: Goldman Verlag, 1991), 57.

23. Helsinki Watch, *Foreigners Out: Xenophobia and Right-wing Violence in Germany* (New York: Human Rights Watch, October 1992), 6.

24. Michael Schmidt, T*he New Reich. Violent Extremism in the New Germany and Beyond* (New York: Pantheon, 1993), 149–151. *Bild's* inflammatory headlines are calculated to play on the jealousies and resentments of Germans whose lives have been disrupted by foreigners. To list a few: "Refugees in the Community—Who's Supposed to Pay for Them?"; "Living Space Requisitioned: Family Must Take in Refugees"; "Refugees Now in Schoolyards"; "Germany's Most Unbelievable Help-Wanted Ad: Refugee Home Seeks German Cleaning Lady."

25. Schmidt, *New Reich*, 146-151.

26. *Ibid.*, 151.

27. *Ibid.*, 183–184. The full quotation: "We are not a welfare office for the Mediterranean. We want to protect the German people's ecological *Lebensraum* against foreign infiltration."

28. Pfahl-Traughber, *Rechtsextremismus: Eine Kristische Bestandsaufnahme*, 184–185.

29. *Real existierender Sozialismus*, or "real existing socialism," was the official term for the SED's brand of socialism. This term was invoked at every opportunity to underline that true socialism had been achieved in the GDR. Since unification, the term is used sarcastically to represent all the worst aspects of state socialism.

30. Article 6, paragraph 1, of the GDR constitution declared, "True to the interests of the people and its international obligations, the GDR has eradicated German militarism and Nazism."

31. Kurt Hirsch and Peter B. Heim, *Von Links nach Rechts*, 48.

32. Klaus Farin and Eberhard Seidel-Pielen, *Krieg in den Städten: Jugendgangs in Deutschland* (Berlin: 1991), 50.

PART THREE

German Unification:
Comparative Legal Issues

Introduction

A. Bradley Shingleton

With the ratification of the Unification Treaty on 21 September 1990, the dissonant legal systems of the Federal Republic of Germany (FRG) and the German Democratic Republic (GDR) were formally harmonized. Unlike united Germany's cultural, social, and economic integration, the legal unification of the two Germanies was, at least theoretically, achieved immediately. In reality, the implementation of legal unification is a continuing process.

Though the accession of the former GDR to the FRG pursuant to Article 23 of the Basic Law (Grundgesetz) yielded constitutional unity, it did not alter the existing legal system of the five new states, which was based on a socialist conception of law as an instrument of the ruling party.[1] Constitutional accession was the basis for legal harmonization, but did not create it by itself.

Although a great number of technical measures were necessary to establish a unified legal system for united Germany, legal unification did not require a treaty. Much of the task could have been accomplished by legislation. The Unification Treaty, however, provided a comprehensive and efficient means of dealing with the massive task of legal harmonization, and also served as a symbolic act of political accommodation.[2]

Unification had consequences in three legal realms: (1) public international law, (2) constitutional law, and (3) domestic law. The Unification Treaty addresses all of them, although it is primarily concerned with domestic law.

Public International Law

Unification had significant consequences in public international law. First, it rendered academic the long-standing question of legal successorship to the German Reich. Constitutional accession of the five states of the

I wish to thank Dr. Peter Ries and Stefan Krüger for their assistance in preparing this introduction. The errors remain mine.

former GDR to the FRG vindicated the Bonn Republic's long-standing claim that it was a continuation of the German state established in 1867–1871, which encompassed the territories of both the FRG and the GDR.[3]

Second, it raised the issue of responsibility for the GDR's international obligations. The postunification rights and obligations of the FRG and the former GDR under international law are briefly treated in Articles 11 and 12 of the Unification Treaty. Existing treaties to which the FRG at the time of unification was a party have continued in force; the FRG's membership in international organizations also continues. Under Article 11 of the Unification Treaty, the rights and obligations flowing from those international treaties and memberships are, with few exceptions, binding on the new federal states. As for treaties to which the GDR was a party, Article 12 of the treaty simply provides that they will be reviewed on a case-by-case basis to determine whether they will be adopted by the FRG or not. As a result of that review, most of the treaties to which the GDR was a party have been terminated.[4] The GDR's state property, international obligations, and domestic debts were, under uncontested rules of international law, assumed by the FRG.[5]

The obligation of unified Germany to make war-related reparations is less clear. Normally, reparations are governed by a peace treaty. But the treaty reached between the four Allied powers, the FRG and GDR of 12 September 1990 (the Two-plus-Four Treaty) is, in deference to German wishes to avoid a "second Versailles," an instrument establishing a "final settlement" of Allied responsibilities with respect to Berlin and Germany as a whole, and was not characterized as a peace treaty. Of course, reparations were exacted from all four occupied zones of Germany between 1945 and 1949, and, in addition, the FRG has paid tens of billions of marks in compensation to victims of the Third Reich. Throughout most of its history, the GDR refused to discuss any such payments, and that refusal is one of the moral and legal obligations inherited by unified Germany.[6]

German unification had other fundamental consequences in international law. The definitive recognition of Germany's border with Poland in the Two-plus-Four Treaty and in the postunification treaty between the FRG and Poland removed a legal and political problem that has lingered during the postwar era.[7] Unified Germany's continued membership in NATO was an epochal event, and, according to the FRG, German unification would not have occurred without it.[8] German unification depended on and simultaneously precipitated a host of dramatic changes in the postwar international legal order, which, taken together, removed the remaining limitations on German sovereignty and answered the long-standing German question.

Constitutional Law

The rapidity of German unification was directly facilitated by the procedure for accession contained in the Basic Law. In its inception, the Basic Law was envisioned as a provisional, quasi-constitutional law, expressly providing for its own replacement by a subsequent constitution to be adopted by all Germans. At the same time, the Basic Law also provided for accession. The constitutional founders in 1949 viewed accession as a preliminary step that would be followed by the ratification of a new constitution. But in 1990 accession to, and retention of, the Basic Law in the end appeared preferable to the protracted and politically complex process of preparing a new constitution. Not only was accession quicker, but it also more accurately reflected the fundamental political reality that unification would take place on the terms established by the FRG's terms. As Wolfgang Schäuble, the FRG's chief negotiator of the Unification Treaty, remarked during the negotiations to his GDR counterpart: "This is the accession of the GDR to the FRG, not the reverse."[9]

Ultimately, the treaty required only six amendments to the Basic Law to reflect the completion of unification. Two of the amendments involved constitutional provisions directly concerned with unification. The preamble to the Basic Law was amended to delete both the renowned "unification command" and the procedure for accession under Article 23 in order to demonstrate that Germany has no further territorial claims or ambitions. The other four amendments were necessary to implement unification pursuant to the terms of the Unification Treaty.[10] Considerable debate occurred in the unification negotiations over other possible amendments to the Basic Law, involving certain social goals, such as the right to employment. The two sides finally opted to "recommend" that the specific constitutional amendments be considered by the postunification parliament within two years. On 1 July 1994, three amendments were finally approved by the federal Parliament after they had been recommended by a constitutional commission. Those amendments gave recognition to the rights of the disabled, a right to environmental protection, and an expanded guarantee of equal rights between men and women. These amendments fell far short of the incorporation of social welfare guarantees that some desired.

The Basic Law has provided a workable modality for German unification and continues to serve, with minimal alteration, as the legal foundation for unified Germany. This is a testament to its durability, flexibility and soundness.

Domestic Law

Although it was not required by the accession process, the Unification Treaty was, in part, an important exercise in political symbolism. In addition to regulating the vast legal technicalities of unification, it was also an acknowledgment that unification transcended constitutional accession and involved the amalgamation of two political entities with distinct historical experiences.

The bulk of the Unification Treaty is concerned with the task of achieving legal harmonization. Most of the Treaty's 45 articles, and all three of its annexes, address the legal aspects and modalities of unification. The enormous scope and detail of the Unification Treaty flow from the complexity of adapting two divergent legal systems while balancing the interests of the FRG and GDR with respect to existing laws and regulations.

The fundamental principle for legal harmonization was simple. Article 8 of the Unification Treaty provides that the federal law of the FRG applies to the new federal states to the extent it is not limited to specific federal states or parts of the Federal Republic of Germany, "and to the extent that this treaty, in particular Annex 1, does not otherwise provide."[11] This approach, the subject of some dispute initially, required the treaty to list all of the exceptions to that principle, and the exceptions comprise hundreds of pages of the treaty.[12] In some cases, GDR law had to be retained because it addressed some unique geographic, social, legal,or economic circumstance. In other cases, specific laws dealt with legal matters of political sensitivity, ranging from abortion to drunk driving laws. And in some areas, such as environmental law, transitional provisions gradually introducing FRG law were necessary, often for economic reasons.

Some areas of the law, such as abortion, were considered so politically difficult to harmonize that they were left to the all-German Parliament to resolve.[13] Other subjects, including seemingly trivial ones such as highway speed limits, nevertheless also touched on political sensitivities and obviously required a political resolution. Some, but not all, of these issues, such as the employment rights of women in certain professions, have since been successfully resolved, bringing the full legal unification of Germany closer to fulfillment.

One of the most difficult new legal problems arising out of unification involved rights to property expropriated by the GDR. Two alternative solutions were under consideration; one involved the return of property to its true owner, and the other envisioned the payment of monetary compensation in lieu of restitution. Clearly, the problem entailed difficult moral and financial considerations as well as legal ones. Even the western political parties disagreed on the preferable alternative. After protracted negotiations, it was agreed that restitution would have priority over compensation, with significant exceptions where restitution would hinder investment.[14]

Other tasks were enormous. The lack of an independent judiciary in the GDR required creation of a new judicial system congruent with FRG law. The GDR lacked an independent, competent judiciary and legal profession, and the resulting systemic deficit has been a huge administrative challenge for the new Germany. In large part, it has been carried out in the same way as the rehabilitation of administrative and governmental agencies of the new states—by transfers of large numbers of western officials. The rehabilitation of the law faculties in the universities in the former GDR has been a difficult and painful process, resulting in the discharge of a vast majority of the preunification professorate.

German unification also forced a coming to terms with crimes committed by officials of the GDR. The criminal prosecution of former GDR officials—including judges—for state crimes presents a troubling moral challenge to the German judicial system. It has provided an opportunity that some wished Germany had at Nuremberg in 1945: the opportunity for Germans to sit in judgment on their fellow citizens. On the day the Unification Treaty was signed, however, the Bundestag passed a law granting amnesty to all former secret police agents who had not been already pardoned or who could be charged with crimes that carry a punishment of up to three years. The treaty itself provides, in general terms, for the prosecution of preunification criminal offenses in the GDR but is conspicuously silent about the criminal responsibility of former East German officials for state acts.[15] In 1991 the first prosecutions of GDR border guards for killings along the internal border began, but the trials have for the most part resulted in mild sentences or acquittals. The trials of former high officials, such as the late Erich Honecker, for the criminal acts of the GDR have been morally inconclusive due to, among other things, numerous procedural hurdles facing the prosecution.[16]

The postwar German judiciary has had some experience with the adjudication of war criminals and Nazi party members. Most of these trials conducted by German courts occurred in the late 1940s after the Nuremberg trials and later trials conducted by the Allies. The trials by German courts of war criminals generally produced mixed results.[17] Of course, other trials of war criminals have occurred sporadically during the history of the FRG, but aging defendants and the unavailability of evidence and witnesses have greatly complicated the rather intermittent efforts of public prosecutors.

The legal confrontation with the GDR's heritage of political crimes has stirred abiding doubts rooted in the German judicial system's failure to confront the Nazi past. That effort, as a whole, has received withering scrutiny.[18] Numerous members of the Nazi-era judiciary continue to occupy prominent legal, academic, and political positions, and the FRG's postwar judiciary has been tainted by conspicuous numbers of judges— now mostly dead or retired—who once swore a personal oath of allegiance to the Führer and implemented his regime's murderous directives. Ironically, this year Germany commemorated, through its highest political figures, the fiftieth anniversary of the attempted coup against Hitler on 20 July 1944. This is the same state that, through its judicial organs, has found no legal objections to the trial in 1944, by the notorious Peoples' Court, which resulted in brutal executions of the coup's participants.[19] With German unification, German justice-both east and west-must again confront the past.

Law was instrumental to the success of German unification, enabling Germans to secure political and diplomatic achievements that may otherwise have proved evanescent. Perhaps most importantly legal unification has restored the rule of law to a part of Germany where it has been absent for over fifty years.

•

Although the three chapters that follow are not directly concerned with unification, they illustrate some of the philosophical notions about the relationship between citizen and state that characterize the German polity. In her chapter, Sylvia Becker shows that German advertising law embodies restrictive notions of what constitutes commercial competition and permissible commercial speech. Christopher Visick provides a comparative overview of German and American employment discrimination laws, and suggests that the German laws reflect Germany's limited experience, as a society, with protection of minority rights. In her contribution on competition in the German legal profession, Ingrid Lenhardt argues that the residency requirement for German lawyers has effectively prevented meaningful competition in the legal field. Together they show the pressures German law must confront as a result of unification and European integration.

Notes

1. This was clear from the second sentence of Article 23 of the Basic Law— deleted by the Unification Treaty—that required the Basic Law to be "put in force" in the acceding territory. Therefore, accession required additional steps for legal unity.

2. There were limits, however. The FRG's chief negotiators made it clear during the negotiations that the process was not one of unification of two equal states.

3. Jochen Frowein, "The Unification of Germany," *American Journal of International Law* 86 (1992); pp. 152, 157, n. 30.

4. The GDR was a party to approximately 1800 treaties. Roughly 80% of them were terminated after unification. See Material Regarding German Unification Report of the federal government to the Bundestag of 4 February 1994, p. 36.

5. Articles 23–24 of the Unification Treaty.

6. The FRG did reach an agreement in May 1992, with the United States settling (for $160 million) for all claims of U.S. citizens for expropriation of property by the GDR. See *Frankfurter Allgemeine Zeitung*, 16 March 1994.

7. Article 1(1) of the Two-plus-Four Treaty affirmed that unified Germany's boundaries are those of the preunification FRG and GDR.

8. Article 6 of the Two-plus-Four Treaty affirmed Germany's right to belong to alliances.

9. Quoted in Konrad Jarausch, *The Rush to German Unity* (New York: Oxford University Press, 1993), p. 170.

10. They were: Article 143 (transitional law for the new states), Article 135(a)(2) and Article 51(II) (voting rights in the Bundesrat), Article 146 (term of the Basic Law).

11. Unification Treaty, Article 8.

12. See, for example, the statement of (then justice minister, now foreign minister) Klaus Kinkel that he enthusiastically supported this approach over some opposition. Klaus Kinkel, "Deutsche Rechtseinheit-Eine Standortbestimmung," *Neue Juristische Wochenschrift* 6 (1991), p. 341.

13. The first all-German parliament enacted a unified abortion law after a bitter political struggle, but it was declared unconstitutional by the Federal Constitutional Court on 28 May 1993 (BVerfG E 88, 203).

14. See, generally, Bradley Shingleton, Volker Ahrens, and Peter Ries, "Property Rights in Eastern Germany: An Overview of the Amended Property Law," *Georgia Journal of International and Comparative Law* 21 (1991): p. 345.

15. See, generally, Guy Christiansen, "American Influence on the Law Governing the Prosecution of Former East German Border Guards," *German American Law Journal* 3 (1993); p. 71.

16. The proceeding against Erich Honecker, the GDR's leader until shortly before the fall of the Wall, was discontinued due to his failing health.

17. See Matthew Lippman, "The Other Nuremburg: American Prosecutions of Nazi War Criminals in Occupied Germany," *Indiana International and Comparative Law Review* 3 (1992); p. 1; and Ingo Müller, *Hitler's Justice*, (Cambridge: Harvard University Press), 1990.

18. See generally Müller, *Hitler's Justice*, pp. 240–260.

19. Decision of 12 March 1971 of the Landgericht (Regional Court) Berlin.

10

"Let the Advertiser Beware": Restrictions on Comparative and Misleading Advertising Under German Unfair Competition Law

Sylvia Becker

To an American observer, the rigor of German advertising law is astonishing. German law sows a virtual minefield of restrictions and prohibitions regulating the manner in which products or services can be marketed. Particularly striking, from an American point of view, are the broad strictures on advertising imposed by the German unfair competition law, under which courts have developed the strictest advertising laws in all of Europe.

Two distinct areas of German advertising law stand in stark contrast to that of its European neighbors and the United States—namely, comparative advertising, which is essentially prohibited, and "misleading" advertising, which is far more broadly defined and regulated in Germany than elsewhere.

Unfair Competition

The German statute against unfair competition—*Gesetz gegen den unlauteren Wettbewerb* (UWG)—dates to 1909.[1] Its basic aim is to secure what is referred to as *Leistungswettbewerb*, which is understood to mean "a positively oriented competition based on the quality and value of one's own performance."[2] The law is based on the principle that rivals should compete "next to each other, not against each other."[3]

This peculiarly German approach to competition in a social market economy is reflected in the economic principles set forth in the Basic Law *(Grundgesetz)*, which guarantees each business the right to assert itself in the marketplace against other businesses through free, performance-based competition. The freedom of each enterprise is protected vis-à-vis not only the state but also other enterprises.[4] Although limiting the freedom of individual enterprises, the law seeks to ensure the conditions necessary for the development of the economic order envisioned by the German constitution.[5] The UWG's goal of promoting fair competition is believed to justify the imposition of limits on the freedom of expression guaranteed by article 5, paragraph 1, of the German constitution.[6]

Consumer protection was not the original purpose of the unfair competition law. It was initially conceived strictly as a means to regulate relations among competitors; its purpose was to protect individual competitors from unfair competitive methods.[7] After 1930, however, German law in this area has increasingly emphasized the general "public interest" in fair competition. Under contemporary law, the protection of all market participants, particularly the consumer, has become a focal point.[8] This shift in focus has had significant impact on how a given competitive practice is evaluated under the statute.

German unfair competition law is largely based on case law, and in this respect resembles American law. This case law orientation is not typical of German law, which is generally characterized by detailed statutory language that leaves little room for judicial interpretation. The major provisions of the UWG, however, are broad and vague and have acquired content only through judicial pronouncements in case law.

The key provisions of the UWG for the purposes of this chapter are sections 1 and 3. The case law interpreting these two UWG provisions imposes the most exceptionally restrictive limits on German advertising.

Guten Sitten and Section 1 UWG

Section 1 UWG is the core provision of the statute against unfair competition. It prohibits competitive practices that offend against *guten Sitten*, or public policy. Section 1 provides a cause of action for injunctive relief in the form of a cease-and-desist order and for damages against a competitor who undertakes such a practice.[9]

Like its English equivalent, the term *guten Sitten* is ambiguous. The case law teaches that a practice contrary to *guten Sitten* is one that contradicts the sense of decency possessed by "right and proper thinking people."[10] In determining whether a particular practice is against *guten Sitten*, the case law calls for a case-by-case balancing of all interests concerned—those of the competitors as well as those of the public, including consumers.[11] This is clearly a highly subjective judicial task, leading one commentator to remark wryly that, for the purposes of unfair competition law, an unethical ad is one that contradicts the sense of decency of the German Bundesgerichtshof (federal supreme court).[12]

The cases interpreting section 1 UWG have prohibited many forms of advertising. For example, section 1 UWG has been held to prohibit tasteless advertising (*geschmacklose Werbung*). For instance, advertising a funeral home on the jerseys of a soccer team is illegal because it is considered tasteless. Section 1 UWG also prohibits strongly emotional advertising (*gefuhlsbetonte Werbung*)—i.e., that exploits such emotions as fear, sympathy, obedience to authority, gratitude, or sexual curiosity, if not directly relevant to the product or service being advertised. For example, "McHappy Day," a promotional gimmick whereby a contribution would be made to a child welfare organization for each hamburger sold, was held to be illegal.[13] Such advertising is considered contradictory to the principle that consumer choices should not be influenced by any considerations other than the quality and value of the product or service at issue.

The case law under section 1 UWG has also imposed severe restrictions on comparative advertising; this is discussed in greater detail below.

Comparative Advertising

There are essentially two types of comparative advertising positive and negative. The former attempts to draw a favorable comparison to a successful product or service of a particular competitor (e.g., "Our product is as good as product X"). The latter is critical of a competitor's product or service (e.g, "Product X is not as good as ours" or "Our product is better than product X").

Under the applicable case law, both types of comparative advertising (*vergleichende Werbung*) are generally considered against *guten Sitten* and are therefore not permissible in Germany. Such advertising is considered inconsistent with the basic principle that goods and services should be promoted only on the basis of their individual quality and value. Thus, as a rule, one may not make any comparative reference (whether positive or negative) to the goods or services of a competitor when promoting one's own goods.[14]

This prima facie ban applies only to references that identify one or more particular competitor(s). The competitor(s) need not be identified by name; it is sufficient that the audience is able to recognize the reference to the particular competitor(s).

The prima facie prohibition under the case law applying section 1 UWG is not limited to untrue or misleading statements about competitors; such statements would fall at any rate under section 3 UWG's prohibition of misleading advertisement. The general prohibition applies even to statements of fact and to objectively correct value judgments. Thus, even perfectly accurate comparisons regarding, for example, the price, durability, convenience, reliability, compatibility, energy efficiency, of one own's product to that of a competitor would fall under the prima facie ban.

Truthful comparisons are not prohibited if there is "sufficient cause" for the comparison *and* the comparison remains within the bounds of what is relevant and necessary. The advertiser bears the burden of proving that these conditions have been met.[15]

Whether or not an advertiser has sufficient cause *(hinreichender Anlass)* to justify a comparative reference is decided on a case-by-case basis, and is usually allowed only in narrow, exceptional circumstances.

Several of the categories of cases that have been held to constitute exceptions to the general ban on comparative advertising relate to specific consumer interests in being informed *(Aufklarungsinteresse)*. One may, for instance, draw a comparison to a competing product or service on the specific request of a customer *(Auskunftsvergleich)*. If, for example, a customer in a store asks specifically why a particular product in the store is more expensive than a product seen in another store, then a salesperson may, in response to the question, refer specifically to disadvantages of the competing product relative to his own product—e.g., the competing product has a shorter warranty period. To justify such specific reference to the competing product, however, the customer must have made a direct request. Absent such a direct inquiry regarding the competing product, the salesperson would not be permitted under German law to mention the competing product's shortcomings in an attempt to sell his own product.

Comparisons that are necessary to explain an otherwise inexplicable technical advance are also permitted *(Fortschrittsvergleich)*. Comparisons between different systems *(Systemvergleich)* or different types of products are also permissible, as long as no reference to a specific competitor is made. An advertisement may, for example, compare in a general manner catalog shopping and store shopping or gas heat and oil heat or a water-cooled motor and an air-cooled motor.

Aside from consumer information interests, defense against an illegal attack by a competitor may provide sufficient cause for comparative advertising *(Abwehrvergleich)*. Thus, comparative advertising may be permissible to correct misleading statements made by a competitor. This defensive use of comparative advertising may also be used preventively. To justify a comparative reference to a competitor on this basis, however, one must show that the resort to comparative advertising was absolutely necessary—i.e., it was the only possible means of preventing or correcting the harm caused by the competitor's unfair practice.[16]

Even a comparative advertisement justified by sufficient cause must be true and not exceed the scope of what is relevant and necessary in light of the justifying cause. Thus, even if the narrow circumstances described above are met, they do not allow an advertiser to direct sweeping general slogans against specific competitors.[17] Examples of such slogans rejected by German courts as too general in scope include "We offer more," "Stronger is better," "Fresh beans taste better," "The Stone Age is over," and "Because no one likes to pay too much."[18] Such advertisement, common fare in the United States, are illegal in Germany if targeted against a specific competitor.

Excessive denigration of a competitor will also render an otherwise justified (by sufficient cause) comparison impermissible under German law.[19] Statements that fall far short of slander have been held excessive under German law—e.g., "One does not go to *any* hairdresser. One goes to Master L."[20] To pass muster under German law, negative statements about competitors must be correct and objectively verifiable.

Comparative advertising (even if disparaging of competitors) is generally lawful under U.S. law, provided that it is not misleading. Indeed, the government agency primarily responsible for enforcement of U.S. advertising law—the Federal Trade Commission—has officially approved of comparative advertising and has stated that industry self-regulation should not restrain the use by advertisers of truthful comparative advertising.[21]

The European Context

Germany's restrictions even on comparative advertising that is truthful are also considerably broader than those of other European countries. Truthful comparisons that are not slanderous or highly derogatory are tolerated in most other European countries, including Austria, Great Britain, Ireland, Portugal, Spain, and Switzerland.[22]

After having tried unsuccessfully in the early 1980s to formulate Europe-wide guidelines concerning comparative advertising, the European Commission prepared a draft directive in late 1991 on the subject that, if adopted, will amend the existing European directive regarding misleading advertisement.[23]

The new directive would allow comparative advertising (defined as any advertisement that characterizes competitors or their goods or services), provided all essential and verifiable details are compared and that it is not "unfair." Under the proposed directive, a comparative advertisement would be considered "unfair" if it leads to market confusion among the advertiser and his competitors or if it degrades a competitor or his goods or services.

If adopted, the directive would set a maximum standard, which member states would not be allowed to exceed. Whether this would require Germany to alter its comparative advertising law is debatable. One could argue on the one hand that the directive is consistent with German law because it allows comparative advertising only when it is not misleading and "unfair."[24] On the other hand, the proposed directive reflects the European Commission's basic perspective that comparative advertising, so long as it is truthful, provides consumers with useful information and that a blanket prohibition is not reconcilable with Union law.[25]

A blanket prohibition of all truthful comparative advertising would raise questions under article 30 of the Treaty of Rome, which prohibits discriminatory limits on the movements of goods within the EU and requires even generally applicable regulations to be necessary and reasonable.[26] The European Court has already recognized that limits on advertising can hinder the free movement of goods in contravention of Article 30.

The European Court's *Yves Rocher* decision in May 1993 is the most recent in a series of decisions questioning Germany's ability to impose its strict advertising law in ways that hinder trade with member states. The *Yves Rocher* case involved a German business that was selling products imported from another EU member. The European Court held that the application of a German unfair advertising law prohibiting eye-catching juxtaposition of previous and current prices, whether truthful or not (UWG section 6e), contravened article 30. Noting that the German regulation prohibited even truthful juxtaposition of prices, the court determined that its application could not be justified as necessary for protecting consumers or for permitting fair competition (purposes that would permit restraining the movement of goods within the Union). A blanket prohibition of such truthful comparative advertising also poses serious questions under article 10 of the European Human Rights Convention, which guarantees the right to free expression.[27]

Although German law regarding comparative advertising cannot accurately be described as a blanket prohibition, it comes rather close to that. For the sake of European legal harmonization, it may well have to be adjusted (e.g., relaxed standards for a showing of "sufficient cause").

Section 3 UWG: Misleading Advertising

Another exceptionally restrictive area of German unfair competition law is that regarding misleading advertising. Though prohibitions of deceptive or misleading advertising apply in all European countries (and in the United States), they are not generally applied as broadly and as specifically as they are in Germany.

Section 3 UWG is the key German statutory provision concerning misleading advertising. It prohibits all misleading statements (*irrefuhrende Angaben*) about commercially relevant circumstances made in a commercial context for purposes of competition.[28] Unlike section 1 UWG, section 3 does not require that an offense against *guten Sitten* be shown. Section 3 UWG lists several specific characteristics of products or services about which "in particular" no misleading statements may be made—e.g., condition, origin, means of production, source, and so forth.

The case law under section 3 UWG is vast and far-reaching.[29] Misleading "statements" prohibited under section 3 UWG can be oral, written, or pictorial. They may appear in brochures or other forms of advertisement or in the name or trademark of a company or product. Even the make up of a product may constitute a misleading "statement." Although technically only factual statements are covered by section 3 UWG, opinions or value judgments are also covered if based on ascertainable facts.

A false statement may be considered misleading under section 3 UWG. This is a straightforward category of cases. Such false advertising is prohibited under other European advertising law as well as under U.S. advertising law. A statement need not be untrue, however, to be considered misleading under section 3 UWG. An ambiguous statement, even if objectively correct, can be a violation of section 3 UWG if it could be misunderstood. An incomplete statement will also be considered misleading if the omission of essential information leaves the consumer with an incorrect impression.

To be "misleading" under German law, a statement need not have misled a single consumer. Subjective intent on the part of the advertiser to deceive is, by the same token, not necessary to prove a violation of section 3 UWG. The challenged statement need only be relevant to consumer decision making —i.e., that it is aimed at influencing market decisions— and that it has an objective potential to mislead.

Who must be potentially misled? Under German law, a statement is "misleading" if it has the potential to mislead a "not insignificant portion" (*nicht unbeachtlicher Teil*) of the audience to whom it is addressed. German case law generally considers a percentage as small as 10 percent (or 10–15 percent) to be a significant enough portion to trigger section 3 UWG. In certain cases—for example, advertising for medicinal products or services—the threshold is set even lower, at 5 percent.[30] The consequence of setting the threshold proportion of potentially misled consumers so low is to prohibit even advertising that would mislead only relatively unsophisticated and unintelligent consumers. Such low threshold percentages stand in sharp contrast to the laws of other European countries, which tend to prohibit only those advertisements with the potential to deceive a "significant" portion of the targeted audience, as distinguished from a "not insignificant" portion.[31]

German law is also exceptional in how it views the "average" observer in an advertisement's audience *(Durchschnittbetrachter der angesprochene Verkehrskreise)*. This is important because the determinative question for the court is is how this "average" observer perceives the given advertisement as a whole. Under German case law, the "average" observer is considered a superficial *(fluchtiger)* observer who is easily misled.[32]

One may question the appropriateness of the German courts' view of the "average" German consumer as naive. The recent entry, however, into the German market of consumers inexperienced in the ways of capitalism may provide new justification for the courts' protectiveness.

Other European countries tend to ascribe less gullibility to their citizens. Spanish literature regarding advertising law, for example, describes the Spanish public as more skeptical and critical vis-à-vis advertising than its German counterpart.[33] Most European countries measure an advertisement's deceptive potential with regard to the normally educated citizen. In France, for instance, "misleading" is judged with regard to an average consumer of average intelligence and attentiveness—the so-called *bon pere de famille*, who is not careless with family finances. Other Europeans do not understand the German legal interpretation of the "average" consumer in this and other areas of unfair competition law. This incomprehension is illustrated by the following remark made by a litigant before the Court of the European Communities and cited by that court in one of its cases: "German unfair competition case law is based on a guiding image of an average consumer as an absolutely unsophisticated, verging on pathologically stupid, careless, and inattentive average consumer."[34]

Determining how the "average" consumer reacts to a given advertisement is an empirical process under German law. Although German judges often simply rely on their own understanding, the court sometimes commissions an opinion survey on a particular question. This reliance on opinion surveys, which are inevitably expensive, also distinguishes German legal thinking in this area. Other European countries consider the determination of consumer reaction an abstract inquiry capable of evaluation by the court.

Comparison with U.S. Law

At first glance, the United States has fairly strict and comprehensive laws that prohibit misleading advertising. At the federal level, there are two general prohibitions—the Lanham Act and the Federal Trade Commission (FTC) Act.[35] In addition, there are myriad state and local laws, most of which mirror the FTC Act. The three principal elements common to actions challenging deceptive advertising are (i) false or misleading representations (whether express or implied) (ii) that are actually or likely deceptive (to a substantial segment of the intended audience) and (iii) that are material to buying decisions (i.e., likely to affect consumer conduct or decision).[36]

Theoretically, the prohibition of misleading advertisement under U.S. law is quite broad and could potentially encompass much of what German law forbids. In practice, however, U.S. law draws a clear distinction between objective claims and subjective claims. The Lanham Act explicitly limits its proscriptions to misrepresentations of fact and therefore does not apply at all to opinions. The FTC Act requires substantiation of objective product claims before such claims are made. Subjective claims are permissible without substantiation, however, because they are considered mere "puffing."

This distinction applies specifically to the use of superlatives. Claims concerning tangible qualities that can be tested or measured against accepted standards and that therefore leave no room for differences of opinion are subject to FTC action.[37] On the other hand, enthusiastic descriptions and claims of superiority expressed in essentially subjective terms—e.g., "the world's finest" or "the best tasting" or "the most beautiful"—are permissible. Thus, in the United States it is commonplace to contend that one's product is "the best," that it "beats the rest," etc. American consumers are expected to be able to assess such "puffing" skeptically. German courts shield German consumers from such hyperbole.

U.S. governmental enforcement of the laws against misleading advertisements have focused primarily on specific, objective claims made about the performance and/or tangible qualities of an advertised product. For instance, unsubstantiated claims that a product can achieve a particular result will be challenged as deceptive.[38] The FTC has expressed particular concern about the advertisement of weight reduction programs and products, challenging unsubstantiated weight loss and weight loss maintenance claims and testimonials.[39] Another focus of FTC enforcement action has been on claims that products are "fat free" or "low fat."[40] In particular, the FTC has targeted advertisements that make such claims while depicting the product at issue being used in quantities that belie the claim.[41] Claims for the nutritional value of foods have also been the target of FTC action.[42] Touting the health advantages of a product without disclosing health disadvantages has also been deemed deceptive.[43] The FTC has also been vigilant regarding environmental (or "green") marketing claims, such as assertions that a product is "ozone friendly," "biodegradable," or "recyclable."[44]

U.S. enforcement activity focuses almost exclusively on the regulation of objective, factual statements and is testimony to the clear consumer protection orientation of U.S. advertising law. The stated objective of German law in this area—promotion of pure competition—is not apparent.

German Law in the European Context

All European Union member states have laws regulating misleading advertisement. As discussed earlier, German law in this area is, stricter in practice than that of its European neighbors. The relative strictness of German law stems primarily from the German legal view of the "average" consumer as easily misled and that an advertisement is misleading if as few as 10 percent of its audience may be misled. These aspects of German law make its standard for misleading advertisement the strictest among all western European states.[45]

The European Union has made efforts to harmonize European law in this area. In 1984 the European Commission issued a directive for the harmonization of laws and administrative regulations concerning misleading advertisement.[46] The directive set only a minimum standard, however, so Germany's restrictive standards were left intact. Member states are free to maintain stricter requirements. As noted above, however, a proposed directive would impose a maximum standard.

Article 30 of the Rome Treaty may limit extreme applications of German law on comparative advertising. Such limitations could prove very significant in view of pan-European distribution networks and cross-border television transmissions. The prospect of disparate treatment of advertisements of German goods versus those from other European countries also poses the risk that German law will disadvantage German producers. This might at some point lead Germany to consider easing some of the most restrictive aspects of German misleading advertisement law.[47]

The Constitutional Right to Free Speech and German Advertising Law

How is German advertising law to be reconciled with the constitutional right of free speech? Article 5 of the Basic Law (Grundgesetz) provides that "everyone shall have the right freely to express and to disseminate his opinion through speech, writing and illustration, and to inform himself from generally accessible sources without hindrance." This right has been held to extend to advertising.[48] The legislature may, however, enact laws that limit the right of free expression and free access to information when other important interests are at stake. In balancing the competing interests, the courts consider, among other things, the purpose of the communication at issue—i.e., whether the purpose is to promote economic interests or to contribute to public debate. The latter purpose argues in favor of the priority of Article 5. Advertising is likely to be viewed, however, as advancing economic interests, and therefore German courts have in this context assigned priority to the interest promoted by the UWG—i.e., fair competition—over the rights protected by Article 5.[49] This approach is not unlike that of the United States, which affords less free speech protection to "commercial" speech.

•

Even a cursory examination of these two key areas of German advertising law—comparative and misleading ads—reveals a considerably more severe approach than that taken by its European neighbors and the United States. Comparative advertising, even if truthful, is prohibited except under unusual circumstances. Misleading advertisement is defined so broadly in Germany as to prohibit statements that in other countries are not worthy of prohibition either because they do not have the potential to deceive a sufficient proportion of consumers or because they constitute harmless exaggeration. German law in this area reflects a view of the average consumer as gullible and seeks to protect even the least sophisticated and least intelligent members of society.

The process of European unification and harmonization of laws in Europe may lead to relaxation in German advertising law. As yet, however, there are no European guidelines that would clearly oblige Germany to ease its advertising restrictions. Therefore, for at least the near future, the German law of advertising is likely to remain conspicuously restrictive.

Notes

1. While the term "unfair competition law" is often understood in the United States to refer to antitrust law (i.e., law aimed at preventing monopolies and unfair restraints on trade), the German law at issue here should not be confused with German antitrust law *(Kartellrecht)*, which is governed by a separate statute *(Gesetz gegen Wettbewerbsbeschrankungen*, or GWB). For a discussion of the relationship between German unfair competition law and antitrust law, see Adolf Baumbach and Wolfgang Hefermehl, *Wettbewerbsrecht*, 16. neubearbeitete Auflage (Beck, 1990), at 61–65.

2. Quotation in text translated from German *(ein positiv ausgerichteten Wettbewerb, der mit der Gute und Preiswurdigkeit der eigenen Leistung wirbt)*. Otto-Friedrich von Gamm, *Neue höchstrichterliche Rechtsprechung zum Wettbewerbsrechts*, 3. neubearbeitete Auflage (Koln: Kommunikationsforum 1985). Before his recent retirement, Otto-Friedrich Frhr. von Gamm was presiding justice on the German

Supreme Court and is widely recognized as a leading authority on the unfair competition law in Germany.

3. Quotation in text translated from German *(nebeneinander nicht gegeneinander)*. Wilhelm Nordemann, *Wettbewerbsrecht*, 6. Auflage (Nomos, 1989).

4. See Wolfgang Gloy, *Handbuch des Wettbewerbsrechts* (Beck, 1986), p. 2.

5. Ibid. Gloy also points out that while the German constitutional court has contended that the Basic Law does not dictate any particular economic order, some commentators maintain that the German constitution precludes a purely individualistic as well as a collectivist economy and thus guarantees a social market economy.

6. Christian Loeffler, "Verstoesst die 'Benetton-Werbung' gegen die guten Sitten i.S. des sektion 1 UWG?" Afp 2/93, 536–541 p. 537; Michael Kloepfer and Gerhard Michael, "Vergleichende Werbung und Verfassung," *GRUR* 1991, p. 177.

7. See von Gamm, *Neue Rechtsprechung*, p. 6; Nordemann, *Wettbewerbsrecht* p. 32 (citing 1929 legal commentary referring to notion that German unfair competition law protects the public or the consumer as a "fundamental and irrepressible error").

8. von Gamm, *Neue Rechtsprechung* pp. 6–7; Gloy, *Wettbewerbsrecht*, p. 17.

9. The German text of section 1 UWG is as follows: "Wer im geschaftlichen Verkehr zu Zwecken des Wettbewerbes Handlungen vornimmt, die gegen die guten Sitten verstossen, kann auf Unterlassung und Schadenersatz in Anspruch genommen werden."

10. Baumbach and Hefermehl, *Wettbewerbsrecht*, p. 122.

11. Ibid., p. 128; Von Gamm, *Neue Rechtsprechung*, p. 11.

12. Nordemann, *Wettbewerbsrecht*, p. 47.

13. BGH, *GRUR Int.* 1987, pp. 534, 535.

14. The leading legal commentary on German competition law suggests that it is overly simplistic to think of the ban on comparative advertising as a "rule" because each individual allegation of an unfair competitive practice under section 1 UWG requires a balancing of interests. Baumbach and Hefermehl, *Wettbewerbsrecht*, p. 494. Many respected commentators do, however, recognize the case law as setting forth a general rule against comparative advertising. See, e.g., von Gamm, *Neue Rechtsprechung*, p. 50.

15. Von Gamm, *Neue Rechtsprechung*, p. 50; Nordemann, *Wettbewerbsrecht*, p. 163.

16. Nordemann, *Wettbewerbsrecht*, p. 180.

17. See Nordemann, *Wettbewerbsrecht*, p. 179, providing examples given in text, among others.

18. BGH, *GRUR* 1968, at 33, 437 Westphalenblatt II; BGH, *GRUR* 1963, at 371, 375, in the case of detergent; OLG Hamburg, *WRP* (1979), 133; OLG Munchen *WRP* (1980), 356, in an advertisement for ready-made homes; and OLG Dusseldorf, *WRP* (1987), 673, 674.

19. See Nordemann, p. 180, providing examples given in text, among others.

20. OLG Hamm, *WRP* (1980), 499.

21. Policy Statement in Regard to Comparative Advertising, 16 *CFR (Code of Federal Regulations)*, Section 14.15(a).

22. See Baumbach and Hefermehl, *Wettbewerbsrecht*, pp. 518–520, Kloepfer and Michael, "Vergleichende Werbung", pp. 170–180, (noting that Switzerland and Austria have recently promulgated regulations specifically permitting such advertising and citing a French Supreme Court decision explicitly permitting price comparisons).

23. Official Journal no. C180, 1991, at 0014. For a discussion of the proposed directive, see Kloepfer and Michael, *GRUR* 1991, p. 170 (citing view of German advertising industry interest group).

24. See Kloepfer and Michael, "Vergleichende Werbung", p. 170 (citing view of German advertising industry interest group).

25. Ibid., 170.

26. For detailed discussion of the impact of Article 30 on German unfair competition law, see Gert Meier, "Einschränkung des deutschen Wettbewerbsrechts durch das Europaische Gemeinschaftsrecht," *GRUR Int.* (1990), pp. 817–820.

27. For a discussion of whether or not German restrictions on comparative advertising violate the provisions guaranteeing freedom of expression in both the German Constitution (*Grundgesetz* Article 5(1)) and the European Convention on Human Rights (Article 10), see generally Kloepfer and Michael, "Vergleichende Werbung."

28. The actual text of the provision is as follows:

Wer im geschaftlichen Verkehr zu Zwecken des Wettbewerbs über geschaftliche Verhaltnisse, insbesonde über die Beschaffenheit, den Ursprung, die Herstellungsart oder die Preisbemessung einzelne Waren oder gewerblicher Leistungen oder des gesamten Angebots, über Preislisten, über die Art des Bezugs oder die Bezugsquelle von Waren, über den Besitz von Auszeichnungen, über den Anlass oder den Zweck oder über die Menge der Vorrate irrefuhrende Angaben macht, kann auf Unterlassung der Angaben in Anspruch genommen werden

29. Misleading advertisement is hotly litigated in Germany, resulting in a plethora of cases. The number of misleading advertisement cases in all of Italy in a given year is roughly equal to that in the Landgericht München. Gerhard Schricker, "Die Bekämpfung der irreführenden Werbung in den Mitgliedstaaten der EG," *GRUR Int.* 1990, 112–21.

30. Marshall, *Unlauterer Wettbewerb: Materielles Recht und Verhalten in Wettbewerbssachen*, 1. Auflage (Deutsche Anwaltverein Rehm, 1989), 74; von Gamm, *Neue Rechtsprechung*, p. 113.

31. For a detailed comparative discussion of misleading advertisement law in European countries, see Schricker, "Die Bekampfung."

32. Schricker, "Die Bekämpfung," p. 116.

33. Schricker, "Die Bekämpfung," p. 119, note 73.

34. Quotation in text translated from German rendition in Nordemann, *Wettbewerbsrecht*, p. 54, citing EuGH, *GRUR Int.* 1984, at 291, 293.

35. See 15 U.S.C. section 1125(a) and 15 U.S.C. sections 45, 52, 55(a)(1).

36. James Maxeiner and Peter Schotthoeffer, *Advertising Law in Europe and North America*, (Cambridge: Kluwer 1992).

37. For example, a respondent was prohibited from representing that its face powder "will spread farther than other competitive face powders of comparable quality" when a test demonstrated that a competitor's powder spread farther and that a number of other competitive powders were equal to the respondent's product in this respect. Similarly, various stipulations have included provisions against claims of superiority, such as that a respondent's air rifles are "more accurate than any firearms" or that a certain spring water "is the purest natural water on the American continent or known to scientists." Better Business Bureau, *Do's and Dont's in Advertising Copy*, section 2, margin note 256.

38. See, e.g., FTC action against Pyraponic Industries II in connection with claims regarding the ability of its "phototron" indoor greenhouse to remove air contaminants (FTC file no. 912 3035); FTC action against a claim by MACE Security International Inc. that MACE formula would instantly stop assailants when actually the formula takes several seconds to work (FTC file no. 912 3374); FTC action against Pollen Company regarding claims that bee pollen could induce weight loss, permanently alleviate allergy symptoms, and reverse the aging process (FTC file no. 902 3145); and FTC action against Silueta Distribution Inc. regarding a claim that its product would break down and reduce cellulite or fat (FTC file no. 922 3343).

39. In connection with weight-loss programs, for example, the FTC recently brought action against Diet Center, Inc. (FTC file no. 902 3178), Physicians' Weight Loss Centers of America (FTC file no. 3185), Nutri-System Inc. (FTC file no. 902 3159), Jenny Craig Inc. (FTC file no. 902 3188), and Weight Watchers International Inc. (FTC file no. 902 3195).

40. See, e.g., FTC action against Klondike Lite Bar (FTC file no. 912 3067) and Clorox Company Take Heart fat-free salad dressings (FTC file no. 912 3337).

41. See, e.g., FTC action involving Presto Food Products (FTC file no. 912 3400), in which Presto ads claimed its products are "lowfat" or "low in saturated fat" when used over cereal or fruit or in cooking when, in fact, the products were not low in fat when used in the quantities required for such purposes.

42. See, e.g., FTC action involving Kraft Singles (FTC docket no. 9208), which concerned claims for the calcium content of individually packaged cheese slices.

43. The FTC challenged an advertisement that linked the low-cholesterol content of Campbell's soup to a reduced risk of heart disease but that failed to disclose that the soup was high in sodium, which increases the risk of heart disease (FTC docket no. 9223).

44. See, e.g., FTC action involving Archer Daniels Midland Co. (FTC file no. 902 3283), which concerned claims for the biodegradability of plastic products containing a cornstarch additive.

45. Schricker, "Die Bekämpfung", p. 115.

46. 84/450/EWG, ABl. 1984 Nr. L 250/20, reprinted in *GRUR Int.* 1984, p. 688.

47. For a detailed discussion of this point, see Winfried Tilmann, "Irreführende Werbung in Europa—Möglichkeiten und Grenzen der Rechtsentwicklung," *GRUR* 1990, pp. 87–93. The article also provides a very useful discussion of principles of private international law that may limit the application of German law in cases involving foreign advertisers from outside the European Community.

48. The quotation from the Basic Law is translated from the German ("Jeder hat das Recht, seine Meinung in Wort, Schrift und Bild frei zu aeussern und zu verbreiten und sich allgemein zugaenglichen Quellen ungehindert zu unterrichten"). *Grundgesetz*, Art. 5(1); see Kloepfer and Michael, "Vergleichende Werbung," p. 174.

49. Such reasoning was applied in a decision of the Hamburg Oberlandesgericht in November 1990, which held that Article 5 did not protect the radio station's newspaper advertisement that suggested that its competitor public radio station was controlled by party representatives and therefore provided "party proportional," rather than independent, programming. OLG Hamburg AfP 2/91, p. 539. See also Loeffler, AfP 2/93 criticizing the decision of the Frankfurt Oberlandesgericht holding that Article 5 did not protect a Benetton advertising campaign held to violate *guten Sitten*.

11

No More Strangers, but Fellow Citizens: Minority Protection Laws in the United States and Germany

Christopher S. Visick

War in Bosnia, rioting in the United States, attacks on foreigners in the unified Germany—today as ever, prejudice and ignorance are causing argument, alienation, and death. As recent history has thrown the people and nations of the world dramatically closer together, old distrusts and anxieties have been awakened in countries and peoples both new to and familiar with democratic communal life. One common method of dealing with these tensions among populations is for government to legislate against particular types of discrimination. This chapter will look at the efforts of two countries that have attempted to do just that, the United States and Germany.

United States Equal Employment Law

Although the United States is a relatively young country, it has a long and varied history of dealing with equality issues. Although never achieved, the equality of people before the law is a core American value. The American Revolution was itself largely a consequence of the belief that "all men are created equal," having "inalienable rights" that the British crown had unfairly denied to colonial citizens.[1] The United States Constitution memorialized these beliefs by creating a government deriving its powers from the consent of the governed, drawing its officials from the ordinary citizenry and constrained to honor certain "rights" of individuals.

Notwithstanding these ideals, the Constitution was marked by the reality of discrimination. By 1789 slavery was already an important economic factor in the United States, and as a result, the Constitution, unlike the Declaration of Independence (and, as we shall see, the German Basic Law), does not state that all persons are equal. Instead, in an infamous compromise, the Constitution provides that for purposes of apportioning taxes and determining the number of representatives from any given state, a black person should be counted as only 3/5ths a single person and Native Americans not at all, and grants only to white men the right of suffrage.[2]

Not until after the Civil War did Congress and the states act to remedy the discrimination drafted into the Constitution. In 1865, Congress passed the Thirteenth Amendment to the Constitution prohibiting slavery. The Fourteenth Amendment was passed shortly thereafter, guaranteeing all persons due process and equal protection of the laws (1868), and the Fifteenth Amendment extended to all races and "colors" the right to vote (1870). These three amendments were joined by the Civil Rights Act of 1866 which provides that

> All persons within the jurisdiction of the United States shall have the same right in every State and Territory to make and enforce contracts, to sue, be parties, give evidence, and to the full and equal benefit of all laws and proceedings for the security of persons and property as is enjoyed by white citizens, and shall be subject to like punishment, pains, penalties, taxes, licenses and exactions of every kind and to no other.[3]

Unfortunately, state and local governments, and private business, found it easy to keep disfavored minorities from voting by imposing literacy tests or creating other barriers to the voting booth. Furthermore, the Fourteenth Amendment forbids only governments from discriminating, and the Thirteenth Amendment, though applicable to both states and citizens, forbids only slavery. These amendments were therefore unable to address discrimination in areas such as employment, private commercial transactions, and accommodations.

Much changed in 1948 with the decision of the U.S. Supreme Court in *Shelley v. Kraemer.*[4] In *Shelley,* a neighbor filed a lawsuit asking the court to enforce a racially restrictive covenant on land. The Supreme Court refused to do so, holding that the Fourteenth Amendment's guarantee of equal protection of the laws would be violated if a court, as one of the branches of government, were to enforce the racially discriminatory terms of a private agreement. In so ruling, the Supreme Court extended the Fourteenth Amendment's promise of equality into the field of private actions—even though the amendment had been previously viewed as restricting purely governmental action only—by ruling that judicial enforcement of a discriminatory covenant in a private agreement constituted unconstitutional discrimination by the government.

With *Shelley,* the promises of equality made in the Thirteenth and Fourteenth Amendments to the Constitution began to bear fruit. Progress came slowly, however, until Congress, after having considered similar legislation every year beginning in 1945, passed the Equal Pay Act of 1963 ("EPA") prohibiting employers from paying different wages to men and women for essentially the same work.[5] Although the debate continues over equal pay for equal work, the EPA remains a legislative landmark in rendering a form of private discrimination in the United States illegal.

The EPA was followed the next year by the single most important piece of American anti-discrimination legislation, the Civil Rights Act of 1964 ("CRA"). Consisting of eleven "titles," the CRA represents "the commitment of American society in the mid-1960s to the ideal of equality"[6] in areas ranging from voting rights to use of public accommodations and facilities to access to public education and federally assisted programs to equal employment opportunity. Although each title is an important element in Congress's effort to combat discrimination, this chapter will address only the last aspect, the right to employment opportunity.[7]

Title VII

The cornerstone of Title VII is Section 2000e-2, which directs employers that

a. It shall be an unlawful employment practice for an employer

1. to fail or refuse to hire or to discharge any individual, or otherwise to discriminate against any individual with respect to compensation, terms, conditions, or privileges of employment, because of such individual's race, color, religion, sex, or national origin; or

2. to limit, segregate, or classify his employees or applicants for employment in any way which would deprive or tend to deprive any individual of employment opportunities or otherwise adversely affect his status as an employee, because of such individual's race, color, religion, sex, or national origin.[8]

According to Section 2000e-2(e), however, an employer is allowed to make an employment decision "on the basis of ... religion, sex, or national origin" if any of these is a "bona fide occupational qualification [a BFOQ] reasonably necessary to the normal operation of that particular business or enterprise."[9]

Title VII has been elaborated in significant ways by judicial interpretation. A recent amendment of the CRA, the Civil Rights Act of 1991, amends CRA to codify and preserve several court decisions favored by Congress.

According to the courts, an "unlawful employment practice" may consist of either "disparate treatment" or "disparate impact." "Disparate treatment" occurs when an employer treats people differently because of their race, religion, or sex; "disparate impact" takes place when "employment practices that are facially neutral in their treatment of different groups ... in fact fall more harshly on one group than another and cannot be justified by business necessity."[10] Thus, an employer who refused to hire women merely because they are women would be guilty of disparate treatment, while an employer who used an employment test that had no correlation to a person's ability to perform the job but tended to eliminate women from consideration for the job would be guilty of disparate impact discrimination, regardless of the employer's intent in using the test. Although "either theory may ... be applied to a particular set of facts,"[11] the two theories have distinct legal requirements.

Disparate Treatment

The landmark disparate treatment case is *McDonnell Douglas Corp. v. Green*, which held that a plaintiff must

> establish ... a prima facie case of racial discrimination. ... by showing (i) that he belongs to a [protected] minority; (ii) that he applied for and was qualified for a job for which the employer was seeking applicants; (iii) that, despite his qualifications, he was rejected; and (iv) that, after his rejection, the position remained open and the employer continued to seek applicants from persons of complainant's qualifications.[12]

If the plaintiff makes this showing, she creates a presumption of unlawful discrimination in employment under Title VII.[13] The employer may rebut the presumption, however, by "articulat[ing] some legitimate, nondiscriminatory reason for the employee's rejection." The employer need not prove that it was "actually motivated by the proffered reasons,"[14] but once the employer offers such a reason, the plaintiff must then "show that [the employer's] stated reason for [plaintiff's] rejection was in fact pretext,"[15] that is (according to the Civil Rights Act of 1991), that the unlawful discrimination was at least *a* motivating, if not the sole or primary, factor underlying the actions of which the plaintiff complains.[16] A plaintiff failing to do this will lose the lawsuit.

Disparate Impact

The United States Supreme Court outlined, in a series of early decisions, the elements necessary to prove the discriminatory impact of an objectively neutral employment practice. Responding to recent Supreme Court decisions that Congress perceived as a retreat from those decisions, Congress codified in Section 105 of the Civil Rights Act of 1991 the elements necessary to prove an unlawful employment practice based on disparate impact.

In disparate impact cases, the division of procedural burdens is similar to that in a disparate treatment case, that is, the plaintiff must first establish a prima facie case of discrimination, after which the employer has the opportunity to demonstrate that its motivation was not discriminatory. The elements required to prove discrimination, however, are different.

To carry its burden of proof in a [disparate impact] case, a complaining party must first make a prima facie showing of discrimination. This is established when it is demonstrated that a defendant's employee selection practices, while perhaps facially neutral and lacking in intent to discriminate, have a discriminatory effect or disparate impact on minority hiring.[17]

As with the disparate treatment cases, "if a prima facie case is established, the burden of proof shifts to the defendant to show the criteria are 'job related',"[18] that is, not motivated by illegal discrimination.

German Law

In large part because of its fairly homogenous population, the Federal Republic of Germany has had relatively less experience in dealing with discrimination against minority populations.[19] The German constitution, the *Grundgesetz* or Basic Law, was, however, written in the shadow of the National Socialist era. As a consequence it contains strong promises of equal treatment for all people, beginning with the first nineteen articles of the Basic Law, the *Grundrechte* or "basic rights."

The Basic Rights

According to the *Bundesverfassungsgericht* (Federal Constitutional Court), the German counterpart to the United States Supreme Court, the basic rights are an essential element of the Basic Law and represent the core of a free democratic order.[20] As such, the basic rights express the principles and ideals upon which the German constitutional norms are based—principles and ideals that demand recognition even when they have not been reduced to concrete legal expression.[21] Thus, the basic rights constrain and direct the activities of the state in all its forms.[22]

The first basic right is that of human dignity:

Article 1. (Dignity of Man ...)
(1) The dignity of man is inviolable. To observe and protect [this dignity] is the obligation of all state authority.[23]

The right of human dignity is foremost among the values expressed in the Basic Law and can be neither forfeited nor limited.[24]

To say that human dignity is inviolable, however, is more inspirational than instructional. Thus there is some debate over Article 1(1). Does it state a right upon which people can rely or does it merely declare the aspiration according to which the state must conduct itself?[25] Of course, Article 1's broad declaration has clear application in cases involving torture, slavery, or genocide, but offers little direction in discerning the contours of the right. Consequently, Article 1(1) is in essence a statement of broad principle that gains meaning from the following portions of the Basic Law. Indeed, Section (3) of Article 1 reinforces this view by stating that the rights following Article 1 bind the legislative, executive, and judicial branches of government as directly effective law.[26]

Although several articles of the Basic Law operate at least peripherally to provide protection against inequitable treatment,[27] Article 3 is the right with most direct application:

Article 3. (Equality before the Law)
(1) All people are equal before the law.
(2) Men and women have equal rights.
(3) No one may be disadvantaged or privileged because of his sex, line of descent, race, language, homeland and origin, beliefs, or religious or political views.[28]

This right to equality is enjoyed by all natural persons and is directed against the state. It requires not just equality *before the law*, but *of* the law because it binds the legislature as well as the judiciary and executive. Because discrimination is a private as well as governmental phenomenon, however, the efficacy of Article 3 in addressing discrimination depends at least as much on its ability to address private actions as it does on its ability to control the state.

Are basic rights, particularly Article 3, directly binding on private persons in their dealings with other private persons? This question has not been answered definitively, although one noted authority, Professor

Dürig, expresses the position of most commentators when he states that the basic rights in general, and Article 3 in particular, are not binding on private persons.[29] Dismissing the argument that the basic rights have direct application to private transactions, he argues that this view creates an unnecessary and impermissible conflict among basic rights. Consequently, the requirement of private persons to observe Article 3 in their dealings with others creates an unconstitutional limit on individual freedom, such as that of personal development in Article 2 and the freedom of opinion in Article 5 of the Basic Law.[30]

But, to the extent it still exists, this dispute is largely academic. The Federal Constitutional Court has held, and the commentators seem to agree, that while the basic rights have indirect application to private transactions, they do not apply directly to them.[31] This means that no individual may assert his right of equality against another in a purely private matter. But it also means that if citizens ask the organs of the state to intervene in their private matters, these organs must act in accordance with the basic rights in issuing, executing, and adjudicating the laws. Thus, for example, a court must observe these rights when asked to interpret private agreements in light of, say, the Federal Civil Code.[32] The full effect and limits of this indirect application are not fully clear, however.

Thus, one might argue that as a practical matter Article 3 requires employers to treat employees equally—that is, without regard for race, sex, religion, or place of origin. This follows because laws regulating German employment relationships, which provide every employee with a more or less formal employment contract, consist of certain rights created by the Civil Code and enforceable in the courts. Consequently, because the government must observe and implement the basic rights when issuing, enforcing, or interpreting laws, employees should be able to invoke the protection of Article 3 when enforcing their employment rights. Unfortunately, this *Shelley v. Kraemer*-like argument founders when it is based on a general right to equality rather than a specific statutory right. Furthermore, this argument might be seen as merely a variant of the argument that commentators such as Dürig dismiss for creating an impermissible collision of rights, and thus, may not lead a court to extend Article 3 to private employment matters. For now, however, the issue is unresolved.

Civil Code Section 611a

Other than the provisions of the Basic Law just mentioned, Germany has few laws ensuring equal rights in any particular sphere of activity.[33] One which does is Section 611a of the Civil Code (the *Bürgerliche Gesetzbuch*), which seeks to create equality between the sexes in the workplace and avoids the debate over the direct or indirect applicability of Article 3 to private actors through means similar to Title VII of the CRA of 1964.[34]

Like Title VII, Section 611a prohibits an employer from discriminating against (literally, "disadvantaging") an employee "because of" the employee's sex.[35] Again as Title VII, it permits an employer to discriminate on the basis of sex if the agreement or measure in question involves the type of activities undertaken by the employer and a particular sex is an "indispensable requirement" of the activity.[36] Furthermore, like Title VII, Section 611a provides for a shifting burden of proof. Section 611a(1), sentence 3, states that in an action seeking damages for illegal employment discrimination, an employee has the initial burden of establishing facts that create an inference of discrimination. If the employee meets this burden, however, the employer may then prove that the treatment considered offensive is justified somehow or that gender is an indispensable requirement of the activity.[37]

But Section 611a makes recovery of damages more difficult than does Title VII. A leading authority on the law has observed that an employee-plaintiff must show that discrimination is "more likely than not" to have occurred.[38] This standard in and of itself is no great hurdle. In defense, all the employer need do to counter this showing is to state an objectively valid, nondiscriminatory reason for its action. The employer need not prove that its actions were entirely free from discriminatory motive.[39] Although this was once enough in American law, the CRA (Section 107(a)), unlike Civil Code Section 611a, now provides that the employee prevails if he or she can demonstrate that illegal discrimination was at least part of the employer's motivation in affecting the employee's employment.

Section 611a seems to have been drafted with at least one eye on Title VII, if not modeled outright on the U.S. law: both laws prohibit discrimination "because of" sex, both laws require complainants to establish facts that create an inference of discrimination, both laws allow the employer to justify its actions with nondiscriminatory reasons after the complainant creates the required inference, and both laws use similar language in assigning the burden of proof. In addition, both laws contain exceptions for gender-relevant job requirements.

Comparing the Laws

It is evident that, despite dissimilar histories, Germany and the United States are pursuing similar legal courses in addressing private discrimination. In both countries, the courts initially interpreted constitutional prohibitions of discrimination narrowly to grant equality only in matters of state action. Subsequently, courts and commentators interpreted these constitutional guarantees of equality to apply to private transactions whenever the transactions involve public authority. Then, each country enacted legislation prohibiting particular acts of private discrimination, making employment discrimination based on sex illegal regardless of state involvement.

At this point, however, the two histories diverge. Throughout the postwar period, and particularly in the 1960s, the United States has been forced—in ways that Germany has not since immediately after the war—to see private discriminatory prejudices as a threat to democratic society. As a result, the U.S. Constitution's promise of equal treatment came to be more liberally construed in order to address many types of private as well as public discrimination. Congress also began to pass laws specifically aimed at eliminating particular types of private discrimination not yet addressed in Germany. In contrast, with the exception of Civil Code Section 611a, Germany has yet to extend Article 3 to the more troublesome sphere of private discrimination, in particular to discrimination based on factors other than sex and in areas other than employment.

Although Section 611a is a promising beginning, it is unclear whether it will develop into a robust tool like Title VII. The law appears to have been only rarely used, narrowly applied, and enjoys virtually no case law and little interpretive commentary. One can only speculate on its likely evolution. For instance, because the law refers to *Arbeitnehmer* (employees), it is not clear whether the law provides a cause of action to applicants for employment and not only actual employees. Furthermore, it is uncertain whether the law requires a plaintiff to make a strong initial showing, or whether German courts will recognize and prohibit, or even distinguish between, disparate treatment (which is intentional) and disparate impact discrimination (which may not be). In time, the law could be fleshed out. In addition, it could spawn similar laws for other forms of discrimination or lead to entirely new methods for controlling discrimination. For the time being, however, the question remains whether and how the promises of equality made in Article 3 of the Basic Law may be invoked and interpreted to prevent employment discrimination despite the Basic Law's limited applicability to private actions.

A first step in addressing the tensions between the aspirations and the reach of the basic rights would be for Germany's Federal Constitutional Court to strengthen Article 3's indirect application to private parties in a manner similar to that undertaken in *Shelley v. Kraemer*. Academic commentators have resisted application of Article 3 to private persons because of a perceived collision of basic rights. Even though any attempt to ensure equality among individuals by regulating private autonomy inevitably limits individual freedom as well, the argument, advanced by

Dürig, is erroneous and something of a red herring. Dürig states that if Article 3 had direct application to private actors, no proprietor could earn more than another, presumably (although Dürig does not say so) because no person would be permitted to discriminate among proprietors by choosing to frequent a particular shop or restaurant more than another.[40] This argument is dismissed by Article 3, which provides only (1) that people are equal before the law, not that they are equal in matters of private choice or convenience; (2) that men and women have equal legal status, not that each man and each woman is equal to every other man or women in every way; and (3) that distinctions between persons may not be based on particular characteristics unrelated to a person's ability to contribute to society, not that no distinctions at all may be made for any reason, such as location, technical competence, price, convenience, or service.

Furthermore, neither equality of and before the law (as promised by both the German and U.S. constitutions) nor equality of opportunity (as promised by the United States' Civil Rights Acts) means equality of result. These laws are intended to allow all people the same chance, not guarantee them the same life. Thus, in the United States, one may hold and express within limits, discriminatory opinions—a right protected by the First Amendment to the Constitution and highly valued by Americans. But this right does not mean that one must necessarily have the freedom to act on these opinions to the detriment of others. Indeed, similar limits on individual autonomy already exist in Germany. In fact, both rights cited by Dürig as conflicting with Article 3—the right to free development of the person (Article 2) and the right to free opinion (Article 5)—expressly admit of limitation. Article 3 does not permit its own limitation. In addition, Article 18 of the Basic Law provides that anyone who uses certain of his or her basic rights, including that of freedom of opinion, to "fight" the "free democratic order" in Germany "forfeits" these rights.[41] Certainly German history bears abundant evidence of the fact that acts of discrimination, including even some nonviolent acts of private persons, may imperil democratic order. There seems to be no reason why Article 3 could not be applied more generously to combat private acts of discrimination.

A second step in addressing potential discrimination in Germany would be to extend Civil Code Section 611a to apply to discrimination based on factors other than sex, such as race or religion, and to make clear that the law extends to persons other than employees. The law as now drafted is similar to Title VII in its approach, and as Title VII has amply demonstrated, the basic approach of Section 611a can be applied to a wider range of circumstances. With these two steps, Germany could quickly, easily, and dramatically increase its ability to promise persons living within its borders equal opportunity in their search for a better life. While they may not offer a complete solution to the increasing instances of private discrimination, they should be implemented.

On this point, perhaps, German antidiscrimination legislation falls lamentably short of its American counterpart, despite the latter's complexity and blemishes: despite obvious problems and a difficult history, most private discrimination in Germany remains beyond the pale of legal recourse. For historical reasons, it may have been more pressing for the United States to combat private discrimination than it was for a homogenous Germany. But with Germany's growing international prominence and ethnic diversity, stronger legal remedies will be necessary.

Conclusion

As this short examination of equal opportunity laws in the United States and Germany has demonstrated, different cultural and historical experiences have resulted in different protections for minority rights and remedies for discrimination. Frictions between majority and minority populations would seem to have increased in most countries recently, and one of the great tasks of the coming years will be learning to ease these frictions. For all their shortcomings, the American laws against discrimination are far more comprehensive than those of most countries. Whether the United States has developed the best legal approach to the complex of problems is debatable in light of the persistence of discrimination. Nonetheless, it remains for countries such as Germany to build on the U.S. experience in seeking ways to integrate their diversifying populations, perhaps finding inspiration for solutions not yet imagined in the United States or elsewhere.

Notes

1. *Declaration of Independence* 4 July 1776.

2. *U.S. Const.* art. I, Section 2, cl. 3. The constitutional compromise regarding slavery is further reflected in art. VI, Section 2, cl. 2, requiring "free" states to return fugitive slaves upon request of the owners and art. I, Section 9, cl. 1, which provided for a twenty-year period of continued importation of slaves. Similarly, although a few states such as Utah and Wyoming had long allowed women to vote, prior to the adoption in 1920 of the 18th Amendment to the Constitution, no universal national right of suffrage existed.

3. 29 U.S.C. Section 1981.

4. 334 U.S. 1.

5. 29 U.S.C. Section 206(d).

6. M. A. Wood, G. Gee and S. G. Wood, *Fair Employment Practice and Standards* (Charlottesville: Michie 1981), 9.

7. 42 U.S.C. Section 2000e et seq.

8. An "employer" is any "person engaged in an industry affecting commerce who has fifteen or more employees for each working day in each of twenty or more calendar weeks in the current or preceding calendar year, and any agent of such person ..." 42 U.S.C. Section 2000e(b).

9. 42 U.S.C. § 2000e-2(e)(1).

10. *Teamsters v. United States*, 431 U.S. 324, 335 n.15 (1977).

11. Ibid.

12. 411 U.S. 792 (1973).

13. See e.g. *Texas Dept. of Community Affairs v. Burdine*, 450 U.S. 248 (1981).

14. Ibid.

15. *McDonnell Douglas*, 411 U.S. 792.

16. Civil Rights Act of 1991, Senate Bill S. 1745, Congressional Record dated October 25, 1991, at Section 107(a)(m) (hereafter "CRA of 1991").

17. *EEOC v. Navajo Refining Co.*, 593 F.2d 988 (10th Cir. 1979).

18. Ibid.

19. Most estimates place the minority population in Germany at approximately 7 percent. "Minority" in these case refers to non-German people residing in the Federal Republic. Remarks of Liselotte Funke, former commissioner of the German Federal Government for Foreigners, at a meeting with fellows of the Robert Bosch Foundation, 13 September, 1991.

20. Decision of the Federal Constitutional Court (hereafter BVerfGE) 37, 280; BVerfGE 31, 73.

21. BVerfGE 1, 18; BVerfGE 2, 403.

22. K. H. Seifert and D. Hömig, *Grundgesetz für die Bundesrepublik Deutschland—Taschenkommentar* (Baden-Baden: Nomos Verlaggesellschaft 1991) 4th. ed. at 26 (hereafter Grundgesetz). See also *Basic Law* Art. 1(3).

23. "Die Würde des Menschen ist unantastbar. Sie zu achten und zu schützen ist Verpflichtung aller staatlichen Gewalt." (All translations from German are the author's.)

24. BVerfGE 27, 6; BVerfGE 45, 229; Seifert and Hömig, *Grundgesetz*, p. 36.

25. Compare, e.g., Apelt, *Juristenzeitung* 51, 353; Kiefersauer, *Juristische Rundschau* 52, 81 and Münch, *Die Menschenwürde* with Neumann, Nipperdey, Scheuner, *Die Grundrechte*, Band II, Hamann, *Kommentar*, and Löw, *Die öffentliche Verwaltung* 58, 516.

26. Art. 1(3): "Die nachfolgenden Grundrechte binden Gezsetzgebung, vollziehende Gewalt und Rechtsprechung als unmittelbar geltendes Recht."

27. See, e.g., Article 2 (General Right of Personal Freedom, a right limitable by its express terms), Article 6 (Protection of Marriage, Family, and Illegitimate Children) and Article 33 (Equality of Citizens; Public Service).

28. The original German is: Artikel 3. (Gleichheit vor dem Gesetz)

1. Alle Menschen sind vor dem Gesetz gleich.

2. Männer und Frauen sind gleichberechtigt.

3. Niemand darf wegen seines Geschlechtes, seiner Abstammung, seiner Rasse, seiner Sprache, seiner Heimat und Herkunft, seines Glaubens, seiner

religiösen oder politischen Anschauungen benachteiligt oder bevorzugt werden.

29. T. Maunz, G. Dürig, R. Herzog, R. Scholz, P. Lerche, H. J. Papier, A. Randelzhofer. E. Schmidt-Assmann, *Grundgesetz Kommentar*, vol. 1 (C.H. Beck'sche Verlagsbuchhandlung 1991) at 134 (hereafter *Kommentar*).

30. Seifert and Hömig, *Grundgesetz* at 52.

31. BVerfGE 7, 198; BVerfGE 30, 199; BVerfGE 73, 269.

32. Seifert & Hömig, *Grundgesetz* p. 28. See also BVerfGE 7, 205 ff.; BVerfGE 60, 239; BVerfGE 61, 6; BVerfGE 62, 242 ff.; BVerfGE 63, 184; BVerfGE 66, 135.

33. There are antidiscrimination laws other than Civil Code Section 611a, such as the *Schwerbehindertengesetz*, which requires employers with at least sixteen employees to employ handicapped employees as 6 percent of their workforce, and the *Gleichberechtigungsgesetz*, which makes men and women (in particular marriage partners) equal in the civil law. But these laws are limited to very specific circumstances. Similar exceptions include the *Beschäftigungsförderungsgesetz* Section 2, prohibiting discrimination against part-time workers, the *Seemannsgesetz* Sections 92 and 93 regulating the employment of women on boats, the *Verordnung über die Beschäftigung von Frauen auf Fahrzeugen* concerning employment of women in the transportation sector, and the *Mutterschutzgesetz* intended to protect mothers and expectant mothers. But again, each of these laws is narrowly limited, and one can debate whether these laws are in fact intended either to achieve equality or combat discrimination. In fact, one such law, the prohibition against women working at night found in the *Arbeitzeitordnung* Sections 16–21, was recently declared by the Federal Constitutional Court to be both unconstitutional and a violation of EU law. Two further laws were recently enacted (on 21 April 1994) regarding sexual discrimination. One law requires employers to adopt affirmative action-type measures for the advancement of female employees. The second law prohibits sexual harassment in the workplace. Both laws were criticized by the parliamentary opposition on the grounds that they do not go far enough

34. Palandt, *Bürgerliches Gesetzbuch Beck'sche Kommentar*, vol. 7 (C. H. Beck'sche Verlagsbuchhandlung 1991) 50th ed. at § 611a (hereafter *BGB Kommentar*).

35. The language in the original is: "Der Arbeitgeber darf einen Arbeitnehmer … nicht wegen seines Geschlechts benachteiligen."

36. The original language is: "Eine unterschiedliche Behandlung wegen des Geschlechts ist jedoch zulässig, soweit eine Vereinbarung oder eine Massnahme die Art der vom Arbeitnehmer auszuübenden Tätigkeit zum Gegenstand hat und ein bestimmtes Geschlecht unverzichtbare Voraussetzung für diese Tätigkeit ist."

37. Section 611a explains: "Wenn im Streitfall der Arbeitnehmer Tatsachen glaubhaft macht, die eine Benachteiligung wegen des Geschlechts vermuten lassen, trägt der Arbeitgeber die Beweislast dafür, daß nicht auf das Geschlecht bezogene, sachliche Gründe eine unterschiedliche Behandlung rechtfertigen oder das Geschlecht unversichtbare Voraussetzung für die auszuübende Tätigkeit ist."

38. "Überwiegend wahrscheinlich" *BGB Kommentar*, vol. 7, at 611a(3)(a).

39. *BGB Kommentar* at 611a(3)(b)(aa).

40. *Kommentar* at 228.

41. "Wer die Freiheit der Meinungäusserung ... zum Kampfe gegen die freiheitliche demokratische Grundordnung missbraucht, verwirkt diese Grundrechte."

12

Legal Ethics as Market Interference: The Example of the German Residency Requirements

Ingrid L. Lenhardt

The rules governing legal ethics in Germany have at times been challenged as unethical. Some of the rules, it is argued, maximize the well-being of lawyers rather than that of their clients and the legal system. Especially under attack are rules that purport to protect lawyers from competition. One of most significant of these ethics rules—that every lawyer reside and maintain an office in a jurisdiction where they are admitted to appear before a court—will be analyzed in this chapter First, the requirements, as well as recent legal challenges to them, will be described. Arguments in favor of maintaining such requirements will then be analyzed from a market-oriented perspective. This chapter will conclude that the residency requirements effectively protect German attorneys from competition, and that they must soon be moderated owing to European Union and international pressures.

Although this chapter focuses on the German residency requirements, these comprise but one aspect of a comprehensive set of prohibitions that limit competition among attorneys. For example, the Federal Bar Association (Bundesrechtsanwaltskammer) also imposes a total ban on advertisements and client solicitation, which limits a client's ability to obtain necessary market information. In 1987 the Bundesverfassungsgericht (hereinafter the Federal Constitutional Court) held that the federal bar association lacked the authority to promulgate various ethics rules, but these rules are to remain intact for proceedings before the disciplinary courts for attorneys *(Ehrengerichtshöfe)* "so far necessary for a workable administration of justice."[1] Therefore, the extent to which the ban will continue in the future is still being vigorously debated while remaining in force. These bans have led to curious limitations on calling oneself an attorney (Rechtsanwältin). Recently, *FOCUS*, a news magazine, declared its intention to publish a booklet on a series of articles about the best five hundred attorneys (of seventy thousand) in Germany but was enjoined from doing so. The conduct of those attorneys who actively participated by making photos available or giving statements was held unethical.[2]

Another professional obligation with anticompetitive consequences concerns legal fees. Under the federal statute on attorneys' fees (*"Bundesgebührenordnung für Rechtsanwälte"* or "BRAGO"), legal fees are highly regulated in minute detail, proscribing the "basic fee" in a scale of charges (*Gebührentabelle*) for an attorney in most cases litigated and setting a cap on reimbursement for litigation expenses incurred by the prevailing party.[3]

Legal Challenges to German Residency Requirements

The practice of law in western Germany is governed primarily by the *Bundesrechtsanwaltsordnung* (commonly and hereinafter referred to as BRAO), a federal statute enacted in 1959, which reflects the peculiar historical German understanding of competition.[4] Because of the 1987 Federal Constitutional Court case mentioned above, BRAO was not extended to the new *Länder* because the federal bar association had previously promulgated detailed ethics rules to assist in interpreting and clarifying BRAO. Thus, one of the last acts of the German Democratic Republic's Volkskammer was to pass the *Rechtsanwaltsgesetz* (commonly referred to as RAG) until BRAO takes effect in the new *Länder*.[5] Nevertheless, RAG is in large part identical to BRAO.

Section 18 BRAO, which sets forth the core of the residency requirements, requires each member of the bar to be admitted only at a court of a certain district (*Lokalisationsprinzip*), a restriction that dates from 1878. This requirement suggests the traditional German link between attorneys and the courts. Members of the bar must maintain an office (*Kanzleipflicht*) and live (Residenzpflicht) in that district.[6] They are also prohibited from holding regular business hours outside that district.[7] Basically, attorneys may practice only in the district to which they are admitted. Some exceptions apply, however, to specific areas of the law, such as labor, criminal, and administrative law.

In contrast to the U.S. court system and its mostly undifferentiated subject-matter jurisdiction, the German court system is highly specialized and decentralized, and, hence, very complicated. Germany has no fewer than five different sets of courts, each with its own special jurisdiction—namely, ordinary jurisdiction in civil and criminal matters (*ordentli-*

che Gerichtsbarkeit), labor, administrative, social matters, and tax. Generally, each set of courts has a court of first instance and a state court of appeal, which are courts of the *Länder*, and are subject to the federal supreme court. Ordinary jurisdiction is most commonly invoked and includes almost all matters of civil and criminal law.

Civil cases are commenced either in the *Amtsgericht* (the local court), the court of first instance in minor criminal and civil cases, or the *Landgericht* (the regional court), the court of first instance in major criminal and civil cases as well as the court of appeal for the cases rendered by the local court. The *Oberlandesgericht* (the higher regional court) is the court of appeal for regional court decisions in civil and some criminal matters, while appeals of major criminal matters are heard in the *Bundesgerichtshof* (the federal high court of justice), the highest court in criminal and civil matters. Finally, decisions of the federal high court can, under certain limited circumstances involving questions of constitutional law, be reviewed by Germany's supreme court.

Germany is divided into approximately 500 to 550 districts, each of which has a local court. This means there are approximately 100,000–150,000 inhabitants per local court district. Rural areas, however, would have a number of districts with fewer than 20,000 inhabitants. Several of these local court districts constitute one district for the regional court, which has approximately one hundred districts. Several regional court districts in turn constitute one of about thirty Higher Regional Court (*Oberlandesgerichte*) districts. There is, on average, one attorney for every 1,027 inhabitants in western Germany.

An attorney will usually be limited not only as to the district where she may practice but also to certain courts in that district. Any lawyer admitted to the local court is eligible for admittance to the regional court of that district.[8] A lawyer admitted to the regional court, however, is usually not eligible for admittance to the higher regional court (*Singularzulassung*).[9] Section 226 II BRAO contains an exception allowing lawyers to be admitted at the regional and higher regional courts in the following six *Länder*: Hamburg, Berlin, Bremen, Bavaria, Saarland, and Baden-Württemberg (*Simultanzulassung*).[10] Moreover, the *Singularzulassung* is unknown in the five new *Länder*, but this will change as the higher regional courts are established there. This particular distinction has its roots in the historical development of court practice in the various *Länder*. The *Singularzulassung* is frequently justified on grounds of confidentiality and the desire to financially secure rural law offices.

Residency requirements do not, however, prevent a lawyer from representing a client in any proceeding that does not require legal representation. This applies in particular to the local courts, which basically have jurisdiction over claims valued at DM 10,000 or less (approximately U.S.$

6,000).[11] Representation by counsel is mandatory in only a few cases before the local courts. In 1987, for example, only 14 percent of the proceedings in the first instance involved cases that mandated representation by an attorney in North Rhine–Westphalia, is the most populous German state.[12] Thus, the residency requirements apply in only a few cases in the first instance. These cases, however, involve appeals or higher amounts in dispute and are therefore the most lucrative for an attorney.

Here is how the residency requirements apply in typical cases: Lawyer X lives in the City of Moers, which belongs to the local court district Moers, the regional court district Kleve, and the higher regional court district Düsseldorf. If X decides to be admitted to the local court, she may practice at the Local Court in Moers and is eligible to practice at the Regional Court in Kleve. X is also eligible to practice in any Local Court in the country other than Moers, but she may not practice at any Regional Court other than Kleve.[13] Moers is located in the state of North Rhine–Westphalia, therefore X is not allowed to practice at the higher regional court in Düsseldorf.

These requirements have grave implications. Once an attorney chooses the district and the court in which she wants to practice, her practice becomes quite limited. In many cases the lawyer representing a client at trial is not able to represent his client on appeal.[14] In addition, the attorney selected by the client might not be able to serve if that the court, to which the attorney is admitted, is without venue (i.e., is not the proper location of the case under the rules of procedure). Furthermore, Section 18 I and II BRAO prevents the attorney from gaining flexibility in his practice by giving up his local court admittance. Unless the attorney is then admitted elsewhere, she is no longer permitted to work as an attorney in the Federal Republic.

The legality of the residency requirements have been called into question after the European Court of Justice decided *Commission v. Germany* in 1988.[15] In *Commission v. Germany*, the court invalidated legislation that essentially prohibited lawyers from other member states of the European Union (EU) from practicing law in the Federal Republic. The court, inter alia, held that foreign lawyers must be permitted to represent clients in proceedings which do not, by law, require the appearance of counsel. Therefore, foreign lawyers may appear in most proceedings before the local courts, because such courts usually do not require representation.

Moreover, the decision held that lawyers residing in other EU member states may, under certain circumstances, appear in matters requiring representation by counsel before a court. This conflicts with the residency requirements, which prohibit a German lawyer from appearing before any court to which she is not admitted. The decision thereby invalidated some aspects of the residency requirements on a European level.

The decision dealt, however, only with "occasional" appearances in German courts and probably cannot justify the appearance of a foreign attorney who establishes a practice of representing clients in German courts.[16] Foreign attorneys might nevertheless be able to appear before a court to which they are not admitted, although members of the German bar are prohibited from doing so. It can be argued, therefore, that the residency requirements violate the nondiscrimination clause found in European Union law and are invalid.[17] If the residency requirements are held to violate EU law, they would be void.

Prior to its decisions in *Commission v. Germany*, the Federal High Court of Justice in 1988 has upheld the constitutionality of the residency requirements.[18] Since then, the requirements have been subject to an intense national debate, yet the discussion has primarily been focused on altering the statutory framework rather than on the unconstitutionality of the residency requirements *per se*. The requirements may also violate the EU's nondiscrimination clause, but this seems to be of less concern to the German bar than the effect that dropping the residency requirements would have on competition.

The establishment of branch offices has been one of the most intensively debated issues involving the residency requirements since the decision of the European Court of Justice in *Commission v. Germany*.[19] Under Section 28 BRAO (*Zweigstellenverbot*) lawyers are often obliged to refer clients to other lawyers because the limitations as to district also prohibit her from setting up a branch office elsewhere.[20] This prohibition on branch offices is probably the main reason why, until recently, German law firms are much smaller than U.S. firms[21] but in April 1989 two major German law firms, one in Düsseldorf and the other in Frankfurt, decided to merge, creating the first German law firm with offices in more than one German city.[22] This merger, it has been argued, violated Section 28 BRAO.[23]

The first merger was nevertheless followed by several others. Innumerable German law firms now have offices in more than one city.[24] This is particularly true for cities in the new *Länder*, where many of the new law offices are actually branches of firms in the old *Länder*. (Most western German lawyers were reluctant to relocate to eastern Germany or to give up their practices in the West, so branch offices were often opened). In fact, at least twenty law firms now have offices in four or more German cities (with at least one eastern German office) along with one or more foreign offices.[25] Lawyers that work in a particular branch also live and work in the district where the branch is located, therefore complying with the residency requirements.[26]

In the meantime, under certain conditions a law firm may maintain offices in more than one German city. This was first permitted by the Federal High Court of Justice in 1989 and has since been reaffirmed.[27] Section 39 RAG, passed by the Volkskammer in September of 1990, took the recent Federal High Court of Justice case law into consideration and permitted the establishment of branch offices in eastern Germany, causing an outcry by the federal bar association.[28]

As of 3 October 1990, the new *Länder* assumed most of the laws of the old *Länder*.[29] As mentioned above, however, BRAO does not apply in the new *Länder* for the time being.[30] As the German Democratic Republic (GDR) had few attorneys to begin with (about only six hundred), virtually none with a comprehensive knowledge of the Federal Republic of Germany's laws, the demand for FRG lawyers boomed. Originally, the legal profession in the GDR, as in the FRG, consisted of sole practitioners. In 1953 the SED-Regime began to collectivize the profession into so-called *Anwaltskollegen*. As of 1979 almost all attorneys were in such *Anwaltskollegen*. They could appear before all courts but were to contribute to "further strengthening socialist lawfulness" and "further developing the citizens' socialist sense of the law."[31] At the beginning of 1990 it became possible to be an independent attorney once again.[32] All those with a diplom-jurist degree from a GDR university and two years of legal experience could practice in the new *Länder* as well as those who passed the western German first and second state examinations (usually at the ripe age of thirty two).[33] Because of the need for western lawyers following unification, the branch office phenomenon has progressed too far during the past four years to be halted, and few seem to be interested in stopping it.

Arguments in Favor of the Residency Requirements: An Analysis

The decisions reviewing the legality of the residency requirements contain several rationalizations.

Two arguments are forwarded in support of the benefits that such requirements bring to clients. First, the lawyer is better able to serve the client not only because he is available for expedited proceedings (she is close to the office and the court) but also because she knows the judge as well as the opposing counsel. This makes him better able to both assess the likelihood of success and develop the best strategy for a case. Second, the residency requirements make it easier for the client to select a trustworthy lawyer because lawyers are well known in the community.

These arguments are not convincing. With the exception of the new *Länder*, an overabundance of lawyers is quite willing to step in for expedited proceedings, if necessary. Furthermore, if clients need to hire counsel familiar with the court and practicing close to it, they are free to choose such counsel. In order to satisfy demand, lawyers will specialize as they see fit. Alternatively, the client might prefer outside counsel because he may be involved in various legal matters, which he may want to put in the hands of a single lawyer, completely independent of the location of any of the controversies. The residency requirements, far from taking these legitimate interests into account, hamper the freedom of clients to choose legal representation.

The residency requirements are also purported to benefit the legal system and therefore society as a whole. This benefit is said to derive from the close relationship among attorneys, judges, and their community, a relationship that forces lawyers to be circumspect in every proceeding, compelled to maintain high standards of trustworthiness, competence, and reliability, which in turn creates a more productive working environment. Higher productivity means lower cost for legal services and reduces the resources society must allocate to the legal system.

This argument also has several flaws. First, independent of any market condition, it assumes that the residency requirements actually create the small town atmosphere with close relationships. In light of the anonymity of today's large cities, this assumption seems questionable. Second, residency requirements actually interfere with the market, creating inefficiencies in and of themselves. Requirements that prevent an attorney from representing his client on appeal result in inefficiency. Another must then be hired to spend the time and energy, reflected in legal fees, to acquire the knowledge already possessed by previous counsel. The benefit-to-society argument fails to take these inefficiencies into account and weigh them against the putative gains in productivity.

Moreover, these productive efficiencies should not even occur. The core of the argument is that the intimacy allegedly created by the residency requirements facilitates the flow of and access to information about the market participants. This flow of information causes the participants to be concerned with their reputation and makes them accountable to the community, thereby shaping the participants' conduct. In an ideal market, however, all market participants are perfectly informed, and hence it is not necessary to facilitate the flow of information.

Conclusion

Assuming a functioning market, the residency requirements do not benefit either the clients or society as a whole. The requirements do, however, benefit the members of the bar in that they protect them against competition and ensure their livelihood. This aspect has actually been offered in support of the residency requirements. Hence, the argument that such requirements are unethical, because they are primarily designed to ensure the well-being of attorneys, is well-founded.

However, the assumption of this analysis, a functioning market, is questionable in a system that allows no advertising and regulates prices.[34] An analysis that does *not* assume an ideal market might very well find justification for residency requirements for reasons other than the well-being of the bar members.

Interestingly enough, the residency requirements first came under fire at a time when the restrictions posed a threat to the competitiveness of German law firms in the international markets—that is, at a time when the residency requirements no longer served the well-being of the bar. In 1993 the first draft of the bill to reorganize the law governing the legal profession was debated before the federal parliament and is still in the hands of the parliament's committee on legal affairs. This draft permits the establishment of branch offices, allows those *Länder* with a *Singular-zulassung* system to develop their own rules on concurrent admission to both the regional and higher regional courts, and loosens up somewhat on the *Lokalisationsprinzip* by letting attorneys appear throughout Germany before the regional courts in civil matters. The various bar groups, legal experts, and other interested parties have requested many conflicting changes to the draft. Some amendments will surely be made, making passage of a bill during this year's legislative period less likely and risking its amendment into ineffectuality.

Notes

1. Federal Constitutional Court decision reported in *Neue Juristische Wochens-chrift* (1988) at 191; hereafter cited as *NJW*.

2. Regional Court decision printed in *NJW* 1994, 331; see Rüdiger Zuck, "Focus-Hocuspokus: die 500 besten Anwälte," *NJW* 1994, 297.

3. Germany follows the so-called English Rule (the loser pays all) and not the so-called American Rule (each party bears its own costs). An agreement to pay a contingency fee *Erfolgshonorar* is void as contrary to public policy. BGHZ *Entschei-dungen des Bundesgerichtshofs in Zivilsachen* 39, at 142; hereafter BGHZ.

4. Under the German system, only attorneys in private practice can be admitted to the bar. Accordingly, in-house counsel are not subject to the regula-tions discussed herein and their ability to act as attorneys is restricted.

5. Thomas Kaiser, "Berufsrecht im Gebiet der neuen Bundesländer–Das Recht-sanwaltsgesetz von 13.9.1990," *AnwaltsBlatt* (1991), at 133.

6. Section 27 BRAO *Bundesrechtsanwaltsordnung*; see Federal High Court of Justice decision reported in BRAK-Mitt. *Bundesrechtsanwaltskammer-Mitteilungen* 1984, 195 (a full-time employee cannot properly carry out a secondary occupation

as an attorney if she works 55–60 km from the law firm and 45–50 km from the court, requiring a commute time of about 35–55 minutes).

7. Section 28 BRAO.

8. Section 23 BRAO.

9. Section 226 I BRAO.

10. In contrast to the United States, lawyers practicing before the Federal High Court of Justice must be admitted to the court and may not practice before any other court. On the other hand, and also in contrast to the United States, any lawyer admitted to any court in the Federal Republic of Germany may practice before the Federal Constitutional Court. Section 22 BVerfGG *Bundesverfassungsgerichtgesetz.*

11. Section 23 GVG *Gerichtsverfassungsgesetz.*

12. This percentage may be even lower today as the amount in controversy for access to the regional courts was recently increased.

13. Note the exceptions stated above whereby X may represent clients in labor, criminal, and administrative cases at any court. She may also represent the client in front of the Federal Constitutional Court.

14. This is of particular importance in the German court system because review on appeal is often de novo, that is, the court engages itself again as factfinder. Thus, the counsel on appeal is not limited to arguing legal issues but must participate in the fact-finding procedure as well.

15. European Court of Justice decision reported in *NJW* 1988, 887. In order to comply with the decision, the federal parliament enacted a law at the end of 1989 which allows foreign attorneys from member states of the European Union to establish law practices in Germany and render legal advice in international law, the law of their home country, and European law. Foreign lawyers from non-member states might, under certain circumstances, be permitted to open up a law practice as well. For a description of the new statute, see Wolfgang Knapp, "Erleichterte Niederlassung für deutsche Rechtsanwälte in den USA und für amerikanische attorneys-at-law in der Bundesrepublik,"*Deutsch-Amerikanische Juristen Vereinigung Newsletter*, p. 10, January 1990.

16. As of 1990 lawyers from other European Union member states can take a qualification test *Eignungsprüfung* for full admission to the German bar. Since then, all of twelve (of fourteen) candidates have obtained such qualification. Deutsche AnwaltAkademie application form, 1994. Supposedly a thousand foreign colleagues are preparing themselves for the test according to the president of the Deutscher AnwaltVerein. See Erhard Senninger, "Deregulierung und Selbstbestimmung–Die Anwaltschaft im Spannungsfeld zwischen ihrer Stellung als 'unabhängiges Organ der Rechtspflege' und den Entwicklungen des Europäschen Gemeinschaftsrechts," *AnwaltsBlatt* 1990, 238. With Austria joining the European Union this year, these figures may dramatically change.

17. The nondiscrimination clause prohibits a member country from discriminating against the citizens of another member country. Arguably, the clause also prohibits a country from discriminating against its own citizens. Because such nondiscrimination clause is sourced in EU law, it is supreme to the law of the Federal Republic of Germany. Accordingly, if some of the residency requirements violate the nondiscrimination clause, then these requirements are invalid.

18. See Wilhelm Feuerich, "Die überortliche Anwaltssozietät–Wunschtraum oder zulässige Partnerschaftsform?"*AnwaltsBlatt* 1989, 360.

19. See Wolfgang Stefener, "EuGH–Dienstleistungsurtoil—Auswirkungen auf Lokalisation und Zweigstellenverbot,"*AnwaltsBlatt* 1988, 367; Erhard Senninger, AnwaltsBlatt 1989, 298; Wilhelm Feuerich, "DieAnwaltssozietät," p. 360; Eghard Teichmann, "Die überortliche AnwaltssozietätUat–Fine Chance für die kleinere Praxis?" *AnwaltsBlatt* 1989, 368; Hans-Jürgen Papier, "Die überortliche Anwaltssozietät aus der Sicht des Verfassungs und Gemeinschaftsrechts," *Juristische Zeitschrift*, 1990, 253; Hanns-Christian Salger, "Überortliche Anwaltssozietäien in Deutschland," *NJW* 1988, 186.

20. Technically, the limitations only apply to the territory of the Federal Republic. A German attorney can set up an office in another European Union member state without residing there and an attorney from another European Union member state can also set up an office in Germany without residing there. European Court of Justice decision reported in *AnwaltsBlatt* 1984, 608.

21. There is already a handful of law firms with one hundred or more attorneys. Although still small in comparison to U.S. law firms with over one thousand attorneys, this is changing rapidly—two of the largest law firms in Germany are to merge shortly, creating a law firm with more than two hundred attorneys.

22. Already prior to the merger, some German law firms maintained branch offices abroad in cities such as Singapore, New York, or Beijing. In the past, the German attorneys working in such offices had to give up their bar membership to avoid violating the duty to maintain an office in the district to which they are admitted.

23. See Wilhelm Feuerich, "Die Anwaltssozietät," p. 360. Prior to the Federal Constitutional Court's decision invalidating many of the ethical rules adopted by the bar itself rather than the Federal legislature (supra n. 1), the interpretation of Section 28 BRAO, as preventing any firm from having offices in more than one district, had not been called into question because the ethical rules—as interpreted by the disciplinary courts for attorneys competent to rule on them—were explicit on this point. See Federal High Court of Justice decision reported in *NJW* 1981, at 2477 (dicta).

24. Thomas Kaiser, "Berufsrecht," p. 133.

25. Laura Covill, "German Survey: Time To Consolidate," *Lawyer International* 19, April 1994, pp. 8–11.

26. See Wilhelm Feuerich, "DieAnwaltssozietät," p. 360.

27. BGHZ 108, 290; Federal High Court of Justice decision reported in *Anwalts-Blatt* 1993, at 130; BGHSt *(Entscheidungen des Bundesgerichtshofs in Strafsachen)* 37, at 220, 223; Federal High Court of Justice decision reported in *NJW* 1991, at 2780, 2781.

28. Thomas Kaiser, "Berufsrecht," p. 133.

29. Article 8, Reunification Agreement, 31 August 1990 *(Einigungsvertrag)*.

30. See notes 2 and 3 above, and accompanying text.

31. Johannes Wasmuth, "Entwicklungen des anwaltlichen Berufsrechts in der DDR," *BRAK-Mitt.* 1990, at 122.

32. *NJW* 1990, 1588: "DDR–Verordnung über die Tätigkeit und die Zulassung von Rechtsanwälte mit eigener Praxis von 22. 2.90."

33. Section 4 RAG.

34. See supra, p. 197.

PART FOUR

Alumni Conference Speeches

13

Germany in a New Europe

Kurt Biedenkopf

In speaking about Germany in a new Europe, one has to make clear that it is a *new* Germany in a *new* Europe because they are interlinked in many ways. When the coup failed in Moscow on 21 August 1991, Russia returned to Europe, remaking Europe as a result. On 23 August 1990, the Volkskammer, the parliament of the German Democratic Republic (GDR) under the able guidance of its minister-president De Maziere, decided to join the Federal Republic of Germany (FRG), in accordance with Article 23 of the constitution, which permits the joining of parts outside of Germany that were German and wanted to return. As a result of this decision, Germany became a new Germany.

This process of Europe returning to its history started early after World War II, showing that Germany's division, which also was a division of Europe, was a historic development. The stations on the way to overcome this division of Germany and Europe are well known. The first outstanding one took place in June 1953 with the uprising of workers in East Germany against what they felt were inhuman demands on their labor. There followed the uprising in Hungary in 1956; in Czechoslovakia in 1968; in Poland in 1980–1981 followed by martial law; and finally, the process that was put into motion by *glasnost* and *perestroika* in the Soviet Union beginning in 1986–1987.

Another important event was the selection of the present Pope, then a Polish cardinal, in the fall of 1978. With a Pole as pope, who declared that human rights would be one of his most important tasks, it became clear

Speech delivered to the Sixth Annual Conference of Robert Bosch Alumni Association, 14 September 1991 in Washington, D.C.

even in 1978 that the division of Europe would not stand, that a community of pan-European culture, religion, and thinking would ultimately prevail.

The division of Europe and Germany ended simultaneously in the fall of 1989 when the Hungary's foreign minister cut the barbed wire at the border dividing Hungary and Austria. At that time some bystanders observed that the Wall has just tumbled, it just does not know it. With the opening in Hungary, it was evident that the division of Europe as well as of Germany could no longer be sustained. Remarkably, this revolutionary process occurred without bloodshed. Although it was a negation of the entire order that had been in place since the end of World War II, not a single shot was fired. Gorbachev and Yeltsin both testified to the end of this epoch in live broadcasts linking U.S. viewers with the Kremlin. Yeltsin stated, "The experiment on our soil was a tragedy for our people." Gorbachev observed, "The model has failed, this is a lesson to all peoples."

Had we been assembled only two years ago [in 1989] and someone predicted that the leaders of the Soviet Union and Russia would make these statements on American television to testify to the end of the Stalinist empire and Communist rule, even in our wildest dreams we wouldn't have thought it possible.

Germany is now undergoing unification because of the events described above. But Germany's political union must be understood on its own, apart from the country's social and economic union. The political union was completed on 3 October 1990; actual unity was achieved the minute the Wall was opened and the government in East Berlin allowed its population—its up-to-then incarcerated population—to move freely into the West. This opening of the Wall represented de facto unity and was irreversible. It was de facto unity because West Germany had never recognized the citizenship of East Germany, so when the Wall opened, everyone in East Germany became a German citizen. They could cross the border and ask for a passport. They could cross the border and enjoy all the rights bestowed on German citizens by the constitution, by social legislation, by the legal order. And they did. In fact, they, not politics, determined the speed of unification.

Economic union was restored even before political union. Namely, on 1 July 1990 when the Treaty on the Currency and Economic Union between the FRG and what was then still the GDR went into effect. I will never forget this day. It was a Sunday and I was flying into Leipzig. When we entered the airport terminal, the police guards that controlled the airport asked the passengers to assemble in a circle. Then, one of the officers presented the female passengers with flowers, welcomed them and said that this was the last day that they were serving in their duty as guards. From then on, Germany and Germans would again be united.

The monetary and economic union taught us a lot, which could be useful in the future for the integration of Eastern Europe. In January and February of 1990 a dispute erupted over how to accomplish economic union. Our Council of Economic Advisors issued a special opinion on 20 January 1990 recommending the adoption of the following policy:

> Step number one: for a number of years the GDR would be permitted to reconstruct its own economy and convert it into a market economy; strengthen it with substantial support and aid from the West; and develop it to a stage where convertibility between the D-mark and the mark in East Germany would be possible.
> Step number two: after an additional lapse of time, the two parts of Germany would slowly integrate; the two currencies would become convertible; and then a common currency would be developed.

This opinion was called the "crowning theory" because the application of the Deutsche mark in both parts of Germany was to "crown" the end of a process lasting several years. That was the learned opinion of the economists.

The people, however, saw it quite differently. Their solution was mass movement from east to west. Both the chancellor and the finance minister had at first welcomed the opinion of the economists because they both felt this was a sound base on which to build. But on 3 February, the chancellor was informed that 68,000 people had moved from east to west in January. It became apparent to him that this policy could not be implemented because the population wasn't willing to support it. It was obvious that with the opening of the Wall, the GDR had lost its legitimacy, which would be impossible to restore even for the purpose of establishing an orderly transition to a market economy. To the great dismay of many learned economists the chancellor offered to negotiate immediately with the GDR on a currency union—to be completed as soon as possible. We did not *end* with convertibility and a common currency, we *started* with convertibility and a common currency.

Yesterday at the World Bank, we discussed what we can learn from this. And we may learn from this that it is impossible to maintain a socialist economy if that economy has lost its legitimacy. Similar methods of integration might be necessary in Czechoslovakia, Hungary, and Poland as we approach the question of how we are going to integrate these economies into western Europe. The currency, and thus convertibility that we instituted was extended to East Germany without first establishing the proper economic conditions. A *strong* economy was extended to a territory with a very *weak* economy. Mobility and the people are what forced this step. We are now seeing the consequences.

In October 1990 political union was completed and the new Länder came into being—an exciting event. On 14 October we elected new parliaments in the five new Länder and in East Berlin, together with West Berlin, and these new parliaments began to operate without constitutions. We are going to discuss, draft, and pass constitutions. The people also elected prime ministers without a government. We then had to build governments. When the ministers in the Free State of Saxony were sworn in on 8 November, each one of them had only four to five people working with them while the projected number of state government employees was roughly two thousand. We are now in the process of building an administration, working with this administration, trying to solve all the problems with this administration, including the problems the administration itself presents. We hope to succeed. I can assure you, however, that this has never been done before.

The consequences of this change from old to new are substantial. They engulf both the eastern and western part of Germany. The new Germany is not an extended old FRG even if it may seem that way. Of course, it is an extension of its constitution, of its bill of rights, of its basic structure, but there, already, one hesitates. We now have sixteen Länder in the upper house, not eleven, of which Berlin was only half a member because of the restraints as a consequence of the four-power agreements. If you have sixteen instead of ten fully operating Länder it is obvious that all the old alliances and the coalitions no longer work. We have to rearrange the power structure. Bavaria is a state that reacted quite nervously to this change in the power structure within Germany. We also have new neighbors. All of Germany, not only the GDR, has Poland as a neighbor. We have to cope with new problems. Traffic and thinking is no longer basically North-South. It is again East-West. To think in East-West terms is new for many people in western Germany. This is one of the reasons why the decision of the German parliament to move the government back to Berlin was met with such irritation and surprise. Suddenly there was an awareness that West Germany was directly involved in the unification process, and that we were not only adding poorer brothers and sisters to our country while continuing business as usual.

Even more important, however, unification means for the new Germany the end of the provisional status of a divided Germany. The provisional status of a divided Germany was a cause for the country to keep a low political profile. Helmut Schmidt is said to have observed a long time ago that West Germany was an economic giant and a political dwarf. Many West Germans preferred this because the country could enjoy its economic strength without being burdened with political responsibility in Europe or elsewhere. When asked to apply its economic strength for political reasons outside the country, West Germany could and did point out that it was a divided country with a damaged national identity because of its terrible misdeeds under the Nazis. Now Germany is suddenly finding itself called on by the United States to form a partnership in leadership. This is quite new for Germany, and it is not really prepared for the kind of responsibilities that leadership entails. Germany *is* nevertheless a major power in the center of Europe. As a consequence, the political center of gravity will move east, which doesn't mean that Brussels will move east but, rather, that we now have to weigh the consequences that our political and economic actions have on Poland, on the republics in the former Soviet Union, on Czechoslovakia, on Hungary, and, of course, on southeastern Europe—namely the Balkans.

All one has to observe is the difficulty organized Europe has with the problem of Yugoslavia to see to what extent the new order is different from the old. The Gulf War and the German position in the Gulf War, and our domestic policy discussion on asylum and immigration are other indications that the country's political agenda has changed. This political agenda, of course, has also changed because of the process of social and economic union within Germany. Economic integration is in the foreground of public attention. The economic integration means the orderly transition from a socialist command economy to a market economy. We are learning by doing. This again has never been done before. In a lot of cases market economies were turned into socialist ones under dictatorships, but we never reversed the process under orderly conditions. We are learning how to do it, and, again, the lessons we are learning will benefit those in the eastern part of Europe, in Poland, Hungary, Czechoslovakia, Ukraine, and other areas.

The transfer to a market economy is a very painful process because many establishments that were previously productive cannot stand up to the test of competition. Of all the enterprises in East Germany, perhaps 40 percent will go out of business. Between 20 and 30 percent will prove capable of surviving without too much public assistance. We don't know about the rest. We will try to reorganize and modernize them so they can become competitive.

About two-thirds of the workers involved in production will lose their jobs. And that is an optimistic estimate. Unemployment, hidden unemployment, in the command society is extremely high. About 92 percent of the employable population in the GDR was employed. Under conditions of high productivity in a competitive industrial democracy, the average employment of the employable population is between 60 and 70 percent. This means, statistically speaking, that between 20 and 25 percent of those who had been employed will lose their jobs and never be employed again. Job opportunities, in other words, will be greatly reduced. The consequences will be felt primarily by women.

In a command society in which political repression permeated all areas of public life, the workplace was an important point of social contact and interaction. Until Eastern Germany's infrastructure has been reconstructed, the people will find it difficult to find new social networks. People live in apartments or houses that are neither adequate nor inviting. Adults usually left their apartments in the morning, took their children to child care or school, and then went to work. They came back in the evening to what they considered a niche of privacy in an otherwise hostile environment.

These structures must change. These changes are at least as painful as losing one's job. The fact that the population in the East is bearing these fundamental changes without any revolt, without filling the streets with fierce demonstrations, is an expression of a very remarkable political strength. I am deeply impressed by the capability of that population to bear change, which could never have been asked of the West German population in the same degree.

Restructuring the economy, however, also entails substantial opportunities. First, we are in the process of restructuring the economy by increasing the service sector. The production sector in the GDR employed almost 60 percent of the working population, almost 15 percent more than the employment in production in West Germany. As we know, in all modern industrial societies employment in production, in the more narrow sense, is decreasing, and employment in the services is increasing. There was, however, hardly a workable service sector in the GDR. There was no sophisticated banking system, there was no insurance, there was very little in terms of craft services. If we only had the same kind of employment, prorata, in East Germany, in Saxony in particular, that we have in the building trades and crafts in West Germany we would employ roughly 300,000 to 350,000 people in Saxony, alone. In the crafts we are now employing fewer than 100,000. Substantial changes in the structure of employment need to take place. But that only can occur if workers are retrained. This is one reason why we have comparatively large retraining and qualification programs for the unemployed as well as for the employed.

One of the devastating consequences of socialist economies is the exploitation of everything that you can exploit. Growth took place in the GDR but at a much slower speed than in the FRG. We are now finding out that real growth, in the sense of increasing wealth and capital stock, ended in the GDR around the middle of the 1970s. The growth that took place after that was fueled and financed by exploitation—by the exploitation of the existing capital stock, the environment and the population. It is depressing to find that the lifespan of a worker in a chemical plant in Bitterfeld, is ten years shorter than his counterpart in a factory like BASF or Bayer or Hoechst. This diminished life expectancy is an expression of the exploitation of humans for production purposes. We have to rebuild the capital stock from scratch. That is true with respect to existing enterprises as well as infrastructure. We have to heal and protect the environment—the damage to which is as yet unmeasurable.

On the other hand, again, crisis always entails opportunity. By overcoming environmental damage we are, at the same time, developing new technologies because the currently available technology cannot resolve the problems. We are thus building up a new industry to overcome environmental damage. This industry will have plenty of work in eastern Germany. Unfortunately, it will also have plenty of work throughout Eastern Europe for decades to come.

East Germany and West Germany can grow together only if the states in the former eastern Germany can supply workable administrations to help investors locate partners. Through this process, transfer payments will be supplied from west to east and human transfer will also take place from west to east. Both, of course, are a drain on West Germany. We are now entering a very intensive debate on how medium and long range both transfers should be.

In the first year of unification we had to improvise. One of the consequences of this was that most of the transfer payments from West to East were financed by budget credits. There were also impromptu and improvised temporary transfers of civil servants from West to East. We are now making the adjustment from improvising to permanence—permanence means we will need transfers for a long time to come. The budget of the Free State of Saxony is approximately DM 26 million, of which 27 percent is earmarked for investment. Twenty percent of this budget is paid for by taxes accruing in Saxony, 17 percent by credit, and the rest by transfer payments. The transfer payments will go down, but they will not go down to zero before the end of this decade. Thus we have to incorporate these transfer payments in the all-German financial structure—an extremely difficult proposition even though West Germany has one of the strongest economies in the world.

Why is it difficult? Because in West Germany the gross national product is divided within West Germany, and everybody has a part of it. The participation in the GNP is secured by political and economic vested interests, by coalitions and other structures, and, of course, in many cases, by law. If you introduce into such a balanced situation of social benefits and economic opportunities that are expected to increase with growth, you disturb the balance. It's like a mobile that you suddenly disturb by hooking a new weight onto one part. The entire structure becomes unbalanced.

The rebalancing of this entire structure is a formidable political task because all of the vested interests want to maintain their position. A shakeup of the political structures and vested interests is an inevitable product of internal unification. But perhaps this is one of the most welcome consequences of German unification. If we do it well, it will present an opportunity to modernize all of Germany. We will find different ways to do things that West German vested interests would not permit us to do in the past—reorganizing the transportation system; employing private enterprise and private investors in the provision of public works; and having private investors plan Autobahns and railroad systems and tunnels and develop communications systems.

Modernization will also extend to the political arena. East German political parties do not follow the kind of confrontation rituals that their western cousins have developed in order to maintain their identities. The roundtable culture that developed in the process of the peaceful revolution has been maintained, and we do not mind voting across party lines in the East German parliament, even though this is considered the devil's work in West German Länder parliaments.

What does this new Germany mean for our neighbors in the new Europe? One thing is certain, as I mentioned before, the West German federal system has assumed a broader character through the addition of five new states. On the state level, we are very interested not only in maintaining this federal system but also in using it as a solution for European problems. To give you an example: the State of Saxony, the Czech Republic and Poland are considering, with the support of the European Union, forming what we call a "Euro Region," including Upper Bohemia, Saxony, and Upper Silesia, to jointly develop these traditional industrial areas. Both Upper Bohemia and Saxony are very highly developed industrial areas and were considered among the richest industrial areas in Europe after World War I. Much of this industrial and cultural tradition still exists, and once we have cleared away the rubble, in Saxony we would say "the silver will shine through again." By working together with these other regions in Czechoslovakia and Poland, we can begin to prepare them for eventual entry into the European Union. We can also begin to cooperate across national borders in areas including the environment, reconstruction of production facilities, and the building of roads and transportation systems. We have set up commissions to work on this and we will receive support from both the federal German government and the European Commission.

German Länder are not permitted to enter into treaties crossing national borders, so we do not call these arrangements treaties. We call them agreements. We do all kinds of things in this connection on an informal but very effective basis, and other Länder in Germany are joining us.

North Rhine–Westphalia recently entered into an agreement with Czechoslovakia on the exchange of scientists and information on the cultural level. We are trying to establish schools of higher learning at which we teach Germans, Czechs, and Poles in order to make sure that the younger generation learns to cooperate, learns the other side's language, and receives training in technical arts and sciences and business administration and economics. When it comes to joining the European Union, these countries will have already been exposed to competitive processes within Europe.

The larger consequences of these integrating processes are, first, after the disappearance of the bipolar structure, which in both pacts led to a high degree of centralization, we are now setting free forces of decentralization. This is true both in the East and in the West. This means that the regions integrated into the bloc system are now demanding more autonomy and more independence and are beginning, if not to fractionalize, at least to regionalize Europe. This process of regionalization is very strong in Eastern Europe because the pressures to centralize were very high. We see it in Yugoslavia in a very unhappy way. We see it in the former Soviet Union; we see it elsewhere. This regionalization will be a very important element of future European development. It is interesting that all regions do not look at the former nation-state as a platform of cooperation and economic integration, but rather to the European Union. This is true not only for the Baltic states and Ukraine but also for all of the regions in Eastern Europe. Also in the West we are beginning to have a revitalization of the regionalization drive. The Basques are asking for autonomy, the Catalans are asking for autonomy. We have a new dimension of debate even within certain regions of France, Italy, Southern Tirol, and others. Europe has never been very tranquil. It is again awakening to its old liveliness, and I hope we have developed the institutional prerequisites to manage this complexity in the years to come. This, by the way, will be one of the most important security aspects of the new development.

Our old security setup was built on a very tidy bipolar structure. It was a clear situation and there was little complexity. After the elimination of the bipolar structure, the security objective changed. While the old security objective of NATO and the Atlantic Alliance was to maintain the status quo in Europe and thus secure peace and stability, the new objective is to manage rapid change and the increased complexity of Eastern Europe. We still have to learn to do this. Some of the problems we have right now in western Europe have very much to do with this process in Eastern Europe. For instance, it is difficult for France, Great Britain and Spain to accept regional autonomy because of their fear of repercussions in their own territories, in their own areas of jurisdiction. Thus, the dispute on how to handle events in Yugoslavia. It is also beginning to show that France, Great Britain, Spain, and to a lesser extent Italy are willing to accept regional autonomy if not to grant independence. We will have to learn how to manage these processes. The new threat to security in Europe is no longer nuclear arms or marching armies, but chaos and a lack of understanding of how to manage complexity, especially in the former Soviet Union.

The most important and most immediate security risk is the large-scale movement of people from the East to the West in order to avoid the dangers of hunger and deprivation. It is of urgent importance, therefore, that we assist Eastern Europe and the republics of the former Soviet Union in managing the complexity that has been created through the "big bang," as it was recently called, of the failed coup and the resulting centrifugal forces. We have to provide not only money, but also know-how. Here the East German states can make a very important contribution. Hundreds and hundreds of eastern inhabitants are specialized workers, engineers, managers, and organizers who speak Russian and have a lot of experience with the former Soviet Union. I have suggested to my colleagues in the eastern German states that we tap these resources to provide help and assistance to Eastern Europe and the former Soviet Union, in cooperation, of course, with western Europe and the United States because the task is tremendous. If we do not involve ourselves to the greatest extent possible, we will risk very substantial political and economic costs. After the coup had just failed, we met with the Polish minister of interior and he told us that, according to government estimates, had the coup not failed, 2 to 4 million people would have left the former Soviet Union to come West. This would engulf all of Europe in chaos and instability.

These are the new challenges. We are finding that as you solve one problem, you create a new one. Thus there will always be a contingency of problems to be solved. But one thing we can say: we are now solving these problems under conditions of freedom. We are solving them as open societies, willing and eager to rejoin Europe and to learn from experience how to build structures that will enable us to manage complexity and plurality without losing the unity of a common European culture. At the center of these developments, Germany will try to balance its own federal structures that are imbedded in many relationships crossing national borders, not only to make sure that recentralization in Germany is impossible, but, in a positive vein, to make sure that by transgressing national borders we help in reducing the importance of the nation-state and open the way to a politically united Europe.

14

Pan-European Policy After the End of the East-West Conflict: German Foreign Policy Needs New Concepts

Karsten D. Voigt

West German foreign policy from 1949 to 1989 rested on one pillar: the firm inclusion in the free societies of the West, namely the European Community and the Atlantic Alliance. On this basis, in 1969, the Social Democratic chancellors initiated *Ostpolitik*, i.e., the politics of pan-European and of course "Pan-German" orientation, with the ultimate aim of overcoming European and German divisions. The treaties with our eastern neighbors and the Conference on Security and Cooperation in Europe (CSCE) process were most visible expressions of this policy. (The CSCE process is defined as a multilateral diplomatic forum involving 53 states across Europe and North America. CSCE negotiations focus on military security, economic cooperation and human rights.)

In the 1970s, these treaties and the CSCE process were instituted against the heavy opposition of the conservatives in Germany. In the 1980s, however, conservatives came to see that both elements of West German foreign policy belonged together and that each had its role to play with regard to the imminent fundamental changes in Eastern Europe and the Soviet Union.

There can be no doubt: at the end of the 1980s we witnessed a broad consensus over the fundamental questions of foreign policy within West Germany. This consensus was an essential condition for the great suc-

Speech given at the Robert Bosch Alumni Association Annual Meeting, San Francisco, California.

cesses of foreign policy in the years 1989 and 1990 and especially for the end of German partition.

Lack of Orientation After Unity

Since unification German foreign policy has appeared disoriented. A few catchwords to illustrate this may suffice: the Gulf War; attempted coup in the Soviet Union; Yugoslavia.

As for security policy, in the eyes of NATO mistakes have been made. The main catchwords: Franco-German Corps; "out-of-area" missions of the West European Union; and inflation of "intervention troops" without a clear concept of how they should interact.

Continuity and Change

We need a sober assessment of the new framework of conditions for foreign policy and a precise answer to the question: how much continuity and how much change; that is, how much conceptual renewal does German foreign policy need?

Despite the burdens brought by unification, the overall weight of the Federal Republic of Germany has increased in the international arena. This has brought with it not only new expectations, but also old anxieties about our neighbors, friends, and partners.

Likewise, the international environment has changed radically. The bipolar world order of yesterday has made way for the multipolar world of today. Great chances and great risks lie together closely. Two fundamental yet, contradictory trends are of particular importance.

Given the political, economic, technological and ecological challenges, that face us, international cooperation and supranational integration (including long-term visions of a "world government" in the framework of the United Nations) are of ever increasing relevance.

Yet political disintegration is becoming pronounced. This is marked by the deepening rift between North and South; by the danger of protectionism between the continents; by increasing ethnic and religious conflicts throughout Africa, Asia, and Eastern Europe; and, of course, by the emergence of new states after the end of the Soviet empire. Disintegration frequently continues on a subnational level—armies are out of control, organized crime takes over. In this situation everything calls for continuity in the basic orientation of German foreign policy.

This means above all, that we continue the policy of cooperation and integration, i.e. multilateralism, as members of the European Union, the Atlantic Alliance, the CSCE and the United Nations. On this basis, however, we need a conceptual renewal. For the area of pan-European policy, the renewal should be along the following lines.

Elements of a New Foreign Policy

There is no doubt that in a first phase of pan-European policy following the end of the East-West conflict, it was correct to attempt to use all the proved and tested institutions, either as indirect stabilizers or, as in the case of the CSCE, as a "catching frame" for the disintegrating parts of the Soviet empire. These institutions have thus been reshaped "in full flight" for new purposes. Eastern Europe and many of the former republics of the former Soviet Union are connected with the West with some success through the CSCE, the North Atlantic Cooperation Council (NACC), and the special treaties of the European Community (EC, now formally known as the European Union, or EU). For a certain time we will have to live with a certain amount of institutional pluralism or even institutional competition.

As Europe grows together "whole and free," however, it is not enough to interpret continuity on an institutional basis, in the sense of "EC, NATO, and CSCE forever." There can be no doubt that in the second phase of pan-European policy, after the end of the East-West conflict, which is now beginning, we have the duty to narrow our focus and to keep realities and wishful thinking more clearly apart.

This goes, first, for our own country, where increasing public debt leaves increasingly less room for an active foreign policy. We are forced to set priorities. Priorities are set right if, for example, in the case of agricultural protectionism, we make the GATT negotiations a success and if we consider the legitimate requests of Eastern Europe in the area of market access. As Americans say epigrammatically: "Trade beats aid."

Realism is needed not only with regard to our own country, but also with regard to Eastern Europe and in the CIS (Commonwealth of Independent States). It would be a terrible mistake if we took the signature of CSCE obligations as a guaranty for pluralistic democracy, for effective renunciation of force, and for human and minority rights. The great war between East and West is eliminated as a risk. But more wars are raging in Europe now than in the past forty years. Therefore, as important as it may be to have foreign policy visions, it is also necessary to focus on this sobering reality. Visions can become reality only when economic crises and national and border conflicts are analyzed more realistically as threats to a stable and democratic development.

We therefore need a foreign policy, which combines realism and responsibility and concentrates on the following essentials:

One: The creation of the European Union (EU) first with the countries of the European Free Trade Area (EFTA) and as soon as economically possible with the central and east European countries. Only with a strong European Union can political and economic stability in Europe and the world be achieved and secured. European integration will go down a dead end street, however, if it is not connected with a fundamental democratization of the EC and if the EC does not become more transparent and closer to the individual citizens.

Two: The prevention of a new "continental drift" between Europe and North America. We have to change the transatlantic relationship from its mainly military orientation to a new, broad basis that focuses more than before on cultural and economic shared values and interests.

Three: The economic and social stabilization of central, eastern, and southeastern Europe and the CIS. We need to talk about Western markets and Western aid. But what we need even more is a clear, transparent coordination of bi- and multilateral aid, especially with regard to the CIS countries. Fair burden sharing is also indispensable. For this we need close cooperation not only within the EC but also with North America.

Four: In the interest of all the people who are directly or indirectly affected by wars and civil wars, the CSCE should concentrate on protecting human and minority rights and security in the more narrow sense. Member states should follow the direction taken at the CSCE summit in Helsinki in July 1992 and try to build the CSCE as a "small United Nations" with the ultimate aim of developing a collective security system.

This would extend first to the central competencies of the CSCE in the areas of disarmament, security partnership, and comprehensive conflict prevention. It would then extend to the necessary network with other regional security systems. Finally, it would extend to:

- Nonmilitary sanctions "within," if CSCE-norms are violated;
- Peacekeeping forces; and
- Defense with regard to aggression by third parties without automatic assistance.

While it is important to begin to move toward this framework, it must, nonetheless, be understood that during this transition period, and within the foreseeable future, such a CSCE cannot replace NATO.

15

The Need for Civil Courage

Yilmaz Karahasan

Three reports recently appeared in one of Germany's biggest daily newspapers, the *Frankfurter Rundschau*, on 31 August 1993: (1) "During the weekend unknown persons pasted right-wing posters on two primary schools in Frankfurt-Oder. The local police reported that the posters bore titles such as "Stop the Foreigner and Asylum Invasion," and "Germany for Germans"; (2) "The Jewish cemetery in Worms was desecrated by unknown persons. According to a police report, more than one hundred tombstones were sprayed with swastikas"; (3) "On Monday night, suspected right-wing activists set fire to a house in Idar-Oberstein. Slogans hostile to foreigners had been painted on the door and one of the walls."

Such incidents are certainly worth mention in the newspaper but have become customary and normal. According to official figures, the number of criminal acts against foreigners more than doubled in the first six months of 1993. From January until the end of June 1993 the Federal Office for Criminal Matters registered 3,365 criminal acts involving hostility to foreigners; in the same time period in 1992 there were 1,443 acts—an increase of more than 130 percent.

We must ask: what is the source of this hate and violence against human beings of a different background or skin color? What goals do the right-wingers serve? Who is interested in inciting Germans and non-Germans against each other? Why do right-wing slogans have such a positive reception among so many people? Above all else, what can we do as

Abbreviated version of a speech delivered in German to the Eighth Annual Conference of the Robert Bosch Alumni Association, 18 September 1993 in Washington, D.C.

human beings, in accordance with the ideas of humanity, democracy, and tolerance, do in order that human beings, whether homosexual, incapacitated, Christians, Jews, or non-Germans can live and work together in peace?

In the attempt to find answers for the rightward drift in the German and other European societies, we cannot, in my opinion, look to one-dimensional explanations. We are dealing with a very complex, and partially contradictory phenomena, and it requires a differentiated, yet still comprehensive, approach.

A comprehensive analysis, of course, exceeds the scope of this speech. Nevertheless I would like to concentrate on a few points that appear to me to be central in this context. They are the deracination of a risk-oriented society, globalization of problems, politics oriented to populism and based on right-wing notions of society

•

In the philosophy of social Darwinism, the battle of peoples for survival is a legitimate phenomenon. An example of this kind of thinking, according to which competition assigns each group of people its proper place, was provided recently by a study of young laborers in the south of Germany, which concluded that "the new national consciousness appeals to the solidity of the D-Mark and performance in international competition." The emphasis on competition and success represses other social goals. Many young workers appear to identify themselves as representatives of the products they produce.

The "New Right," colored by a chauvinism based on affluence, is capable of perpetrating distinctions in this way. In the words of one young professional affected by these trends: "My normal way of thinking tells me that I should act in order to achieve profit. But our government acts in such a way as to cause financial losses. A refugee doesn't add anything, he only imposes costs on us."

According to this perspective, the guest worker—the labor immigrant—has a legitimate place in a functioning society of affluence as a modern-day coolie.

•

The centers of the world community consist of highly developed market economies. The globalization of markets for capital, goods and labor, and the presence of corresponding international institutions—the World Bank, IMF, G-7 and GATT evidences this.

A comprehensive report of the UNDP, the development agency of the UN, recently reported that one-quarter of humanity (the rich North) consumes sixty percent of the available food; a quarter of humanity (the rich North) causes three-quarters of all global ecological damage; and for every dollar of development aid provided by the North to the South, 3.5 times that amount is returned in the form of interest payments on debt, and unjustifiable prices for raw materials.

Migration caused by poverty reflects a world becoming more chaotic. It cannot be ignored that the colonially conditioned structures of exploitation continue in effect, and that the causes of the North-South conflict lie in the rich North, the center of the international fabric of society. Right-wing politics react to these global transformations.

This type of thinking does not arise out of a vacuum. It is much more a case that this thinking is an element of normal social consciousness. The perpetrators of violence against foreigners consider themselves accordingly as "executors of the people's will."

Populism on the Right

For more than ten years, Germany has been ruled by a CDU-FDP coalition with a neoconservative, economically liberal orientation. Its *Wende-politik* (policy of change), resulting in the massive transformation of the social welfare state into a pure entrepreneurial state, has been characterized by a policy of massive redistribution from the have-nots to the haves, and the reduction of workers' rights. As a result, on 1 January 1994 the top corporate income tax rate will be reduced from fifty three percent to forty seven percent, the rate for retained corporate earnings will be reduced from fifty percent to forty five percent, and for distributed earnings it is reduced from thirty six percent to thirty percent.

This amounts to policies based on the principle that the state should withdraw from social responsibility and from securing employment, and it should only serve to protect the interests of capital. In other words, this means that the most important factors are the optimal use of resources, and guaranteed high profits, even in times of crisis. This has very little to do with rationality, and much to do with the interests of industrialists. Protection of the rich does not result in economic growth.

In particular, the situation of the eastern part of the FRG has intensified so much that the people living there experience a "risk-oriented society" as a society of shocking riskiness. A self-proclaimed right-wing radical described it poignantly: "The great problem for young people at present in eastern Germany is unemployment that is rapidly increasing. And in addition, we know so little of what to do with free time, which we have a lot of ... young people are dissatisfied and must release their frustration."

One should not overlook the moral and spiritual changes that occurred in the early 1980s with the advent of the Kohl government. The taboo against right-wing government policies was shattered by the general attitude toward history that encourages its uncritical sanitization instead of critical engagement. An example of this uncritical approach toward history is the claim that Germans cannot always be "forced to confront" Auschwitz. In addition, the debate about asylum has shown how closely prevailing political thought approaches right-wing extremism. It bears remembering that the fathers and mothers of the Basic Law, as a result of the experience of Hitler's fascism, provided in the constitution that: "Politically persecuted persons are entitled to asylum." Furthermore, almost a million Germans found safe haven abroad during the Third Reich. For several years now, an increasingly negative discussion has surrounded this exemplary provision. Through slogans such as "refuge-seeking imposters" and "economic refugees," complicated circumstances are reduced to mere political symbols with ethnic overtones. These symbols and ways of thinking are current not only with right-wing extremists and neofascists.

Recently the right to asylum in Germany has been limited by a policy of sealing off and walling off to such an extent that the reasons and motives for immigration are no longer in the foreground of the debate. Instead, the focus is on how refugees enter the country. The so-called third-state solution—namely, that if refugees come to Germany through a safe intermediate country they are denied asylum in Germany—has been revealed as a mere pretense for massive deportations. A Fortress Europe in this sense will preserve neither its dedication to the rule of law nor protect its prosperity. This poisonous language has penetrated social and political opinion and has assumed political incarnations. In this sense, the political parties must answer for the fact that their slogans have unleashed criminal and anti-social energies.

That our concept of politics, and also our concept of parliamentary democracy, has become fragile and imperiled by a tendency to fragmentation, is also apparent from the fact that those who do not vote is the largest group of "voters" among young people.

•

As a result of the fact that 22 people have been murdered by right-wing extremists since 1992, disgust, sorrow, resignation, angst and anger has spread among non-German citizens in Germany, particularly among those with Turkish nationality. There have been an increasing number of incidents in factories involving racist and Nazi graffiti. "Turks Out," framed with swastikas and slogans of incitement are the most harmless of these. Several years ago in Hoechst AG there was an incident in which a homemade poster was placed on a factory door, showing the head of a

Turkish worker with the caption: "Wanted: 3000 DM reward if living, 5000 DM reward if dead; dead or living, better dead." A particularly shocking representative example.

Jasemine, a twenty-year old citizen of Frankfurt with a Turkish passport, dreams of a "land in which all people can live who don't know where they really belong—an island, at best." The so-called foreign workers have become, since they stopped arriving in 1973, an essential part of the economy of the FRG. Almost two-thirds of them have lived in the FRG ten years or longer and more than two-thirds of "foreign" children and young people were born in the FRG. People from more than thirty-three different nationalities labor in the Opel car factory in Bochum, and a good quarter of the 19,000 employees there do not have a German passport. Things are, for the most part, harder and more demanding for these non-Germans. Only 50 percent of the households of non-Germans have a bath, a toilet or central heating. In the words of one Turkish girl: "If I stay a while in Turkey on vacation I become homesick because I grew up in Germany, and I feel more strongly drawn to Germany. My home is more Germany than Turkey."

Let us remember: after the Second World War, the economic reconstruction of Germany required labor. The first agreements governing applications for employment was made in 1955 with Italy, in 1960 with Spain and Greece, and in 1961 with Turkey. Others have followed. Shortly thereafter several hundred thousand workers came from Italy, Spain, Greece, Portugal and Turkey to the FRG. They were greeted with trumpets and drums; the millionth worker, from Portugal, received media attention, and a moped.

I recall, in this connection, John Kennedy in the 1960s in Berlin stating "I am a Berliner" and the entire German population cheered. After thirty years I say I am a Frankfurter [a citizen of Frankfurt] and no one notices.

Particularly in the area of employment are the disadvantages of non-Germans evident. They render above-average performance, under conditions of irregular working hours and subject to great demands, health risks, poisonous materials, noise and heavy manual labor. In the event of rationalizations, layoffs are focussed on non-German employees. They are seen as—consciously or unconsciously—as a group that doesn't belong here, who had a limited time period to earn money and now can return home. Every seventh non-German worker is unemployed. Article 1 of the Basic Law states: "The dignity of human beings shall be inviolable. Its respect and protection is the responsibility of state power." Our dignity is however trod upon daily in a million ways.

When it comes to economic production we—non-German citizens— are equal. When it comes to financing the social safety net and the public budget we are not subject to discrimination. We are not excluded from paying our part of the costs of German unity. That is properly so!

What is improper and undemocratic is when we are not allowed to participate in decisions about what happens with the economic benefits of our society; what tax revenues are spent for, and how our common future must be shaped. To be sure, the earnest professions of the responsible politicians about democracy and human dignity are worthless when the political rights of citizens who are a part of this society are withheld.

This brings me to the closing part of my comments—the consequences for a courageous shaping of politics and society.

Civil Courage Is Necessary

Those who live in a civil society have a role in determining its political culture. Decisive opposition against discrimination already has been expressed in many ways: large rock concerts against right-wing extremism, mass demonstrations, moments of silence in factories, and chains of light in which six million people have participated.

It must be our task, however, to make the concept of courage a continual process of opposition. Therefore IG Metall, together with human rights groups and the anti-racism movement have initiated a "Courage" project.

By wearing a button, the personal commitment of wearer is demonstrated: to respond to statements hostile to foreigners, to intervene when foreigners are threatened, regardless whether in the street, the bus, subway or workplace, and to offer or seek help in the event of attacks on the street.

The commitment of courage means the distribution of warning whistles to people who live near refugee housing in order to create a kind of warning system, so that "neighbors protect neighbors." Or to form "courage-groups" who trace racism in its environs, and publicize the names of public establishments that discriminate against foreigners.

Courageous engagement is insufficient alone, but must be coupled with a politics of courage. That means we need a different politics that does justice to the shaping of a multicultural society and promotes social justice. We also need a humane asylum policy and progressive immigration law. Immigration policy must be reformulated. This has long been ignored by the dominant political forces, even though the federal states have long suffered the consequences. Also it is necessary to provide for equal rights for all six million non-Germans through anti-discrimination laws and participation in democratic decision-making through the right to vote. We also need a new law of citizenship that permits dual citizenship. The definition of society should no longer be oriented to a "folk-based" ideology. It is necessary to have an employment policy that finances work and unemployment. It is also necessary to have perspectives, especially for young people, that secure a right to the future, meaning education, social security, and meaningful use of leisure time.

A politics of courage also means that state institutions finally do justice to their constitutional responsibilities and apply the laws in a consistent way in order to clarify the limits of social tolerance on the one hand and to impede the activities of neofaschist organizations.

It is a scandal that those right-wing extremists parties, that are not legally prohibited and can participate in elections and receive subsidies from tax revenues for election expenses. For example, the "Republikaner" received 16 million marks in last elections for the European Parliament.

Also in factories we, the unions, must bring the concept of courage to bear on day-to-day matters. There is a Works Constitution Law (Betriebsverfassunggesetz) that requires action against discrimination in labor relations. This involves more than simply placing a sign on a bulletin board; it is much more a matter of finding a way to address the problem by prompting those affected to think about the problem.

Solidarity is necessary in order to deal with the anxiety of non-German compatriots of being threatened. For example, fellow steel workers at the Hoesch factory in Dortmund organized a "telephone chain" in order to be able to react in case of emergency.

It is also important to make multiculturalism a normal daily experience in the factory. At the VW factory in Wolfsburg an educational project was commissioned and carried out in which a memorial object was constructed with technical knowledge of metal and welding and industrial materials. It was unveiled on 21 March 1993, the UN Day Against Racism. Involvement in tariff negotiations, evaluation of work conditions, and further worker education and development are important parts of the work of a union. Some discrimination can be ameliorated through focused group actions combined with appropriate educational measures for non-German colleagues.

On the social level, an institutionalized process of integration and anti-racist action is necessary. The creation of "Round Table" involving concerned groups—refugee, anti-racist groups, churches, unions and sport association can assist in this process. There must be a process of historical enlightenment in which memorial sites and the confrontation with the past are given a heightened priority in school history classes. An element of a progressive perspective is the securing of the fundamental democratic consensus.

In 1994, we in Germany are confronted with a great challenge. Elections will take place for practically all state parliaments, the federal parliament and the European Parliament. In concrete terms, we must hinder a wide-spread entry of right-wing groups into these bodies.

The historical recollection of fascist terror, persecution and murders of millions of persons—not only in Germany—the fascist war of aggression must make us vigilant. Therefore the question arises whether the contemporary situation is comparable with those times of the fascist seizure of power and terror. I think not. The Weimar Republic was destroyed because there were too few democrats who struggled, and too many people who looked the other way.

In this sense I want to close with words from Martin Luther King:

In every social revolution of triumph and we are favored with a sense of fulfillment, and other times in which the strong winds of disappointment and setbacks blow in our faces. We must not, during this trip across the powerful ocean of life, allow ourselves to be overcome by the unfavorable winds. We must, in spite of the winds, be borne along by the energies and engines of our courage.

—M.L. King in his last speech to his assistants in November 1967

About the Contributors

Sylvia Becker graduated from the Georgetown University Joint Degree Program in Law and International Affairs (JD/MSFS) in 1987. She currently practices law at the Washington, D.C. office of Kaye, Scholer, Fierman, Hays & Handler. As a fellow in the Robert Bosch Foundation Fellowship Program (1990–1991), she worked at the German Foreign Ministry and the Munich court system.

Kurt Biedenkopf has been the minister-president of the Free State of Saxony since 27 October 1990. Saxony is the largest and most populous of the five federal states that replaced East Germany after unification.

Frederick R. Fucci is a graduate of Amherst College in Massachusetts (B.A. 1981 *cum laude* in European Studies) and the University of Paris IV–Sorbonne. His graduate education consisted of a joint Juris Doctor/M.A. degree in 1987 from Georgetown University Law Center and Paul H. Nitze School of Advanced International Studies (SAIS) of The Johns Hopkins University. His professional experience has included a position as a research associate at the International Law Institute in Washington, D.C., and, since 1988, as an associate attorney at the law firm of Reid & Priest in New York. As a Robert Bosch Fellow, he worked in the Eastern Economic Policy division at the Bundesverband der deutschen Industrie (the German Federation of Industries) and at the Treuhandanstalt, the German privatization agency, where he was an adviser to the department responsible for foreign investment in the eastern part of Germany.

Thomas A. Hagemann, a Robert Bosch Fellow in 1991–1992, and is currently a partner in the Houston law firm of Mayor, Day, Caldwell & Keeton. He is a 1978 *magna cum laude* graduate from Rice University and earned his law degree from Yale Law School in 1982. From 1985 to 1991 Mr. Hagemann was an Assistant United States Attorney in Los Angeles, California. He has also been an adjunct professor at both the University of Southern California and University of Houston law schools, and is a frequent contributor of legal articles, book reviews, and opinion pieces to various periodicals.

Mark J. Jrolf was a Robert Bosch Fellow in 1992–1993 and served internships in the Federal Ministry of Economics in Bonn, and the State of Brandenburg Ministry of Economics in Potsdam. In Potsdam Jrolf focused on the role of the state in privatization and economic development in the new federal states with particular emphasis on the region surrounding Eisenhüttenstadt. He received a B.S. in Finance from Babson College in 1986 and an M.S. in Management from the MIT Sloan School of Management in 1992. Jrolf is currently a management consultant with McKinsey & Co. in Washington, D.C.

Yilmaz Karahasan is a member of the Management Board of IG Metall, one of the largest trade unions in Germany.

Ingrid L. Lenhardt received her B.S. in accounting with highest distinction from Indiana University and passed the Illinois Certified Public Accountant examination in 1982. In 1986 she received her J.D. degree from Northwestern University. She has been a recipient of a DAAD fellowship in 1982–1983 at the Technische Universität in Berlin and a Fulbright fellowship in 1986–1987 at Kiel Universität, where she was awarded an LL.M. degree. As a Robert Bosch Fellow in 1990–1991 she was with the Federal High Court of Justice, Deutsche Gesellschaft für Mittelstandsberatung and Lufthansa legal department. She was the foreign resident counsel with Heuking Kühn Kunz Wojtek in Dusseldorf from 1993 to 1994 and has been a lecturer at the Rheinische Friedrichs-Wilhelms-Universität Bonn since 1991, where she is pursuing her Ph.D. in comparative legal studies.

Colette Mazzucelli is completing her Ph.D. in government at Georgetown University. In 1987 she received an M.A. in law and diplomacy from the Fletcher School of Law and Diplomacy. As a Robert Bosch Fellow, 1992–1993, Mazzucelli worked on the ratification process of the Treaty on European Union. She is currently a research associate of The Jean Monnet Council at George Washington University's Elliott School of International Affairs.

Angela Kurtz Mendelson is a Ph.D. candidate in modern European history at the University of Maryland. She has worked as a lecturer on East German literature and history at Georgetown University's School for Summer and Continuing Education; as a staff aide in the offices of the premier of Brandenburg and a deputy leader of the Social Democratic Party in the German parliament, and as a government relations representative for a private corporation. She has degrees in European studies and international relations from Georgetown University and The Johns Hopkins University School of Advanced International Studies (SAIS), respectively.

Adam S. Posen is the 1993–1994 Arthur M. Okun Memorial fellow in Economic studies at the Brookings Institution; he received his Ph.D. in political economy and government from Harvard University in 1994, and was a National Science Foundation graduate fellow there from 1989–1992. As a Robert Bosch Fellow, Mr. Posen had internships at the Deutsche Bundesbank at Deutsche Bank. He graduated *magna cum laude* and Phi Beta Kappa in Government from Harvard College in June 1988. He will begin work in the Research Department of the Federal Reserve Bank of New York in late 1994.

Lauren Stone is associate director of the Foundation for a Civil Society (formerly the Charter 77 Foundation–New York). She worked for the U.S. Information Agency from 1980 to 1992, serving as the assistant cultural attaché in the U.S. Embassy in East Germany from 1990 to 1991. Ms. Stone is a former arts administrator, lighting designer, and state manager from the San Francisco Bay Area.

Karsten D. Voigt has served as a member of the Bundestag since 1976. He serves as the Social Democratic Party's (SPD) spokesperson for foreign policy and is a member of the Committee on Foreign Relations, as well as a member of the Executive Committee of the SPD's Parliamentary Group. Outside of the Bundestag, Mr. Voigt serves as vice president of the North Atlantic Assembly, where he is chair of the Committee on Defense and Security, and as a member of the Executive Committee of the Union of Social Democratic parties of the European Union. Mr. Voigt has been a member of the SPD since 1962.

Christopher S. Visick is a lawyer with the New York office of the law firm of Jones, Day, Reavis & Pogue practicing in the general corporate area. He was a 1991–1992 Robert Bosch Foundation Fellow.

Bradden Weaver is a graduate of the College of William and Mary and the Yale University Center for International and Area Studies. Between college and graduate school he served on both Senate and House staffs. In addition to his time in Germany spent with the Robert Bosch Foundation, he studied at the Muenster Universität on a Rotary International scholarship and interned in the office of Bundestag Deputy Matthais Wissmann on a fellowship from the German Emigree Foundation. He is a doctoral candidate and teaching fellow at the Yale University political science department.

Michael Zumwinkle is employed as a migration policy officer in the Bureau for Refugee programs at the United States Department of State. Zumwinkle joined the Department of State in July 1990 as a presidential management intern, following completion of an M.A. degree in Public Affairs from the Hubert H. Humphrey Institute at the University of Minnesota. He graduated with a B.A. degree in government from St. John's University in Collegeville, Minnesota in 1986. In 1992–1993, Zumwinkle was a Robert Bosch Fellow, and worked at the German Chamber of Commerce and Industry in Bonn and BASF AG in Ludwigshafen and Schwarzheide.

About the Book and Editors

German unification has proven to be a complex, multidimensional process rather than a single political event. Four years after political unification, Germany continues to confront formidable economic, social, and cultural challenges in the unification process. This volume examines some of economic, social and legal aspects of the unification process four years after political unification was achieved.

A. Bradley Shingleton received his J.D. in 1982 from Duke University School of Law and was a recipient of a DAAD Fellowship in 1979–1980 at the Phillipps-Universität in Marburg, Germany. As a 1986–1987 Robert Bosch Fellow, he served at the Federal Ministry of Justice in Bonn and in the Legal Department of Robert Bosch GmbH in Stuttgart. He has published several articles on legal topics in German and in English as well as a chapter in *Germany Through American Eyes* (Westview 1989). He was coeditor of *Germany at the Crossroads* (Westview 1992). He is an attorney in private practice in Washington, D.C.

Marian J. Gibbon received her M.A. in international relations from the Johns Hopkins University School of Advanced International Studies (SAIS) and her B.A. in economics, *summa cum laude* and Phi Beta Kappa from Macalester College. She is presently a Manager in Ernst & Young's International Finance Services group, where she provides financial, strategic planning, and privatization advisory services to diverse corporate and government clients in Russia and the CIS. As a Robert Bosch Fellow from 1991 to 1992, she worked in the European Community division of the Federal Ministry of Economics and for the Leipzig branch of the Treuhandanstalt. Prior to the Bosch Fellowship, Ms. Gibbon worked for two years with Ernst & Young's International Development Group, where she focused on private sector development projects in Africa, Asia, and Eastern Europe.

Kathryn S. Mack is director of the Face-to-Face program at the Carnegie Endowment of International Peace. She is also a senior associate at the Endowment, concentrating on public international law and Asian trade issues. She was recently awarded a Council on Foreign Relations fellowship to work on Asian trade issues for 1994–1995. Before joining the Endowment, she was a corporate attorney with White & Case in Washington, D.C., where she specialized in international transactions and international trade. Ms. Mack received a J.D. degree from Yale Law School in 1985. After graduation, she served as a law clerk to the Honorable Edward C. King, Chief Justice of the Supreme Court of the Federated States of Micronesia. As a Robert Bosch Fellow in 1986, Mack worked in Bonn, Germany, in the Federal Ministry of Intra-German Relations, and in Berlin in the Economics Ministry studying legal and economic relations between the two Germanies.

Appendix A:
Chronology of German Unification

December 1943	Tehran Conference
February 1945	Yalta Conference
7–8 May 1945	German unconditional surrender
5 June 1945	Allied Control Council: Berlin divided into four sectors; Germany divided into four zones of occupation
July–August 1945	Potsdam Conference
January 1947	"Bi-Zone" created by merger of American and British zones
1948–1949	Berlin blockade
23 May 1949	FRG founded
6 October 1949	GDR founded
25 July 1952	Entry into force of the Treaty of Paris establishing the European Coal and Steel Community
17 June 1953	GDR Uprising
23 October 1954	NATO admits FRG to membership
May 1955	Warsaw Pact established, including GDR
1 January 1958	Entry into force of the Treaty of Rome establishing the European Economic Community
13 August 1961	Berlin Wall erected
1970	Treaties by FRG with Moscow and Warsaw
1971	Quadripartite Agreement on Berlin
1972	FRG-GDR Treaty on the Basis of Relations
1 July 1987	Entry into force of the Single European Act on completion of the internal market
Summer–Fall 1989	Exodus of GDR citizens via Hungary (also via embassies in Poland and Czechoslovakia)
7 and 9 October 1989	GDR public demonstrations against SED government in Berlin and Leipzig ("Monday demonstration")
9 November 1989	Berlin Wall breached
28 November 1989	Chancellor Kohl lays out ten-point program to

	overcome the division of Germany and Europe
18 March 1990	First free elections in GDR
5 May 1990	"Two plus Four" talks begin; foreign ministers of Great Britain, France, U.S., USSR, FRG, and GDR meet in Bonn for first talks on German unity
1 July 1990	Economic, monetary, and social union of FRG/GDR
31 August 1990	Unification Treaty between FRG and GDR signed in Berlin
12 September 1990	Treaty on the Final Settlement with Respect to Germany ("Two plus Four") signed
19 September 1990	GDR People's Chamber ratifies Unification Treaty
20 September 1990	Bundestag ratifies Unification Treaty
1–2 October 1990	Document to suspend Four-Power rights is signed
3 October 1990	In accord with Article 23 of the Basic Law, GDR accedes to territory and five new states formed
2 December 1990	First Bundestag elections in unified Germany
17 June 1991	Treaty with Poland signed (guarantee of the Oder-Neisse border)
21 June 1991	Bundestag vote establishing Berlin as the future capital
29 October 1993	Decision to base the European Monetary Institute (precursor of the European Central Bank) in Frankfurt
1 November 1993	Entry into force of the Maastricht Treaty establishing the European Union
January 1994	German unemployment exceeds four million for the first time since World War II
4 March 1994	Legislation introduced in the federal parliament to dissolve the Treuhandanstalt, which had privatized almost 13,000 state-owned enterprises
20 May 1994	Legislation adopted by the lower house of the federal parliament establishing a fund of DM 18 billion to provide compensation for nationalized and expropriated property in the former GDR
9 September 1994	Departure of last American troops from Berlin

Appendix B:
Articles of the German Law with Respect to Unification

Preamble: The German people have also acted on behalf of those Germans to whom participation was denied. The entire German people are called upon to achieve in free-self determination the unity and freedom of Germany.

Article 23: For the time being this Basic Law shall apply to [all West German states plus Greater Berlin]. In other parts of Germany it shall be put into force on their accession.

Article 146: The Basic Law shall cease to be in force on the day on which a constitution adopted by a free decision of the German people comes into force.

Index